"I am extremely impressed with Patt Lind-Kyle's tremendous knowledge, experience, wisdom and her platform for sharing the important subject of life, death, and dying with us. What Patt has done with the scope of this wisdom and application is an epic venture extraordinaire."

—Judith Aston, founder of Aston Kinetics

"*Embracing the End of Life* provides powerful and inspiring insights and guidance along the path to freedom; freedom to face the obvious, inevitable part of our lives we call death; freedom to be fully alive."

—Marc Lesser, CEO, Search Inside Yourself Leadership Institute
and author of *Know Yourself, Forget Yourself*

"Patt Lind-Kyle gently takes our hand and walks us consciously through the death and dying process. In doing so she is a handmaiden to help us discover our true Self, and we learn that we are already the light into which we continue our journey."

—Rev. Jerry Farrell, Unity minister and former hospice chaplain

"An eminently practical guide for dealing with pertinent details, from the prosaic—such as living wills and medical directives—to the esoteric. ... If you think there is a chance you may one day die, we highly recommend this book."

—Donna Eden and David Feinstein, PhD, *New York Times*
bestselling authors of *Energy Medicine*

"In her latest book, Patt makes a major contribution to the field of death and dying, as well as helping us work through how to live our best life until the end."

—Gail Aldrich, Principal, The Aldrich Partnership

"*Embracing the End of Life* is perhaps the most important book about death and dying present today."

—Gary Malkin, seven-time Emmy Award–winning composer and
co-author of *Graceful Passages: A Companion for Living and Dying*

"*Embracing the End of Life* is ... a very useful and practical guide for everybody who is consciously willing ... to live a more happy, vital, and spiritual life by diminishing the fear of one's own death."

—Dr. Pim van Lommel, MD, cardiologist, and *New York Times* bestselling
author of *Consciousness Beyond Life: The Science of the Near Death Experience*

Advanced Praise for *Embracing the End of Life*

"The fear of dying keeps countless people from living fully—as well as keeping countless others trapped in endless suffering. *Embracing the End of Life* will help all of us prepare joyously for the inevitable."

—Christiane Northrup, MD, *New York Times* bestselling
author of *Goddesses Never Age*

"Patt Lind-Kyle has written an essential book for the universal rite of passage that each of us must eventually face. . . . It is high time that the culture claims this passage in reverence, and with proper preparation. This book offers the way to create a peaceful and enlightening death—just as it should be."

—Anodea Judith, author of *Wheels of Life*

"This is the most comprehensive and practical book on preparing to die consciously. How to prepare psychologically, spiritually, and legally all presented in an approachable and usable manner. If you have any questions about healing your fear of death, read Patt's book."

—Dale Borglum, PhD, founder of the Living/Dying Project

"In *Embracing the End of Life*, Patt Lind-Kyle unravels the most important and most misunderstood aspect of life. For within the mystery of dying lies the key to living. This is a must-read for anyone wishing to breathe and live fully."

—Dr. Jacob Liberman, author of *Light: Medicine of the Future*

"In this comforting and practical book, Patt Lind-Kyle clearly lays out the practicalities of dying for us and for those around us. . . . This wonderful resource is our guidebook to the country we're all bound for, transforming death from a terrifying mystery to a conscious transition to the love that lies beyond."

—Dawson Church, PhD, author of *The Genie in Your Genes*

"In a culture such as ours that denies what it doesn't understand, this is an intensely needed book. . . . The author of this book has been stalked by death but has also stalked death herself, and been handed a most valuable gift that she passes on to us in this entertaining guidebook to a hitherto unknown land."

—Emmett Miller, MD, author of *Deep Healing*

"[Embracing the End of Life] . . . is a must-have book for anyone who works with death and dying."

—Linda L. Fitch, shamanic teacher of Dying Consciously

"Drawing on the world's greatest spiritual traditions as well as modern science, author Patt Lind-Kyle pulls back the curtain of death and helps annul the horror that humans often experience in life's final chapter. ... It is difficult to imagine a more important contribution, because our very survival as a species on Earth will largely depend on our beliefs about what happens in the greatest transition of all."

—Larry Dossey, MD, author of *One Mind*

"Patt Lind-Kyle has given us a marvelous manual for preparing the transition we all will make eventually. Brilliantly done, *Embracing the End of Life* provides the reader with many resources and guidelines that one can employ in ending one's life consciously—a major benefit for oneself and one's family and loved ones who remain."

—John Renesch, author of *The Great Growing Up*

"Forty-seven years ago, Elisabeth Kübler-Ross rocked the world with her discussions on death. Her work largely led to the use of hospice. We ordinary mortals need a deeper personal journey to our own preparation for the inevitable march to that couch on which we lie down. Here is a wonderful guide."

—Clyde Norman Shealy, MD, PhD, neurosurgeon
and author of *Blueprint for Holistic Healing*

"In her most recent book, Patt Lind-Kyle has offered a rare gem ... a resource that guides us through the realms of expansive and liberated living that also helps us prepare for conscious dying."

—Roxanne Howe-Murphy, EdD, author of *Deep Living*

"Patt Lind-Kyle's transformational book offers the precise guidance needed for the contemplation of death along with the tools to actually transcend fear and discover the joy of living with full awareness of mortality."

—Karen M. Wyatt, MD, author of *What Really Matters*

"In *Embracing the End of Life*, Patt Lind-Kyle offers readers a multitude of useful approaches to the subject, along with numerous meditation exercises ... and information on advance directives, organ donation, and other issues. This book can serve as a helpful unpacking of Ram Dass's advice, 'I assure you, dying is perfectly safe.'"

—Jeff Kane, MD, author of *How to Heal* and *Healing Healthcare*

"Those who are fortunate enough to have gravitated to this book will find it to be a wise handbook for living."

—Michael Beckwith, founder of the Agape International Spiritual Center
and author of *Spiritual Liberation*

Embracing *the* End *of* Life

Other Books by Patt Lind-Kyle

Heal Your Mind, Rewire Your Brain

When Sleeping Beauty Wakes Up

About the Author

Patt Lind-Kyle, MA, is an author and thought leader. She has taught in the academic world, created a small business, practiced as management consultant and executive coach, and had her own private consulting practice. Patt has been exploring the exciting new brain/mind research and working with the new tools of neuromonitoring to help individuals become more effective with their brain/mind. Patt's current focus is on the awakening process to rewire our approach to death. She was trained as a hospice volunteer and served patients in the Hospice Hospital of Portland, Oregon, and Hospice of the Foothills of California. Patt confronted the deep fear of her own death in a long meditation retreat.

Her book *Heal Your Mind, Rewire Your Brain* won the Independent Publishers Gold Medal Award and a Best Book Award from USA Book News. Patt has written a chapter in *Audacious Aging*, and she is also the author of *When Sleeping Beauty Wakes Up*. Visit her online at www.pattlindkyle.com.

Embracing *the* End *of* Life

A Journey Into
Dying & Awakening

PATT LIND-KYLE, MA

Llewellyn Publications
Woodbury, Minnesota

First Edition
First Printing, 2017

Cover Design by Howie Severson/Fortuitous Publishing
Interior illustrations by Llewellyn Art Department

Llewellyn Publications is a registered trademark of Llewellyn Worldwide Ltd.

Library of Congress Cataloging-in-Publication Data
 Names: Lind-Kyle, Patt, author.
   Title: Embracing the end of life : a journey into dying & awakening / Patt
     Lind-Kyle, MA.
   Description: First Edition. | Woodbury : Llewellyn Worldwide, Ltd., 2017. |
     Includes bibliographical references.
   Identifiers: LCCN 2017032851 (print) | LCCN 2017023883 (ebook) | ISBN
     9780738753836 (ebook) | ISBN 9780738753560 (alk. paper)
   Subjects: LCSH: Death. | Life.
   Classification: LCC BD444 (print) | LCC BD444 .L489 2017 (ebook) | DDC
     155.9/37--dc23
   LC record available at https://lccn.loc.gov/2017032851

Llewellyn Worldwide Ltd. does not participate in, endorse, or have any authority or responsibility concerning private business transactions between our authors and the public.

 All mail addressed to the author is forwarded, but the publisher cannot, unless specifically instructed by the author, give out an address or phone number.

 Any Internet references contained in this work are current at publication time, but the publisher cannot guarantee that a specific location will continue to be maintained. Please refer to the publisher's website for links to authors' websites and other sources.

Llewellyn Publications
A Division of Llewellyn Worldwide Ltd.
2143 Wooddale Drive
Woodbury, MN 55125-2989
www.llewellyn.com

Printed in the United States of America

Disclaimer

Please note that the information in this book is not meant to diagnose, treat, prescribe, or be a substitute for consultation with a licensed healthcare professional. Both the author and the publisher recommend that you consult a medical practitioner before attempting the techniques outlined in this book.

To Don Riso
His Enneagram teaching came from
his heart, and that healed my soul.

Contents

Part III—The Path of Freedom   261

List of Exercises

Chapter 11

Chapter 12

Chapter 13

Chapter 14

Chapter 15

Foreword by Karen Wyatt, MD

In my years of working with dying patients as a hospice physician, I saw ample evidence of the death denial that exists in our society. Many of my patients had never even considered the fact that they would one day face their own death and were totally unprepared when they reached life's end. They had to struggle to heal relationships, find meaning in life, and cope with fears of the unknown in the very last moments of their existence. Most of them had lived life in an unconscious manner as well, and had failed to grasp the deeper lessons of their experiences and engage fully in the entire spectrum life had offered them. These are the people the renowned Buddhist teacher Sogyal Rinpoche referred to when he wrote, "Most people die unprepared for death, as they have lived, unprepared for life."

The fear of death is part of our human nature but doesn't serve us well in our individual lives when we fail to contemplate and embrace our own mortality. In addition, this lack of death awareness has harmed our entire planet, as we have existed without respect for the fragility and fleetingness of all life, have taken more than needed from the earth's limited resources, and have failed to honor the natural balance of the ecosystem. When we ignore the importance of death in the life cycle, we hinder the flourishing of creativity in our own lives and also in the natural world. For our own evolution and the survival of the planet, it is essential to confront the denial of death and transcend the limitations of our fears.

Los Angeles funeral director Caitlin Doughty once mentioned in an interview that the denial of death is a "luxury" of living in a First World nation. She went on to say that had we been born in India we would view death as a natural part of life, as a result of witnessing it on a daily basis: from beggars dying on the streets to family members dying in the home to crematory pyres floating continuously along the Ganges River. But we in Western society have not had this lifelong exposure to death and must intentionally educate ourselves to overcome our intrinsic death-phobia.

Those who recognize their own mortality may be inspired to prepare for the end of life, but have little idea where to begin or how to confront their fears and limited knowledge about dying and death. Fortunately, Patt Lind-Kyle's groundbreaking book *Embracing the End of Life: The Journey Into Dying and Awakening* offers the precise guidance needed for the contemplation of death along with the tools to actually transcend fear and discover the joy of living an awakened and aware life.

With her background in East/West psychology and extensive research in right/left brain function, Lind-Kyle is perfectly suited to guide the reader across the bridge between life and death. She combines her academic knowledge with the wisdom attained from her thirty-five-year practice of meditation in the Theravada tradition to provide a richly interwoven mind/body/spirit approach to death and dying. In addition, her life-changing book is both inspirational and practical, with specific exercises to explore the roots of fear, age-related meditations, and descriptions of Enneagram and brain frequency patterns for various stages of life.

This book informs the reader not only about the physical, psychological, and spiritual aspects of the dying process but also inspires the examination of emotions and beliefs about death through a series of written reflections. These exercises form the guideposts for a journey into deeper and deeper death-awareness that results in expanded consciousness as well. Ultimately the reader is not only prepared for what the dying process may entail, but also equipped with a new mind-set toward death and specific practices necessary for navigating unknown terrain at the end of life. Furthermore, a wealth of practical resources is offered for caregiving, legal document preparation, and support of the dying from various religious perspectives.

Embracing the End of Life offers a beautiful gift for those who follow its recommended exercises: the opportunity to become enlightened about death long before this wisdom is needed. Transcending the fear of death in this way allows much more room for creativity, joy, and the freedom to finally live in a fully awakened state. Patt Lind-Kyle writes, "Death is one of the most precious experiences you will ever have in this life." It turns out, her book informs us, that death is actually the key to life—and there is no more important lesson for us to learn.

As a guidebook for the journey from birth to death, *Embracing the End of Life* serves as a wise companion for those who dare to live deeply into the mysteries of life and death, with eyes wide open and mind fully centered in the present moment. This innovative and comprehensive book has the power to change the perception of death for the individual reader and for society as a whole as we confront the most fundamental question of our humanity: "How do we live while knowing we will die?" Read this book now to transform how you live for the rest of your days, and then keep it on your bookshelf as a resource to consult over and over again on your own "journey into dying and awakening."

—Karen Wyatt, MD, author of *What Really Matters: 7 Lessons for Living from the Stories of the Dying*

Introduction

Why Are We Interested
in the End of Our Life?

If you accept that death is part of life,
then when it actually does come, you may face it more easily.
—HIS HOLINESS THE FOURTEENTH DALAI LAMA

A few years ago, I went through an extraordinary experience of confronting the end of my life. The experience started during a heat wave at home in California. I had a two-hour appointment in a very cold air-conditioned office. When I left the office, I walked out into the afternoon summer heat. When I started my car, the temperature gauge read 99 degrees. I didn't open the windows to let out the hot air, and I drove for a while before turning on the air conditioner. It took me a while to get home, as I made stops for several errands, getting out of the car into the heat and then getting back into the car heat. As I neared home, I started to feel awful. I had a headache, felt fatigued, and had an upset stomach. When I finally got home, I felt even worse.

I searched the Internet and found that I probably had a condition called heat exhaustion. I made a telephone call and was warned by a doctor friend to stay in a cool place, be quiet, drink liquids, and rest because my condition could develop into heatstroke. This meant a heatstroke could damage my brain, heart, kidneys, and muscles, as well as increase my risk of other serious complications leading to death. My doctor friend said that I needed to maintain a balance in my body temperature for at least two weeks.

This news of needing to rest for two weeks was very disturbing to me. Months before, I had made plans for a month-long meditation retreat outside of Boston. I was scheduled to fly from my home in California to the East Coast within the week. Given my heat exhaustion, I was anxious about going on the retreat, as I read that the East Coast was in an intense, humid heat wave.

Even with my condition, I still decided to go. Fortunately, by the time I got on the plane I was feeling better. In the Boston airport, the evening news on a TV monitor announced, "This weather is the most humid heat wave the East has experienced in years." I immediately took an air-conditioned shuttle and arrived at my retreat destination at 8:00 p.m. When I got out of the shuttle, I was stunned by the heat and humidity. The night heat together with the humidity was off the charts, and I could feel my anxiety about heat exhaustion percolate and rise.

The next morning, I began to have the same heat symptoms I'd had at home. My room did not have air-conditioning, but the meditation hall did. As I went back and forth between the heat and the cold, the heat exhaustion symptoms got worse. I was now in the same boat I'd been in at home, but it was not the boat I wanted to be in. My body did not feel good, and I didn't know what to do. I became increasingly anxious and scared. The symptoms were getting worse each day, as was my anxiety.

The third night after arriving at the center, I woke up in a state of terror at about 2:00 a.m. This is the time at the retreat center when there are no teachers and no one else available to contact. I was totally alone. The twenty-five other meditators were in their individual rooms. I had been in many long retreats and had experienced fear and anxiety before as I struggled with thoughts and emotions, but this was different. I felt the tension, fear, constriction of breath, and all the heat symptoms welling up inside of me. I was increasingly confused and full of terror. The question kept coming, *What do I do?*

I tried to meditate, do yoga, sing softly to myself, and listen to my meditation music. Nothing worked. The inner voice kept saying, *How can I stop this terror? What should I do?* Finally, I sat up in bed and questioned myself, "Patt, what is making you so frightened, so anxious, that it's driving you into complete terror?" The answer came quickly: "I am frightened to die." I remember saying to myself, "Well, there is nothing I can do now, so I might as well die." With that, I laid my head down on my pillow, pulled the covers over me, and went to sleep.

I slept soundly until my alarm rang for breakfast. I got up, free of the heat exhaustion symptoms and also of the terror. What happened? After a lot of reflection on this event, I realized that I had confronted pieces of this terror of death in many of my long meditation retreats. With the threat of heat stroke and the physical symptoms growing in me, I finally faced that inner terror, looked it straight in the eyes, and let it go. As I faced the fear directly, I called its bluff and the fear, physical symptoms, and terror vanished. I felt free!

This was not a mental or even an emotional reaction, as I realized in some deep place within that death had been stalking me for a long time. As long as I pushed this unconscious fear of death away, I was stuck in growing terror. In a real way, the heat and terror were my friends to help me face this deep part of my life and open me to sense my inner freedom. The next day, I told my teacher what had occurred, and she supported me that I had been very courageous.

Of course, I am quite aware that someday I will physically die. There is no doubt that death will come for me, as for everyone. I know that my body will get a disease or I will wither away from old age or perhaps die in an accident. What this experience and awareness left me with were burning questions that kept repeating in my head throughout the month-long retreat. *What happens to the mind when I die? Where does it go? What quality of mind is imperative for me to be in as I die?* I remember reading a quote from a spiritual teacher that helped me focus to contemplate these questions. Although I am not a follower of Osho, when I read this quote, it gave me a direction to search out the type of mind we need when we leave the body and go on to our next journey. He said, "Remember, only that which you can take with you when you leave the body is important.

That means, except meditation, nothing is important. Except awareness, nothing is important, because only awareness cannot be taken away by death. Everything else will be snatched away, because everything else comes from without. Only awareness wells up within; that cannot be taken away. And the shadows of awareness—compassion, love—they cannot be taken away; they are intrinsic parts of awareness. You will be taking with you only whatsoever awareness you have attained; that is your only real wealth." [1]

From my research into many spiritual traditions and my own meditation experience as well as scientific research, it has become clear to me that when we die we take only our inner qualities that, hopefully, we have been cultivating all our lives. Osho indicates that meditation is a key and a means to develop awareness of these inner qualities we need for our death and rebirth—whatever that rebirth will be for each of us.

During that month of retreat, I kept asking these two questions: What is this awareness I gain from meditation? How do I continue to develop it? As these questions repeated in my mind, I came to discover that when awareness is found and developed, it cannot be taken away.

In the months after the retreat, a deep yearning pressed me forward to find answers to my questions about death and to find the steps that would help others find their own answers. Something new was arising in me, and I was excited that I was birthing a new process for myself and perhaps for others. I no longer wanted to seek outside myself for inspiration, but rather to follow the inner lead of guidance of this force I was experiencing. Like a flashing mental sign, I kept seeing, "Death is the next big journey in my life." I became conscious that time was of the essence. I wanted to develop those inner qualities of awareness of peace and serenity without a mental struggle and without emotional terror when I came to my dying. This journey to understand and explore the practical and spiritual aspects of death and dying has become my passion and mission for my own sake and to share with others.

Let me pause to say that my exploration of my own death and the passion to help others face their death followed many years of critical illness, long medita-

---

1. Osho Rajneesh, *Meditation: The Art of Ecstasy* (New York: Osho International, 1992), 33.

tion retreats exploring the fears and darkness of my inner world, hospice training in which I volunteered with the dying in a hospice hospital and home hospice, counseling people facing their own death, and being present for the death of both my father and my mother. Now later in life, the opportunity arrived for me to put together my life experience in a manner that could help others face this doorway called death that each of us will walk through.

This guidebook is the result of my journey. Along with the research I did on dying, the moments of death itself, and what is beyond our dying process, this book is also the result of my inner discovery. My research led me to explore and develop a map of the physical, psychological, and spiritual journey of both death and spiritual awakening. Through the descriptions of others, who have explored the process of dying, I discovered that in going through the journey of death we are transformed. What the transformation through death means is to die and awaken to be free of affliction. When you die and the quality of your mind is consciously aware, that gives you inner peace, a feeling of calm, serenity, and a release of fear into a deep comforting of inner love. In the dying process, your mind goes through the most important spiritual experience of your entire lifetime.

What became clear, as I researched the dying process, is the understanding that there is a release or a letting go that we can do to be free and live a fuller life now. Without a doubt, I became convinced that while I am alive I must train my mind to let go both for how I live now and for my death. The purpose of this inner preparation to die is to develop the quality of a conscious mind now.

One of the reasons I was so frightened of dying was that my mind was not prepared for the *process of death*. I had the direct experience that I was frightened of the unknown because of the incredible fear surrounding death that our culture teaches. I felt alienated and disconnected from death. So I avoided the idea of death and kept focused on outer-world activities, believing that some day, without conscious awareness, life would be snatched away from me. However, the Dalai Lama has given us an important reminder: "If you are mindful at death it will not come as a surprise. You will not be anxious. You will feel that death is merely like changing your clothes. Consequently, at that point you will be able to maintain your calmness of mind." [2]

In our culture, we know we will die, but at the same time we all tend to deny it, ignore it, and cover it up in many ways. How to prepare for death is not talked about or focused on even by our doctors, caregivers, and religious teachers. But I also see this "cover-up" changing with the emergence of Death Cafes, conversations about death with dignity laws, and films and books about death. Also, because there is a growing pressure from the aging Boomer generation as death is arriving at their generational shore, there is what is being called a "Death Awareness Movement," or DAM!

Even though there is a growing awareness about death at a cultural and societal level, there are core questions I believe each of us needs to explore at a personal level. Some of these questions you may have already confronted. Other questions may not be in awareness for you. Here are some of the critical questions I've asked myself as I began to write this book and now ask you in order to help you begin to frame your thoughts and feelings as we begin this journey of exploration. One or more of these question may stand out to you now. However, we will explore all of them and more over the course of the book:

- Do you have a fear of death, and, if so, how do you work with that fear?

- What in your life keeps you from dealing with the practical issues of preparing for your death?

- How do you prepare your mind and emotions to confront your dying when it begins to happen to you?

- Would you be willing to give up your power to the medical community to continue heroic methods to preserve your life in ways that keep you from a peaceful and conscious dying process?

- How do you prepare for the actual moment of your death and what may lie beyond your dying, whatever your beliefs?

- What legal preparations do you need to create now for your eventual death?

---

2. Dalai Lama, *The Path to Tranquility: Daily Wisdom,* edited by Renuka Singh (New York: Penguin Books; Reprint edition, 1999), 4.

Those of us in Western society are generally disconnected from ourselves as to what we feel, as well as lost and adrift when it comes to the reality of the meaning of our death and what the process will be of our death. Generally, there is little around us in our families, friends, and society at large to help us understand and make critical choices about the death process, other than medical decisions. The current approach to the dying process centers primarily on the medical model of mitigating pain and not on dealing with the inner fear and suffering that arises in moving through the various stages of death. This medical model highlights alienation from the actual fact of death. That alienation is what you might face if you are not prepared for your dying process. Death is simply one more aspect of being a human being. In our culture, we've made death a taboo.

As our society pushes the fear of death away from us and hides it in hospitals, hospice facilities, and nursing homes, I decided to develop a map of the physical dying process in order to understand what I would face at death. My effort in this research and the accompanying practices I've developed have been done to alleviate my own fear of dying and to help others who are interested in exploring this area of their life.

My previous book *Heal Your Mind, Rewire Your Brain*[3] examined the functions of the brain waves and the wealth of growing research about the brain-mind relationship. As I got deeper into the research on death and what is occurring in the brain and mind, more clarity came on how the mind progresses through the dying stages and how it unravels at death. This discovery answered one of my core questions. The process of my research showed me that as the body goes through a transformation at death, so does the mind. I realized that if the mind is trained to be aware and continually conscious, then the dying process is the most powerful spiritual experience and opportunity of our lifetime. You need to know enough ahead of the time of your death process to be willing to work with your mind and to have challenging discussions with your family, with medical people, and with your friends to prepare you and others for what is to come at your death.

---

3. Patricia Lind-Kyle, *Heal Your Mind, Rewire Your Brain* (Santa Rosa, CA: Energy Psychology Press, 2010).

The Path Toward Death

There are two kinds of courage when you face sickness, aging, and death. The first type of courage is to confront the truth and reality of your mortality so as not to be fearful. The second is to act on the truth you find. The path toward your death is frequently unclear because you do not know what will happen, so it is hard to know what to do. The challenge is to explore your unique path toward your own death and how you want to face it. My dream is that this book will increase your courage to unwind the challenge of your own death and that you will learn and know the truth of your own path for yourself.

In the course of the material I present about death, I will also discuss the journey beyond death. My bias is that there is a "something" that is experienced beyond our physical death. This view comes from my exploration of many spiritual traditions, my own inner experience of traversing many levels of mind states in meditation, the growing body of research of brain states at death, and the experience of people that "return from the dead," called a "near-death experience." Whether or not you believe in an afterlife, however, preparing mentally, emotionally, spiritually, and practically for this inevitable event provides clarity, strength, and understanding for how you choose to approach your dying process and how you awake to your dying today.

The focus of the book assumes you want to learn about your own death process or you are concerned about those in your life who are dying of old age or of some illness. The information and exercises will also be helpful if you or someone in your life has had a sudden health event, such as a heart attack, or lost a loved one in a car accident. Understanding what happens at the moment of death helps prepare for sudden death or protracted illness. In the case of sudden death, information on how to recognize after-death experience is even more vital to this journey into dying and awakening.

I decided to call this book a guidebook instead of simply a book because I want it to help guide you to explore the key questions of your own process and discover the outer as well as the inner conditions of preparing for your death and your awakening to a more vital life now. The book is designed to have you create your own guidebook of how you want to prepare for your dying and living now if you desire to do so. As a guidebook, the exercises, visualizations, meditations, and, if you choose to use them, the bonus videos, will help you explore and question your personal understandings and values about death, how to engage caregivers and family in what you want as you go through the dying process, how to establish practices and ways to give yourself feedback about your inner explorations, and the very practical preparation of financial and legal issues to attend to.

You will be presented with information, questions, and exercises to think and write about. I encourage you to get a notebook or a journal or put a file on your computer that is devoted solely to the exploration of questions, exercises, and "things to do" about your own dying process. This will be your "How I Want to Die Manual" that you can provide to others as you enter your own dying process.

The book also provides practical wisdom on the dying process as well as a step-by-step program on how you can wake up to a place of freedom in yourself while still alive. My intention in this book is to give you a context, a structure, as well as a helpful guide to familiarize yourself with what you need to know and prepare for as you look across the horizon to your own death. This book will also allow you to experience your practical concerns, contemplate how you want to die, and prepare you and your loved ones for the journey.

Besides the exercises in the book, there are bonus videos that can be used with the second part of the book if you choose to do so. These videos can accompany the guided meditations, and they use colors, coded color music, and binaural beats that put you into deep brain-wave experiences as you attempt to go deeper into our own dying and awakening process. You will be provided information in the appendix on how to use these videos.

In this book, I am encouraging you to have a meditation practice as part of death/awakening training preparation. If you don't currently have a practice, you may find helpful my book *Heal Your Mind, Rewire Your Brain* and its accompanying meditation CDs that teach you how to have deep meditation experiences using your own brain-wave patterns. The book and CDs can give you a beginning point to establish a meditation practice for yourself.

Although you will be working individually with the exercises and responding to the material and questions I pose, the book is also intended to be a guidebook for groups who want to come together and explore and support each other. I have found coming together in groups to work with this material provides a cross-fertilization of insight, support, and deep honesty that deepens connection and community. I designed the material to be used by families, circles of friends, churches, meditation groups, and other organizations. The purpose is to create communities of support and guide people in learning how to prepare for their own death and to know how to support each other in the dying process. We prepare for babies, professions, trips, and more, but we do not prepare for the most important experience that will ever happen to us. Within a supportive community of life and death, you are preparing to go home.

The first part of the book is the overview of our death process. In this part, you will explore the process of how you physically, psychologically, and spiritually die and how to work with your fears about death and your dying.

The second part of the book lays out the psychospiritual transformation journey we all can go through long before we die. This part gives the understanding of why you need to train your mind to live fully now and to prepare for your death. Preparing for your eventual death now enables you to release the uncertainty and fear of dying.

The first process is for you to learn how the mind is developed step-by-step and how it develops over time into an identity that I call a *constricted self presence of fear*.

The second process is to learn the steps for unraveling the constricted self. This is done by the incorporation and the transformation of the constricted self into what I call the *expanded self of love*. This transformation awakens your unique awareness. Recall what Osho said, that awareness is consciousness that cannot be taken away at the time of death. My desire for you in writing this book is that you discover this awareness for yourself. It is to discover your freedom!

I am deeply grateful for my teachers through the years who have pointed the way into an exploration of the inner world. For this book in particular, the years of research opened to me the many authors who have explored the dying process. Both within the text and in the bibliography, I acknowledge their contribution to an understanding of what it is to pass through this doorway of death.

It is my hope that this book will serve to further a broader understanding and preparation for the dying process and what it means to awaken to a different life now and beyond through my own experience and the digestion of others' insights. I am excited to begin this journey with you to learn how to prepare to die and discover the process of awakening to a full and vital life now.

Part I

How to Prepare
for Your Death

If we are duly prepared, I can promise that the moment of death will be an experience
of rejoicing. If we are not prepared, it will surely be a time of fear and regret.

—ANYEN RINPOCHE

A central theme or practice in my life for more than forty years has been to meditate. I found it brought peace and calm to my anxious mind. As I look back, it seems magical how I was pulled into meditation. I have never quite understood this deep yearning to connect with something other than the outside world. I question now, in my seventies as I write this book, what quality of mind or nature of mind do I want to be in when I die? I want to familiarize myself with the quality of mind while I am alive so I am prepared for the powerful moment of death, as Osho suggested.

I began my research on the death process by studying the psychospiritual aspect of dying. Psychospiritual pertains to the relationship between the mind and spirituality. The psychological approach works toward an understanding of your personality identity in the context of discovering that it is part of something larger than who you think you are. Psychology is concerned directly with the state of your mind during the dying process. Spirituality relates to the transcendent awareness, to something beyond your normal thinking and reaction patterns. Both the psychological and spiritual aspects of your life will be encountered in the various stages of death.

Most people have some familiarity with Elisabeth Kübler-Ross's psychological stages of dying: denial, anger, bargaining, depression, and acceptance.[4] These stages represent some of the psychological content of your mind as you approach death. What I am calling *spiritual* is what transcends your psychological mind and expands awareness beyond the normal five senses. It is this spiritual part of life that religions, mystical systems, music, art, and poetry open within us. Dying is a journey of turning inward both psychologically and spiritually to confront the resistance, the process of letting go, and the ultimate transformation of your life. Fundamentally, dying is the process of letting go of your beliefs, perceptions, identity, others, nature, and the cosmos itself to move into the vast mystery that is death and beyond.

In my studies on dying, I found that my earlier work and book exploring meditation and brain frequencies applied to the dying process as well. I also found that the energy centers (chakras) of the body, as described in many ancient spiritual traditions, play a part in the dying process. Integrating brain-wave frequencies and chakras began to make sense of what happens when we die. As I wove brain frequencies and chakras together, I had a realization that the process of dying is really the same as the spiritual awakening process that many traditions describe. In the sections that follow, you will be exploring and weaving together these two aspects of your physical and metaphysical body: brain waves and chakras.

Of greatest importance as you begin your exploration is to face your fear and the *natural resistance* that comes with confronting the mystery of death. Note, however, that the more you know about the dying process and the similarity of spiritually waking up to your inner nature the more the fear of dying dissolves. The reduction of your fear of death can change you both psychologically and spiritually. Through meditation practice and other contemplative methods, you

---

4. Elisabeth Kübler-Ross, *On Death and Dying* (New York: Simon and Schuster, 1970).

can reach a quiet space of balance in preparation for the moment of your death. You can also be living a life of freedom and joy now before you die.

The basic fact of your life is you will die. When you will die and how you will die is the unknown. We all carry this unknown within us. As we begin this journey to explore dying, there are two basic questions to consider. The first is *How do I use this absolute fact of my dying in my daily life?* The second is *How do I open up my heart and mind to release my conscious and unconscious fear of death?* In the pages that follow, you will explore how prepared you are to answer these questions. You will also be given the opportunity to consider what is really important for you to do now in your life to prepare for your death. Although we will explore the dimensions of the dying process, we will also explore how to live more fully today.

Chapter 1
The Physical, Psychological, and Spiritual Process of Death

To be prepared for death ... life shall thereby be the sweeter.
—WILLIAM SHAKESPEARE

The view of many religious, philosophical, spiritual, and mystical traditions is that death is one of the most precious experiences you will ever have in this life. You and I may dread death because we don't have the knowledge, experience, understanding, or cultural support that would help us to view it differently as we face this great unknown. We still have a choice, however. We can either live in dark fear or turn on the light. To choose to turn on the light and explore the process of your dying can bring you the greatest personal discovery of your life. The traditions say that you will discover that the moment of your death will be like the moment of birth. Your dying will be a time of your greatest need and uncertainty as well as your greatest joy and fulfillment because you will be moving through the doorway into an incomprehensible life experience.

What I discovered in myself and in working with dying individuals is that conscious preparation, like what we will be doing in this book by focusing on a positive death, can actually help us in our dying. Yet there are still unconscious wants and desires that muddy our mind and emotions. You may have had thoughts like the following or heard others say: "I only want to die in my sleep." "I want to be instantly killed in an accident." "I want a lot of drugs so I don't feel any pain when I die." "I want all my friends and family telling me, 'Don't worry, everything will be okay, you won't go to hell.'" Or finally, "Because of my disease I'll commit suicide so I don't have a prolonged death." If these types of "death plans" don't go as they are supposed to go, then it creates undo fear and uncertainty.

Wanting your dying to be different from what it actually is will create resistance and pain for you as you move through the outer separation from your normal life, and then enter the inner chaotic changes and fear that the final letting go of your physical life will bring to you. I give you this caution as you begin this book with the hopes that you will realize that you can and need to prepare many things before you enter the final stages of dying. This is the work we each must do in order to let go of our resistance to death.

The lesson is learning that we are dying in some way every day. To die into your living now is the true gift of preparing for your final death. Many people have told me that as they confronted the future of their own death and prepared for it, they became more alive and vital in living their lives now. Opening to a new inner life now—what we were born to be—is the same as going through the portal of our death.

What Dies in Us Physically?

Let us begin by understanding the physical part of the dying process. Later in the book, we will look specifically at what happens just before death, at the actual moment of physical death, and after you die. But to introduce the question of what happens at physical death, we will consider for now what goes on in your nervous system, in your brain, and in the rest of your body when you die.

The Nervous System and Death

Our nervous system plays a critical function in how we will approach our death. Death is about letting go. Our autonomic nervous system is responsible for regulating the body's unconscious actions. When we move through the dying process, we shift into one of the two divisions of our autonomic nervous system. The two divisions are the parasympathetic nervous system and the sympathetic nervous system. The parasympathetic nervous system is often considered the "rest and digest" or "feed and breed" system. The sympathetic system is responsible for the "fight, flight, or freeze" response to outward threat.

An older simplification of the parasympathetic and sympathetic nervous systems describes the autonomic nervous system as the inhibitory (parasympathetic) and excitatory (sympathetic) responses. It is the parasympathetic nervous system that takes over during the dying process. Being the inhibitor, the parasympathetic is a slowly activated dampening system of the body. You need this "damping down" as you move into the final stages of dying. The two branches of the nervous system have opposite actions. One system activates a physiological response and the other inhibits it. You can experience this oscillating movement of high activity and then deep sleep as you are in the process of letting go to your death. It is the parasympathetic nervous system that kicks in when you let go in the final stage of dying. When letting go happens in any aspect of life, it results in a relaxed state of mind and body.

The Brain and Death

The growing body of research into the functioning of the brain is revealing new insights about what occurs in the brain when we are dying. One of the areas of research is related to our various brain-wave patterns. When you get close to death, the brain activity settles into a period of slower delta wave frequency.

Delta frequency is the slowest of the four major brain waves (beta, alpha, theta, delta). Delta is the brain frequency that we are in during sleep. The brain frequencies can be recorded to observe the fluctuating electrical changes in the brain as we approach death and afterward. A seminal research study with mammalian brains at the University of Michigan, published in the *Proceedings of the National Academy of Sciences* in 2013, reported that after clinical death, the brain enters a brief state of heightened activity normally associated with wakeful consciousness or so-called gamma brain-wave activity.

Gamma waves are the fastest brain waves and are associated with high levels of concentration. In a variety of other brain research labs, gamma brain waves have been demonstrated and recorded in Tibetan monks and others in deep states of meditation. Using cardiac arrest on animal subjects, the Michigan researchers demonstrated that this "afterlife" brain activity is also highly coordinated across brain areas and different brain wavelengths. Gamma waves are the neural hallmarks of high-level cognitive activity. This activity not only resembles the waking state, it might even reflect a heightened state of conscious awareness similar to what the researchers describe as "the highly lucid and realer-than-real mental experiences reported by near-death survivors." [5] This is a pretty bold claim that critically depends on a person's quality of consciousness to be able to report after-death experience.

The researchers argue that at the final stage of brain death there is actually more evidence for consciousness-related activity than during normal wakeful consciousness. At this point, it is difficult to quantify "consciousness-related activity," but it does support the notion that the more conscious or lucid you are at the time of death, the more you remain in that lucid state to be liberated or freed to experience another state of reality. This corroborates what Tibetan and other religious and spiritual traditions describe as the awareness we have after our physical death and when the brain no longer appears to be functioning.

The Body and Death

As you approach physical death, your body undergoes a variety of metabolic changes. As metabolism slows, your body has more difficulty turning food into energy to keep everything going. A clear sign that you are approaching death is your wanting little or no food or drink. If caregivers try to give it to you, you may become agitated and resistant to being fed.

One of the noticeable changes is the slowness of breathing. There will be periods where there is no breathing for more than a minute and then a surge of fast breathing. The erratic breathing may last several days before you die.

---

5. Jimo Borjigin et al., "Surge of neurophysiological coherence and connectivity in the dying brain," *Proceedings of the National Academy of Sciences* 110, no. 35 (2013): 14432–14437.

Coughing fits can happen as fluid builds up in the lungs. The fluid in the lungs is what often causes the rattling sounds in the breathing.

Body temperature can fluctuate between being very high one moment and then very cold the next. Along with the temperature variations, the skin will begin to change and will feel cold to the touch, followed by the appearance of blotchy patches on the skin. The skin can also change color, moving from pink to a grayish tone.

As you get closer to the moment of death, you will enter into a sleeplike coma. You will become increasingly weaker and lack bowel and bladder control. The kidneys will release urine that is brown or dark red. You will stop producing urine when you are very close to dying.

Vision and hearing become less and less, and hallucinations are common at this point before death. Restlessness may also increase, and often even the weakest person attempts to get out of bed.

All these physical indicators reveal that the body is shutting down. How long your body takes to go through the final stage of physical shutdown will depend on your unique physical and medical conditions.

Psychological and Spiritual Aspects of Our Dying

Throughout history, philosophers and religious persons have reported that *how you respond to the moment of your physical death is mirrored by the life you have lived.* If you are always on the go, busy, independent, and with a strong identity in the world, then dying will be an abrupt change of lifestyle! If this is your pattern, you may resist the shift of your body to slow down and resist letting go of the body as you approach death. Likewise, if you are a lethargic couch potato and have difficulty concentrating your energy on challenges, you may resist the shift to focus on a deeper awareness within you as your body begins to shut down. The struggle to hold on to your life pattern will determine the struggle that will ensue with your dying.

Death has a process of its own. It is a journey where you are not in control. Out of control is scary when you are used to being in control. Control is the hallmark challenge of the letting-go process. Letting go of your mind and body does not have to be terrifying. But rather, understanding what you will experience and having loving support around you will let your passage of death be both peaceful and transformative to you and others.

Let's begin to explore your resistance to being both alive and dying. We begin with a journey of three steps. The following five chapters are divided into three steps. Each step lays out the journey of your dying process. Everyone may not go through these steps, but knowing each step will give you guidance into reducing the fear of facing your own death.

- *The first step* describes what happens when death is inevitable and there is no further treatment possible. The first step explores the general resistance you probably have facing your death. Most of us will try to push away or find some rationale or means to run away from dealing with the issue of death and our resistance to avoid it both mentally and emotionally.

- *The second step* is letting go when you can no longer use every means medical or otherwise to hold on to life and realize you can no longer resist or push away from death. At this step, you finally begin to let go and accept what is inevitable.

- *The third step* is the process of transcendence. This is the experience of our actual death or ending of the body breathing, the heart and mind ceasing, and the journey (whatever it may be) beyond life. In each step on this journey, there are exercises to personalize and explore more deeply how to reduce the fear of dying.

Chapter 2
Step 1:
Stages of Resistance

One who is free of fear knows that at the deepest level
of realization there is no suffering, no birth, no death.
—Roshi Joan Halifax

Sogyal Rinpoche, in his book *The Tibetan Book of Living and Dying,* describes that "two people have been living in you all your life. One is the ego, garrulous, demanding, hysterical, calculating; the other is the hidden spiritual being, whose still voice of wisdom you have only rarely heard or attended to." [6] As the physical aspects of your dying body commence, there is a psychological dynamic that comes to the forefront of your experience.

The dying stage you begin to enter is called resistance. Resistance brings disorder, confusion, and unpredictability as you enter the dying process. The irony is that resistance is needed to break up the identity that must dissolve in order for you to pass through this threshold of death. Resistance emerges in the death process as the ego, which many call the *false self* and I describe as the *constricted self,* begins to break down. The false self or constricted self and the contrasting

---

6. Sogyal Rinpoche, *The Tibetan Book of Living and Dying* (San Francisco: HarperCollins, 1994), 120.

true self or what I term the *expanded self* are less psychological terms than spiritual descriptions.

Thomas Merton was one gateway for many Western searchers confronting the truth of these two aspects of our lives and an announcer of these terms of *false self* and *true self* as part of our spiritual and psychological makeup. From his writings, particularly on Zen Buddhism and Taoism,[7] it is clear that he was influenced deeply by Eastern spiritual traditions. Merton was Catholic, a Trappist monk, and a mystic who wrote more than seventy books. He was friends with the Dalai Lama, D. T. Suzuki, Thich Nhat Hanh, and many other Buddhist spiritual leaders. His writings have influenced legions of spiritual seekers from many traditions all over the world.

These two terms, *false self* and *true self*, have influenced both my understanding and my direct experience on my inner journey. However, I have changed the labels of *false self* and *true self* to *constricted self* and *expanded self* because "false" and "true" give the connotation of the self being either bad or good. The expanded self can be defined as the holistic self. It is the body, heart, and mind in a state of balance and integration that functions at a high level of energy and awareness. The constricted self is fragmented and, in Western culture, mainly focused on fear and anxiety and lacking contact with emotional awareness of the feelings in one's heart.

The reality for most of us is that we live unconsciously in the constricted self until, through therapeutic work, spiritual exercises, or other physical or emotional shocks to our system, we confront our individual suffering and begin moving toward experiencing our expanded self. Dominated by the constricted self, we experience our protective ego identity, but when our identity starts to break apart, it is possible to begin to discover the core nature of our expanded self. Various religious, spiritual, and psychological traditions indicate that at this point of breaking apart our self-created identity, a journey of healing and awakening begins.

One aspect of opening to the expanded self is that we don't create a new identity or personality. The expanded self is the energy, expression, or mani-

---

7. Thomas Merton, *The Asian Journal of Thomas Merton* (New York: New Directions, 1973).

festation of the identity with which we came into this life. When self-presence (toward which our expanded self is evolving) awakens consciously in us, we embody this energy of life flowing directly through us and we feel that we've been reborn.

In the second half of the book, we will explore more thoroughly the relationship between the constricted self and the expanded self in the awakening process of your life. Let me focus a bit here on the constricted self, as that is the part of us that resists our dying. At this point in our discussion, the constricted self and what is psychologically termed "the ego" have similar characteristics.

You know from your own experience what your constricted self is like. The constricted self is full of fear that manifests as anger, loneliness, shame, control, judgment, and so on. This constricted self separates you from loving and trusting the hidden vulnerable nature of what you truly are. In long periods of meditation practice and as I studied the process of my ego's demise, I was amazed at how real I thought my constricted self was in my life. The thoughts kept returning, "How could I live without it? Wasn't my ego my emotions, my body, my accomplishments, my power, my true identity?" Over years of psychological work and meditation, I struggled with the ego personality—the constricted self—I had constructed, with all its thoughts, feelings, and sensations. As many of you have learned and experienced, facing your constricted self is deeply challenging.

Death affects your fragile constricted self in dramatic ways. This constricted self that created your personality structure has lived in a world of its own creation. It has been able to negotiate and navigate your suffering. I say the constricted self is fragile because we get physically weaker, whether by accident, disease, or old age, as we progress toward death, and this weaker, more fragile physical state creates the feeling that life has become uncertain and out of control and often moves us into an emotional chaotic reaction as the time of death approaches. At death, this chaotic emotional reaction is the holding on of the constricted self. This ego, this constricted self, is what you must let go of and leave behind. For some of us, it is a battle, as we hold on; for others, it is a gentle release.

In this chapter, we will explore how resistance is really a gift as we face our death and Elisabeth Kübler-Ross's research more than fifty years ago of her five reactions or "resistances" to dying: denial, anger, bargaining, depression, and acceptance. With each of these reaction patterns, you will have the opportunity to explore them with an exercise for each one.

The Gift of Resistance

The stage of resistance actually provides a hidden gift as we approach our death. Resistance is part of the transpersonal journey each of us will experience as we go through our dying process. Resistance is an emotional state and its movement is unpredictable, disorganized, and confused because the constricted self is beginning to lose control. Most of all, in the stage of resistance, your physical as well as your emotional life is breaking apart. Resistance occurs when there is a holding on or "clinging" to your constricted self. We resist who we think we are and don't want to let go of our identity as a person.

Your identity naturally shifts when you age as well as when you have a disease or an accident. In these events, as in the dying process, the constricted self begins to be dismantled. The constricted self does not know anything about death; it only knows it is fearful of it and it must hold on to its existence. Thus you are in a struggle, feel out of control, are unable to do your normal life, and seem to become emotionally unbalanced. The constricted self becomes resistant to this state because of fear of loss, wanting safety, and needing to give up control to the forces of caretakers, doctors, drugs, or immobility. The entire reality that has made up your life and who you are in the world begins to disappear. This growing disappearance of your constricted self can create more chaos and a downward spiral into anxiety, uncertainty, and fear.

As you begin to die, resistance is primarily marked by emotional turbulence and reaction. Chaotic fear erupts in your life because you are no longer feeling connected to others or to your environment. There is a sense that you are cast adrift and alone. This chaotic eruption of emotions at this stage is driven by and connected to your past. The erupting fear you may experience is psychologically connected to when you were born.

At birth, you and I were disconnected from the safety of our mother's womb. That experience set the drive and underlying fear of whether we could ever feel safe again, both psychologically and practically. The result of that trauma of separation creates a driving pattern throughout your life. One aspect of that pattern is you will try to connect and stay connected to others in your own unique way. Your tendency will be to hold on to people, things, ideas, and experiences so that you won't feel separated or alone. This struggle originally occurred psychologically at the time of our birth, during what is called the *primal catastrophe*.

Don Riso, in his work with and writings about the Enneagram,[8] asserts that the primal catastrophe is activated when we realize we are alone and separate from the world. The Enneagram's overarching message is that how we individually develop our personalities, the constricted self, is a method of compensation to overcome this fear of separation and aloneness. Learning to release our unique compensation pattern heals the separation and leads us to inner freedom and a more expanded life. The Enneagram is an ancient system of personality typing and release practices that we will use in part 2 of this book.

Roshi Joan Halifax, an American Zen teacher and a teacher of the dying process, describes catastrophe as "the essence of the spiritual path, a series of breakdowns allowing us to discover the threads that weave all of life into a whole cloth."[9] I will explore more fully the compensation pattern of the personality/constricted self versus the development of the expanded self in the second half of this book.

In spiritual terms, as well as in your psychological experience at birth, you were separated from your true expanded self. This is the capital "S" Self, the essence that breathes you, that keeps your body alive, and that keeps you healthy and balanced emotionally. Religious and spiritual traditions give many names to the expanded self presence, such as God, Source, or Light. Through meditation and other spiritual practices, you can learn that the inside energetic force that runs you has been disconnected consciously by the deep unconscious separation we've all experienced.

---

8. Don Riso and Russ Hudson, *The Wisdom of the Enneagram* (New York: Bantam Books, 1999).
9. Joan Halifax, *Being with Dying* (Boston: Shambhala, 2011), 197.

Even with constant practice, most of us take an entire lifetime to become conscious of this existential separation and attempt to learn how to reconnect to the Self. If this reconnection to the Self is not your conscious journey, you will try to fill the emptiness and loneliness of your inner separation through all kinds of external means in the material world. You know the story. Emptiness gets filled through some form of pleasure that is based on wanting the newest, best, youngest, and so on. This emptiness, pleasure seeking, and wanting is what the Buddha called suffering. As you get closer to your death, the chaos of this suffering often gets stronger. It is the "wanting" to escape your life and your death.

Resistance manifests differently in everyone. For some, resistance is experienced psychologically in anxiety, alienation, despair, dread of engulfment, loneliness, neediness, despondency, losing control, feeling unloved, and guilt, among other states. The constricted self rushes into these states by bringing to the forefront of your mind past regrets, guilt, or future longings to escape the present moment of your inner pain. You and I attempt to avoid the present because it is only in the present (space and time) that we can confront thoughts of death. Anytime you face some form of loss, you are at the edge of facing a form of your own death.

Elisabeth Kübler-Ross, in her classic book *On Death and Dying*,[10] describes the stages of dying that she observed in her research at the University of Chicago medical school. Interviewing patients and doctors and sitting with dying patients, she observed the reactions of these individuals as they were told that they had a limited time to live. Kübler-Ross noted that the reaction to dying typically generated some form of resistance and turmoil in the patient's life. In the resistance and turmoil of a person dying, she observed five basic reactions. She noted that these five didn't necessarily occur in sequence, nor did all five always occur in every individual. Depending on the physical and emotional state of the dying process, all five reactions, some of them, or none of them would be present. Almost everyone she observed, however, had all or some of these emotional reactions.

---

10. Kübler-Ross, *On Death and Dying.*

Kübler-Ross indicated that the main component that drives any of these reactions is the resistance of fear. Fear, she described, is what fuels the reactions of denial, anger, bargaining, depression, and acceptance. Kübler-Ross understood that with any of these reactions, a person couldn't let go, accept, and surrender into the beauty of their own death until the fear of dying was confronted.

Exercise: *The Mask You Wear Regarding Your Death*

At this time in your life, what are the emotions, beliefs, and behaviors you have about death? On a page of your notebook draw a large outline of a mask in the shape of a face with a mouth and two eyes and on the back side of the page draw another similar mask. If you are working with a group, be prepared to share your masks.

- Write on the front of the mask a list of beliefs/behaviors/emotions that you present to the world in regard to your inevitable death.

- Write on the back of your mask the beliefs/behaviors/emotions that you do not present to the world in regard to considering your death.

Consider from your own life experience the first four reaction patterns to death that Kübler-Ross observed in dying patients. As you read about these patterns in the following pages, notice your own emotional reactions to them. In your notebook or journal or on your computer, make notes on what you received from each of the following reflections.

Denial

According to Kübler-Ross, people first deny that they are ill or that their physical issue is fatal. Denial is a mask for fear. It is pushing away the thought of losing your identity. *Your personality, your constricted self, does not know or believe in death.* Denial serves as a type of emotional anesthesia that clings to resistance. The fear of losing the security of who you think you are is a shock, and with the shock you tell yourself you can't or won't deal with what is happening. The constricted self does not know how to face mortality. It is in conflict between knowing that the body is not immortal and wanting to believe that it is. The power of denial is operational when the constricted self closes off the present moment and focuses only on maintaining a future that asserts you will somehow always be here, however irrational that appears.

Exercise: *Reflection on Denial*

Let your body relax in a sitting position. Close your eyes. Breathe slowly for a few breaths. As you take your next inhalation, repeat this phrase: "Death is inevitable; I will die sooner or later."

As you exhale, let your denial be released with your breath and say: "It is gone."

Repeat these two phrases five or six times and then sit quietly and notice how you feel emotionally, the thoughts you have, and any body sensations. Write this reflection in your notebook.

Anger

Anger is experienced when you realize that your independent boundaries are being broken and you must live as an impotent victim. Anger also arises from fear. As fear becomes more intense, the anger of the constricted self enters into rage, envy, resentment, and violence. The possibility of death blocks your wants and desires, and anger is how you resist loss of control. You can become terrified because you don't know where you are going or what death is like or what it is like after death. Anger becomes one of your defenses against your terror about dying.

Exercise: *Reflection on Anger*

Let your body relax in a sitting position. Close your eyes. Breathe slowly for a few breaths. As you take your next inhalation, repeat this phrase: "Death comes whether I am prepared or not."

On the exhalation, repeat: "My anger is released as I am present in this moment."

Repeat these two phrases five or six times and then sit quietly and notice how you feel emotionally, the thoughts you have, and any body sensations. Write your reflection in your notebook.

Bargaining

Bargaining is laced with fear. Bargaining occurs when you dampen your anger and try to become rational and positive. The reality of your condition will ultimately break through the anger. One type of bargaining is to hope for a miracle by pleading with God. It is also a hope that the medical community will have a miracle drug, procedure, or process that will return you to health.

Bargaining is similar to what a person would do to make a plea before a court of law. The plea is: "If you let me live, I will…" When the bargaining starts, it is the beginning of letting go of the constricted self. When you begin to bargain, there is a realization that there may be something bigger than you that is in control. There is a bit more honesty and a bit more willingness to face the truth of your death at this stage.

Exercise: *Reflection on Bargaining*

Let your body relax in a sitting position. Close your eyes. Breathe slowly for a few breaths. As you take the next inhalation, repeat the phrase: "My life span is not fixed at a certain age."

On the next exhalation, let the fear be released, repeating the phrase: "Death can be on any day, at any moment."

Repeat these two phrases five or six times and then sit quietly and notice how you feel emotionally, the thoughts you have, and any body sensations. Write your reflection in your notebook.

Depression

Depression arises when you face the powerlessness and aloneness of your coming death. After the plea-bargaining insight that you are really dying sets in, the psychological energy may turn from resistance and effort to powerlessness and feeling depressed. Often what you will experience is the absolute knowledge that death is inevitable. There is no hope of escape. *"Death has come for me."* The psychological and metaphysical awareness can bring a deep sense of disillusionment. It is the realization that your identity is an illusion and it is beginning to fall apart. You begin to perceive that your life is now something different from what you believed it really was. Your life is still something real to you, but in many other ways, it also feels false and meaningless. The anticipation of loss and separation from being alive brings grief and heralds the mental acceptance of immanent mortality. When depression hits your consciousness, the realization occurs that you are losing all hope and the situation will not improve. The struggle to let go to your dying may seem to get darker and darker, accompanied by uncertainty and a growing fear of no control over your life.

Exercise: *Reflection on Depression*

Let your body relax in a sitting position. Close your eyes. Breathe slowly for a few breaths. As you take the next inhalation, repeat the phrase: "My body, my friends, and my family can no longer help me."

On the next exhalation, repeat the phrase: "I let go of holding on to this life."

Repeat these two phrases five or six times and then sit quietly and notice how you feel emotionally, the thoughts you have, and any body sensations you feel. Write your reflection in your notebook.

Despair

To these first four reaction patterns to dying that Kübler-Ross described, I want to add the reaction of despair. We will consider her fifth one later on. Despair can come silently and unsuspectingly when you reach the end of your physical and emotional rope. This happens when there is nothing more you can hold on to in order to save your life. All medical treatment has run out or completely stopped, hospice has arrived and is giving palliative care, and doctors, nurses, friends, and family have given up hope that you can survive. As you approach death, you may feel increasingly powerless and pessimistic about your life. You may lose heart, abandon any hope of recovery, and become despondent toward family and friends. Many people know in their hearts they are dying but are not accustomed to facing that thought because it is too terrifying for them. It is truly difficult to grasp in your mind that you are dying. Despair is related to the recognition that nothing can be done to save your life.

All the hope of physical recovery or of a drug to extend your life a little longer or anything else healers can do for you cannot happen now. This conviction can move you to passivity and withdrawal. This state of despair envelops you in a feeling of no meaning, emptiness, and apathy. As the magic of the expectation of your desire to continue to live fails, it is difficult to accept the thought of your dying, even though in the depths of your heart you know death is inevitable.

Exercise: *Reflection on Despair*

Let your body relax in a sitting position. Close your eyes. Breathe slowly for a few breaths. As you take the next inhalation, repeat the phrase: "My body is fragile, I am vulnerable, and my life is almost over."

On the next exhalation, repeat the phrase: "I let go, and I accept what is happening to me."

Repeat these two phrases five or six times, and then sit quietly and notice how you feel emotionally, the thoughts you have, and any body sensations you feel. Write your reflection in your notebook.

Chapter 3
Step 1:
Running Away from Death

We humans cannot bear much Reality.

—T. S. ELIOT

In the Sufi teaching tradition of Islam there is a character, Mulla Nasrudin, who is characterized as the "wise fool." Here is my retelling of one of those stories. Mulla Nasrudin bumped into Death on a street in Mecca. Death registered a look of surprise and the fool's blood went cold. That night, Nasrudin fled on a sleek stallion and rode away from Mecca faster than the wind. The next day, he was in a hillside village far from Mecca. Rounding the bend in the road, he again bumped into Death. In terror he heard Death say, "I was surprised to see you as you were in Mecca. I had an appointment with you in this distant village this very morning." [11]

Many of us will naturally feel afraid when we first face the possibility of dying due to an accident, a catastrophic diagnosis of disease, or simply the process of aging. Like Nasrudin, many of us try to run away from the time of our death. As we face death, we will fear pain and the loss of all that is precious to us about life. This is the normal part of grief we all will feel. We will fear and grieve the

---

11. Idries Shah, *The Pleasantries of the Incredible Mulla Nasrudin* (New York: Penguin, 1993).

loss of our capacities, our possessions, our relationships, and our dignity, and face what is beyond death.

What we often don't recognize is that, in our daily lives, we experience many similar losses. We are unconsciously impacted by fear of death beneath the day-to-day experience of loss in our lives. Many other events confront you daily to grieve as loss, such as a precious artifact from your parents accidentally breaks, your children leave home and "their" room in the house to live on their own, or your long-term relationship ends in divorce. When you confront a disease or fatal illness, however, it finally hits you that now your entire life, your reality as a physical being, is going to leave this life and that everything you know and have experienced will be over and gone. At this point, you can become traumatized, despairing, and even terrified. You try to run away from death as fast as you can. You have no idea what is going to happen to you. Unconsciously and even consciously like Nasrudin, in the previous story, you can feel trapped by death's closeness.

Fear is often what drives you to seek to sustain your life through heroic medical treatments when your physical condition worsens. These interventions often result in a quality of life that becomes disabling and worse than your life before you take the treatment. You and I will attempt the heroic intervention because we view death as an enemy that we must fight and overcome. However heroically we fight death, it will still win. Many of us say that we want to accept death when it comes. Accepting death sounds simple, but there is still fear and it will be a deep challenge for you. Rather than running away from death as the basic option, the challenge is to discover if there is a possibility of facing death differently. Can you find a means or process of facing your fear with courage?

The ancient and famous Tibetan yogi Milarepa, after he left his old path as a robber, was afraid of his death and what would come after his death because he had killed many people. His fear of death led him to a snowcapped mountain cave in Tibet where he meditated on the uncertainty of the moment of his death. Through long years of meditation practice, he reached the true nature of an awakened mind, and his fear of death vanished. Milarepa experienced the triumph over terror. What he teaches us is that it is possible to be fully alive in our bodies, living happy lives and in service to others, and not be afraid of death. This is the option you and I want to discover before we face physical dying.

Life and death are amazing gifts. The Buddhist teachings say that a human life is so precious and the odds and chance of you or I being born into this life are so small that this gift of life is like a blind turtle rising from the depths of a vast ocean to poke its head through a small floating golden ring. Life and death are actually one event. *How you live and how you die are the same thing.* Learning to live and learning to die are the amazing gifts you've been given.

You are like the turtle poking your head through the golden ring of this existence. If you haven't committed to learn to live well and die well, you need to ask yourself and explore inwardly now for help to do it. Life is short and you and I need to take this moment in time to gain the wisdom of our heart as we begin to ask different questions. Roshi Joan Halifax sums up our challenge: "One who is free of fear knows that at the deepest level of realization there is no suffering, no birth, no death." [12]

In this chapter, you can explore through a series of exercises your beliefs about death, the question of suffering and pain and how to confront it, how meaning plays a part as you face resistance to death, the gift of acceptance of your death and how meditation is a significant means to prepare now for dying.

Exercise: *Beliefs About Death*

Reflect on the following questions of belief, knowledge, and practice.

- Intuitively, will my death be painful? If so, how am I to prepare for dealing with the pain?

- What is it like for me to be accepting of my own dying while living? Give some examples.

- What do I believe about whether there is an afterlife of some kind?

- What other questions come to mind about approaching my death?

---

12. Halifax, *Being with Dying*, 132.

Step 1

Write your initial responses in your notebook or computer. If you are in a group, share your answers.

Exercise: *The Constricted Self*

The ego or constricted self has the qualities of resistance when we are living inside it. Examine what you need to know about your constricted self in order to recognize how these resistant qualities can play out in your life. Write your responses in your journal as a way to continue observing your constricted self and how it works in your life. If in a group, share your thoughts.

- Describe what you think your constricted self is and how it plays out daily in your life.
- Make a list of the times when you experienced the constricted self as the dominant force in your life.
- When have you been in resistance and then shifted into self-acceptance about a struggle you've had? Give an example.
- What is it like to be accepting of your own dying while living? Give examples.
- What do you do to avoid or escape the fear of the present moment? Why?

Suffering and Pain

In the classic children's book *The Velveteen Rabbit*, Rabbit asks the Skin Horse, "Does it hurt to be Real?" The Skin Horse says, "Generally, by the time you are Real most of your hair has been loved off and your eyes drop out and you get loose in the joints and very shabby. But these things don't matter at all because once you are Real you can't be ugly except to people who don't understand."[13] Most people are concerned about the pain they will experience as they die. Like the Velveteen Rabbit, we ask: Does it hurt? Is death going to be painful as we

---

13. Margery Williams and William Nicholson (Illustrator), *The Velveteen Rabbit* (New York: Doubleday, 1991), 6–7.

get our hair loved off, our eyes drop out, and we get "loose in the joints and very shabby"? It is true that as we age and as we have physical ailments, we may feel more physical discomfort and pain coming to us at the end of our lives.

Throughout life, we are dependent on the strength of our bodies, but as we age this strength naturally deteriorates or is affected by various ailments and diseases. We become increasingly unable to care for ourselves. The loss of control is difficult to accept, but what is worse is judging ourselves and grieving the loss of the younger, more mobile person we were. To make matters worse, pain may be exacerbated by psychological feelings of helplessness, abandonment, shame, lack of control, and isolation. The reality is that at any age by an accident, disease, or war we may suddenly die. At any moment of our lives we may face the pain of our dying.

As all aspects of your life change, it is easy to feel vulnerable and powerless. It seems as though you will die a thousand little deaths before you physically die. As you experience growing uncertainty and the disintegration of the normal patterns of your life, physical and mental loss begin to tighten your body and increase your emotional reactions. As you experience pain and the dissolution of your body and mind, you may begin to enter an increasing cycle of deepening inner suffering at the loss. *The truth we want to explore, however, is as you move into the various stages of your death, physical pain may become inevitable but psychological suffering can become optional for you.* Remember what the Skin Horse said to Rabbit in the book, *The Velveteen Rabbit*: "…By the time you are Real, most of your hair has been loved off, and your eyes drop out and you get loose in the joints and very shabby … but once you are Real you can't become unreal again. It lasts for always." [14]

The Nature of Pain

Science tells us that pain is really made up of non-pain components. The components consist of sensations, intensity, and rhythmic pulsation. You continually interpret these sensations as pain and you make up a mental story about the experience of your pain. You and I make up these pain stories all the time. For

---

14. Ibid., 6–7.

example, your story may be, "My pain of arthritis grows worse because I have to be on my feet all the time. I can't get rid of this pain!" The pain is neither good nor bad, but the story you made up about the pain creates the distress you have.

Pain is part of the daily drama of being a human. How you approach pain is essential to both your living and dying. If you are willing to explore the elements of your pain, you may come to a realization that you don't have to be so upset and reactive when you are in pain. Pain has a transient nature; it is always changing in one way or another. To explore pain may create a different pattern of thought, such as: "I will sit and notice the pulsation of pain in my arthritic knee and feel myself relax. I offer my pain on behalf of the many that have even worse pain." Consider the notion that the courage to face your pain consciously may actually be a gift of patience, a development of strength to endure when needed, a means to help nourish compassion, and a deeper capacity to open to gratitude and the insight that life is fragile and precious.

Joan Halifax once asked His Holiness the Dalai Lama about what to do when pain can't be worked with through spiritual or psychological means, and he was emphatic that we should always do the best to help relieve pain and suffering, whether with modern pharmacology or meditation and understanding. [15] In that conversation with Joan Halifax, he went on to tell her that if medications are used, they can cloud the physical and psychological mind, but not to worry because the nature of the True Mind—that essence of ourselves beyond the physical and psychological mind—is what is liberated at the moment of death. He affirmed that if the dying person has had a strong meditation practice then even if medications are taken and the person is not very conscious, it is still possible at the moment of death to become one with the nature of the Expanded Mind. Like the Skin Horse says, "Once you are Real these things don't matter at all." [16]

---

15. Halifax, *Being with Dying*.
16. Williams, *The Velveteen Rabbit, 5*.

Exercise: *Confronting Pain*

Either prerecord this exercise to guide you with your eyes closed or have a partner or a friend read it to you. Give sufficient pauses between each statement. Write your reflections in your notebook.

• Close your eyes, take several deep breaths, and consciously take some time to relax your body.

• Remember a time when you were in pain. The pain can be physical or emotional. Imagine now that you are in an intense state of discomfort and pain. Imagine letting yourself be present and simply observing in this situation of your pain.

• Look through and beyond the pain of wanting it to be different and of struggling to push the pain away. Without wanting it to be different, simply acknowledge that you feel and have pain.

• Move your attention into your heart area. Feel the warmth, pulsating, caring, and comforting feeling radiating through your body pain. As you stay centered in your heart, affirm and say to yourself, "My True Mind nature is free from all the pain."

• Breathe into the heaviness of the pain with this affirming heart and exhale the cool light air out of your heart into your body. Continue with this pattern of breathing into the heaviness and breathing out lightness.

• Be present with this pain. Imagine you are breathing through all the pores of your body.

• Watch the pain shift, move, and dissolve. Be conscious of the inner peace and gratitude that you can be with pain and move beyond pain. Rest in this peace.

• Open your eyes and move your body when you are ready to do so.

Exercise: *Confronting Physical and Emotional Suffering*

Consider how you confront both physical and emotional suffering. Contemplate and write in your notebook or on your computer your responses to the following questions. If working in a group, share your answers.

- What would you do if you were in physical pain or discomfort? Would you face the pain, ignore it, deny it, drug yourself, or embrace it?

- Which of the previous options do you choose today to deal with physical pain?

- How would you feel and what would you do if you were not given permission to grieve your life (as you know it now) as you entered the death process? Perhaps if you died suddenly of a heart attack or a car accident.

- How will you react if you are judged by family or friends if you get out of control with any of the reactions that Kübler-Ross and I describe (denial, anger, bargaining, depression, despair) due to your physical and emotional circumstances?

- How will you handle other people—spouse, family, friends, caregivers—when they become upset with you because you begin to withdraw and isolate yourself?

- How will you know when you are acting like a victim to your situation and give your power away to your family or caregivers? Give some examples of how you've responded as a victim up to now in your life.

- What are your strategies for working with the intensity of pain? Examples would be trying to ignore it, using drugs, exercising, or finding alternatives like painting your pain, setting your pain to music, writing about it, softening into the pain mentally by accepting it, or exploring the sensations of your pain mentally (where it is located in the body, its intensity, etc.).

- How do you work with your pain? The following phrases may support your practice in being aware of pain. As pain arises now in your life, experiment with one or more of these phrases as a focus for you.

    * "I am kind to the source of my pain."

* "I realize that my pain is not permanent."

* "I let go of my want to control pain."

* "I know that I am not my pain."

* "My pain is neither a good process nor a bad process in me."

* "I know that the pain does not limit the kindness of my heart for myself."

Life's Meaning as Part of Resistance

I remember my father saying to me before he died, "What have I done in my life that was worthwhile?" My father died more than thirty years ago. At that time, few books about death were available. I did, however, read a book about near-death experiences. The book was Raymond Moody's *Life After Life*. I read it when my father got sick because I had hoped Moody would give me a glimpse of what my father was experiencing.

In this book, Moody described how to relieve painful suffering and how to accept death. Moody suggested that, as we die, it is important to recall our worth, significance, and the meaning of our lives. Because of Moody's insights, when my father asked me the question, "What have I done in my life that was worthwhile?" I was able to have a conversation with him about the qualities I saw in him. I told my father that he was a giving, reliable, and kind man. It was clear to me that my simple sharing shifted his tightness and uncertainty about his dying. My words put a smile of love on his face. My father's simple question is one many of us will ask about our worth and meaning at the end of our lives. I have no idea where he got the question, but it was an important one for his dying process, and I believe it is important for all of us.

The playwright Edward Albee famously said, "What could be worse than getting to the end of your life and realizing you hadn't lived it?" [17] The important question then is: What is meaningful in your life today? In the process of dying, if you have not explored your inner life and what is meaningful for you, you will

17. Academy of Achievement, "Edward Albee—Academy of Achievement." http://www.achievement.org/achiever/edward-albee/#biography.

Step
1

not easily move forward to the acceptance and surrender stage of your dying. You will not move forward to accept your death until you feel safe and have let down your defenses. When you are willing to let down your defenses, you will begin to feel relieved and accept the goodness and beauty in life, no matter your physical condition. If you are willing to change or release even one negative or selfish pattern, you are a step further toward freedom in your dying.

It has been found by psychologists such as Abraham Maslow and Viktor Frankl, among others, that simply existing day by day working at a job, making money, being housed, being fed, and having some form of safety and security is actually unfulfilling, empty, and has little or no essential meaning for one's life. You know that when there is some form of personal sacrifice or devotion to something larger than yourself, your life takes on an inner radiance of purpose and meaning. Life has value if you see yourself as part of something greater than personal survival. This something larger can be found in your spiritual life, your family, your community, and society at large with all its issues and concerns. All this is expressed in some form of service to others. That sense of service to others was what gave meaning and worth to my father's life. Frankl, in his classic book *Man's Search for Meaning,*[18] said, "In some ways suffering ceases to be suffering at the moment it finds a meaning, such as the meaning of a sacrifice." And "Those who have a 'why' to live, can bear with almost any 'how.'"

Exercise: *The Meaning of Your Life*

Remember, you will die. When you go to bed at night, you assume and are convinced you will wake in the morning. But some of us do not wake up in the morning. Also, some part of you is convinced you will live to an old age. But you know that at some point in your life, death will take you and you may not be old and gray. In this exercise, you have the opportunity to look back on your life and evaluate if it has had meaning and value for you.

---

18. Viktor Frankl, *Man's Search for Meaning* (New York: Simon and Schuster, 1984), 22.

Prerecord to listen to and be guided by the exercise or have a partner or friend read it to you. It is best to lie down on a bed or on the floor for this exercise. Give time to reflect between statements.

- Relax your body by tensing and releasing your shoulders, arms, hands, and other parts of your body and then close your eyes and breathe deeply as you focus your breath in your heart.

- In this state of calm relaxation, imagine you are a very old person on your deathbed. Ask yourself your age. Imagine that your face has deep wrinkles, there is stiffness in your limbs, your breath is shallow, your hands and feet are numb, and you feel deeply tired and frail. Your body is ready to die.

- Notice where you are—in a home, in a hospital, where? Is anyone with you? What is this old person like that you are? Ask yourself, "Do I like myself as this older person?"

- As the old person, ask yourself, "What have I achieved in life? What have I done to create a life of meaning?"

- Imagine now that you are ten years older than you are right now and you are lying on your deathbed. How old are you? Who is with you, what have you achieved that is meaningful by this time? Recognizing yourself ten years from now, what can you do today to gain what you want as meaningful for your life? Said another way, ask yourself, "What can I do today to have a meaningful death tomorrow?"

- Imagine that you will die in one year. You are lying in your bed, preparing to die. What can you do right now to support a peaceful death? What would you do differently from what you are doing today? What might you need to forgive in yourself and in others? Who might you need to forgive? Ask yourself, "From what do I need to let go?" Imagine you will die in a month. Who do you want with you to share your last moments of this life? Ask yourself, "What has been meaningful for me as I look at my life in the past six months?"

• As you are falling asleep, you realize you will die tonight. Ask yourself, "What is the biggest gift I have received in this life? With whom will I share this gift before I die?"

Lie still for a while with eyes closed. Absorb these different stages of dying and what has been meaningful for you at each stage. When you get up, record your insights in your notebook or on your computer. Reread the questions in each section to remind you of your reflections.

Exercise: *What Gives Me Meaning?*

Reflect on and answer the following questions. Write your responses in your notebook. If in a group, share your answers.

• What have I accomplished in my life?

• What has given me purpose and meaning throughout my life?

• What have I done to help, support, and serve others?

• How much care, respect, and attention have I been willing to give to my relationships?

• Where in my life have I stretched beyond my limits with courage to heal my psychological wounds?

• Do I have awareness and perspective about my life, and have I accepted myself and my life as I've lived it?

Acceptance

In the eye of the storm after the initial realization that your death is coming for you, there arrives Kübler-Ross's stage of acceptance and surrender. If you as a dying person have worked through the chaos of your emotions and resistance to dying, you can enter into a place of calm and peace. In acceptance, you are giving up and surrendering to your own death.

Many spiritual teachers have been heard to say, "Death happens. It is just death, and how we meet death is up to us." How will you meet your death? In the following list, check off the ones that are appropriate for you now. These statements are some of the acceptance characteristics that you will face as you are dying. As you contemplate them, write in your journal what comes to mind about the conditions in your life that are currently creating your response and feelings. If you are in a group, share your responses.

- I can sense the inevitability of my own mortality.

- My coming death is marked with remorse, regret, and a feeling of inward hopelessness that I haven't fulfilled my purpose in life.

- I can feel that I am close to my death. The sand of my life is rapidly passing through the hourglass toward my death. It is going faster than I thought it would.

- I know I have not touched rock bottom about the inevitability of my death. What I am resisting is …

- I am aware of what calm and peace would feel like in the process of my dying.

- I believe there is still a strong possibility of my continued existence. I am not going to die yet.

- I sense a suicidal panic attack due to not being completely aligned with the physical and psychospiritual aspects of my death.

- I am tired, weak, and want to sleep like a teenager. I want to go unconscious and avoid the threat of death.

- I want to be drugged and not be aware of my dying.

- I have not moved into my interior self because I still fall back into fear of dependence, neediness, and being a burden, and not feeling lovable.

- I still have a strong yearning for what I have not fulfilled at this point in my life. What is it?

- I am terrified of the hidden, unconscious, dark shadow in my mind of dying and losing control of my life.

- I have strong anxiety and fear of being separated from all that I love.

To accept your death is to accept the fear of dying. Not fearing death is all a matter of perspective! The filmmaker Woody Allen famously said, "It's not that I'm afraid to die, I just don't want to be there when it happens."[19]

Exercise: *Accepting Myself*

Respond in your journal to the following questions. Before answering them, become still in silence and breathe deeply so that your mind and heart settle and you can listen to the deepest part of yourself. If in a group, share your thoughts.

- What is it that I am afraid of accepting about my dying?
- Describe everything you think of as "you."
- What is the lifestyle I have lived? Is there another style of life I would have preferred?
- Describe the characteristics of your life that are easy to accept and those difficult to accept.
- What do I most appreciate about my life?
- How do I want to be remembered after I die?

Exercise: *How a Person Dies*

Thus far we have considered some of the challenges we face as we confront the fact of our dying. The following visualization practice is to shift to the positive aspect of what dying can be for you. Record these instructions to guide you or have a partner or friend read them to you. For this exercise, lie on a bed or on the floor. Give time to pause between statements. Record your experience in your notebook or computer.

- Take a few moments to relax your body, breathe deeply, and close your eyes.

---

19. Woody Allen, *Without Feathers* (New York: Random House, 1975), 99.

- Imagine a person—it could be a spouse, family member, or friend—has just died. See them in a bed with eyes closed and not moving.

- As you visualize the body, see their consciousness take the form of a small ball of light moving from the base of their spine up to the top of their head. Observe that light quickly flying out from the body at the top of their head like a shooting star and then dissolving into the heart of a Presence of immense light above the person.

- As you see this illuminated being, ask or pray that the person be freed from suffering as they become merged into the light of this Presence.

- Imagine this small light becomes like a star being released from this Presence into an even vaster luminosity. In this expanding sky of luminosity, the individual entity is no longer present. Become aware that they have merged into the sky of luminosity and there is only this star that is the true luminous nature of their being.

- Remain in this state of awareness for a few moments observing this luminosity. Be aware of any emotional feelings, body sensations, or thoughts you may be having.

This exercise was to give you an insight into the luminous nature of your being as the potential experience of your death. This short practice gives you the experience of the light of the true nature of your own mind and how it can benefit all beings, especially those you are leaving behind. To know and experience before you die the luminous nature of what death holds for you gives you the possibility to accept and be present to your own experience of dying even now before death comes for you. As I will describe in the next section, one of the most powerful ways to keep working with your mind and your own death before you die is meditation.

Meditation

Meditation is a practice that prepares you for death. A daily meditation practice trains you to release and let go of your constricted self every day. The practical function of a daily practice is to train the mind to let go of the busy resistances of daily life. When you are in the dying process, meditation practice prepares you to relax, stabilizes your mind, opens you to compassion, and creates a dynamic shift that reduces your anxiety and fear.

In many ways, meditation is a type of dying. It is first a letting go of your mental patterns, thoughts, and emotions that occupy your daily life. Whether using the breath as a focus or a mantra or a chant that repeats over and over there is a letting go of the mental world and a "falling into" your senses and then a growing expansion beyond the boundaries of your body. As meditation becomes deeper, the sense of your identity weakens and your ego can become frightened just like you will experience as you go deeper into your dying process.

The value of meditation is that beneath the busy mind is a space of peace and calm. Meditation concentration accesses this space of peace and calm by allowing you to let go of your patterns as well as your needs, fears, and wants. The fruit of this practice occurs in an open space of knowing. In this knowing, you realize that you have everything you need within you. Thus the letting go to death is just another letting go of what you practice in meditation. By learning to let go in your daily life, you let death take care of itself as it occurs in the natural course of your life.

Unfortunately, if you have not learned to let go daily in meditation, your resistance to your death may be a time of unrest, confusion, and terrifying emotionality. A developed meditation practice can be the most powerful tool for you when you are dying.

Exercise: *Reflection on Meditation Practice*

Respond in your journal to the following questions. Before answering them, become still in silence and breathe deeply so that your mind and heart settle and you can listen to the deepest part of yourself. If in a group, share your thoughts.

- If you have a meditation practice, describe it. How much time do you spend practicing daily? Consider how you believe it can help you in preparing for your death. Is the practice strong enough for the time when you will die? Do you need to alter or do a different practice or in some way deepen your meditation practice? Simply reflect on the value and daily helpfulness of your practice for your dying.

- If you don't have a meditation practice, decide if you want a practice. If you want to experiment with meditation, seek out a form of meditation practice that would be appropriate for you. My book and CDs can help guide this process as one way to explore meditation.

Sogyal Rinpoche urges that we practice meditation because "We are fragmented into so many different aspects. We don't know who we really are, or what aspects of ourselves we should identify with or believe in. So many contradictory voices, dictates, and feelings fight for control over our inner lives that we find ourselves scattered everywhere, in all directions, leaving nobody at home. Meditation, then, is bringing the mind home." [20]

20. Sogyal, *The Tibetan Book of Living and Dying.*

Chapter 4
Step 2:
From Resistance to Letting Go

The spirit flight, the ecstatic flight of the shaman, is a journey beyond death.
To learn how to die is to learn how to live, for you are claimed for life and never be
claimed for death. In a sense a person of power spends a whole life learning how to die.
—ALBERTO VILLOLDO

Surrendering to your death is losing everything, but it is also gaining the possibility of what you have always wanted unconsciously. Why you fear surrendering to your death is that it feels extremely scary to face the unknown. You do not know what you will be gaining if you surrender to it. You don't want to surrender or confront the fear and the accompanying chaos because your constricted self wants to be in control. It is more comfortable for you to be in the constricted self than to be in the unknown. What is often the case regarding our death is that the constricted self goes into fear, depression, and despair many times before it is willing to let go. *To surrender your physical life is to let go of the constricted self, this personality identity that you've created and lived with all your life.*

What is the constricted self deeply frightened to give up? The constricted self is giving up the connection to the outside world as well as all it has experienced within you. Most important, it is giving up the body that houses it. It does not want to let go into the unknown, into totally new territory. Clinging to the outside world has been a habit developed from birth. The deep challenge of your constricted self is that it has to give up all its habits, judgments, emotions, thoughts, friends, family, and the materiality it has worked so hard to acquire, let alone the body that you believe you are. To your conscious mind, you must give it all up, but this seems impossible. Yet the suffering at the end of physical life becomes so great that you can feel a release is imminent even when you are afraid of it. What is the experience of dying you are releasing into?

Dying brings you so many different kinds of experiences. As your body and mind alter from the physical dissolving, you may have blissful or not so pleasant experiences in the process. You may have various strange hallucinations that are related to the medicines you are taking. You may have reactions to the autointoxication, which refers to your own body toxins poisoning you as the dying process proceeds. As you deepen into dying, you can experience altered states of consciousness. Sometimes there are mystical experiences of encountering deceased relatives, profound insights, and a deep sense of purpose about your life and what lies ahead that can't be shared in words.

If you take a moment and look back at your life, you will notice that there have been points of major changes where you have had to let go of something. When forced to change, you made a shift. All your life, you have had transitional periods. You have made major changes and entered into the unknown. It is important to identify those times.

As difficult and challenging as it may seem, trust that capital "S" expanded Self in you that gives you a knowing that you are more prepared for this major transition of death than you think. Isaac Asimov, scientist and author, ruefully said, "Life is pleasant. Death is peaceful. It's the transition that's troublesome."[21] The transitions are only troublesome when you are not prepared for the dying!

In this chapter, you will understand that birth and death mirror each other and this can create for you a revelation that death fully understood is a natural part of living day to day. I also present eight characteristics of letting go to death

---

21. Isaac Asimov, *Fantastic Voyage II: Destination Brain*, Vol. 2 (London: Grafton, 1988), 275.

that is the key transition process and a wonderful dying preparation for yourself and others called a loving kindness practice.

Transitions from Birth to Death

Birth and death as transitions have similar physical, psychological, and spiritual components. Birth teaches us about death and death teaches us about a new birth.

Even if a woman is wanting to get pregnant, there is often a psychological and physical shock as things change in her body and psyche. Even though we know intellectually that we will die, at the same time there is a denial that "It will never happen to me." When dying begins, we are often shocked and not ready.

The pregnant mother begins to nest and gather all that is needed for the arrival of the baby. A conscious dying person reverses the process, giving things away and getting practical things in order for their family, so as to complete their life.

The pregnant mother can wonder if she can find room in her heart to love another new being. The dying person wonders how to let go of the ones they love.

The pregnant woman may feel the body has a mind of its own as the baby grows. The dying person may experience the dying of the body as someone they can't control.

As the time comes for the birthing of the child, the mother worries about the process of giving birth. "Will it hurt? Will I like the baby when it arrives? What will the baby be like? Will I have supportive, nurturing people to help me?" And so on through many feelings of anxiety. In reality, as the dying person approaches their death, they have the same anxiety with many of the same questions.

The body knows how to give birth if interventions are kept to a minimum. Too often, medical interventions can prolong the dying process and interrupt the natural inner experience of the one dying.

There is a restless, despairing stage in childbirth when, after hours and hours of trying, the woman cannot seem to birth the baby. In the dying process, the intense struggle between holding on to life and letting go may seem endless. In the New Testament, Jesus speaks to his disciples about his death. He says,

"When a woman is about to give birth, she is in great pain. But after it is all over, she forgets the pain and is happy, because she has brought a child into the world. You are now very sad. But later I will see you, and you will be so happy that no one will be able to change the way you feel." [22]

As with the birthing process, fear and confusion can interfere with the dying process, for the one dying and for the family and caregivers. Surrender and letting go are needed in both dying and birthing. In the end, as you go through the positive nature of this transition, no one will be able to change the way you feel. Kahil Gibran, in the book *The Prophet*, said, "You would know the secret of death. But how shall you find it unless you seek it in the heart of life?" [23]

Step 2

Exercise: *Life Transition*

Remember a time when you made a significant transition into a new stage in your life. Contemplate these questions and record them in your notebook. If working with a group, share your answers.

- At what age did you make this important transition?
- What did you have to let go of from the previous stage of life to move through the transition?
- In the transition, what did you feel was pulling you into the next stage?
- What did you need to be receptive to in order to open to a new stage of your life?
- What did you need to respond to even though the outcome was unknown to you?
- What were three actions you took that helped you engage in what was pulling you forward into the next stage of your life?

---

22. *Holy Bible: Contemporary English Version,* John 16:21–22 (New York: American Bible Society, 1995), 1307.
23. Kahlil Gibran, *The Prophet* (New York: Alfred A. Knopf, 1923), 80.

The Revelation

Death can become an amazing revelation to you as you begin to let go to it. As you become more adjusted to and accepting of the prognosis that you are going to die, you become increasingly prepared to accept that dying is part of your living. When you enter into this place of acceptance and surrender to what is happening to you, there is a growing awareness that death is real and you will die. For some, there comes the deep insight that everything dies and this is natural. This awareness begins to open the door of your heart and mind that you will be separating from physical life. From this realization, a shift occurs away from the negative thoughts of the constricted self that has dominated your psychological mind as you struggled in the chaos of resistance.

The Indian saint Shri Nisargadatta said, "The mind creates the abyss and the heart crosses it." [24] In the chaos, you enter a dark night of the soul as your mind goes deeper inward to face death and painfully experience a stripping away of the elements of your constricted self. With this revelation and surrender to your coming death, the outer battle of psychological struggle comes to an end. As you surrender, the mind becomes still. With the mind quiet and stilled, the inner world of your life begins to be revealed without outer distraction.

St. John of the Cross, the fifteenth-century Spanish Catholic priest and mystic, wrote the famous book *The Dark Night of the Soul*. This is John's account of his journey of surrender and awakening spiritually. At one point in the book, he writes about his struggle to surrender and be free: "I will cry out for death and mourn my living while I am held here for my sins. O my God, when will it be that I can truly say: now I live because I do not die?" Finally, in response to his struggle, he says, "That perfect knowledge was of peace and holiness held at no remove in profound solitude; it was something so secret that I was left stammering, *transcending all knowledge*." [25]

As it did with St. John of the Cross, the inner world opens itself to you in a revelation. The inner world reveals that there is no personality, there is no

Step 2

---

24. Nisargadatta Maharaj, *I Am That,* translated by Maurice Frydman, 2nd American (revised) edition (Durham, NC: The Acorn Press, 2012), 8.

25. St. John of the Cross, *Dark Night of the Soul* (Radford, VA: Wilder Publications, 2008), 83.

constricted self; rather, there is only the true expanded self in which you are everything. What seems like a sudden knowledge has in fact taken years to reveal itself to you. All too often, this knowledge comes at our death. For most of us, we have been cut off and disconnected from our expanded self by our constricted self our entire life.

As I've described, this constricted self is not who you are. It formed very early in your life from your interpretations of your experience and the way others described and judged you. This constricted self was created to survive the deep separation you experienced at birth, and you continued to develop it out of your continuing need to survive. This constricted self began and can continue to tighten your consciousness and perception and wider awareness of everyday life as well as spiritual dimensions, if you do not learn a different way. *The truth in this revelation at the end of your life is very clear: You have been alienated from your expanded self all your life, but it is what you really are.* The question you face now before you confront your actual dying is, "What is my expanded self and how do I open to it?" Whether or not you discover this expanded self now, it is this true self-presence that will take you through the transition of your dying.

Exercise: *Who Am I?*

Who you are, your identity, is the ongoing question throughout your life. Contemplate the following questions and add your reflections to your notebook.

- What in me doesn't want to let go?
- What do I need and what could help me the most as I prepare to die?
- What do I fear the most about my physical condition of sickness or dying?
- What is it like to let go of something I have cherished most of my life? What is that something?
- Create a six-month story in which you know you are dying. How would you prepare for your death?
- What is the meaning of your life up to this point? Is this what you want to take into your death?
- Describe how you would answer the question "Who am I?"

Eight Characteristics of Letting Go of Death

When the revelation comes to you that you are going to die, the letting-go process deepens. There are typically eight characteristics that you can observe within you as you move closer to the doorway. These nine are in a general way the normal sequence, but each person may respond differently and have a different unique sequence of responses. These eight characteristics will give you some sense of the process as you move toward your death:

- The stage of resistance ends when the constricted self experiences a feeling of despair, which means that you have no hope of remaining alive.

- The constricted self has been your protection, but as it loosens its hold on your psyche there is a movement into feelings of dread, panic, and even for some a sense of wanting to commit suicide because you feel you are losing your identity as a person. If your expanded self opens too soon into the mind and heart of your being, it can cause the constricted self to contract suddenly back into fear. At this transition stage, you must let the constricted self dissolve in its own timing.

- As the outer battle of resistance ends with the inner release to your dying, the outer world slips away and the expanded self of awareness begins to reveal itself.

- The will to live is strong in you as part of your biological imperative, even as you move closer to death. Even though you begin to let go, you can again resist and let go again and resist again.

- As you move closer to death, the constricted self has no choice and no place to go but to let go or remain in resistance and terror.

- As you surrender, the expanded self emerges in your consciousness. There are often feelings of being engulfed by it, plunging out of control, and a sense of being trapped by this new consciousness as the constricted self tries to regain control and survive.

- As the expanded self emerges in you, it continues to dissolve your ego identity as a personality and you experience your constricted self disappearing into silence.

- As the silence within you grows, a deep inner expansion begins as a gradual movement into a spatial awareness. This awareness of space is the emergence of what is meant as the expanded self.

Dying Preparation for Self and Others

In many spiritual traditions, there are also practices that emphasize compassion and kindness for yourself and others.

- Relationships: The first stage of preparation as you soften into your letting go to your death is to resolve any incomplete issues you have with others in your life. Resolution is necessary because it shifts you out of resistance to others and enables you to come to completion in your relationships. You need relationship resolution in order to embrace your journey into and beyond death with a clear mind and open heart.

- Fears: This phase of surrender is also a time to express your natural fears to family members about leaving them. It is an important time for you to express any sadness, grief, or other emotions that you have held back from yourself and for others. It is a time to admit guilt, shame, and pain and seek forgiveness in such things as not being honest in your life with others, regrets about incomplete relationships, actions and rejections that hurt others, fears regarding any financial burdens that you may be leaving behind for others to take care of, or any spiritual fears about what lies beyond your physical death.

- Family Issues: Most important, this time is to clear any issues between family members and you. Your dying can bring healing between family members, resolving old hurts and eliminating conflicting energy patterns that may have existed for generations. You will want to settle as many inner and outer disturbances as possible so that, as you leave this life, you feel free and complete.

- Interpersonal Contact: As you move into this acceptance stage of healing with others, it is not the time to isolate yourself from family and friends. Contact with others will give comfort, assurance, and support as the journey of your dying deepens. The caution here is to own and affirm to others the limits of interaction and your physical boundaries.

- Self-Care: As you die, you need to be in your own rhythm with family, friends, and caregivers, as you are with yourself. You will need freedom to sleep, eat, pray, and meditate as you remain in a consciously aware state. As endings create sorrow, express to yourself first and then to others around you that you need space in your day to seek inner quiet and solace. Simply having people sit silently with you can bring great comfort. You will begin to discover that those around you will bring a great deal of caring and love for you as you let go of your own resistance to dying. This is a precious moment in your life.

- Good-byes: Most of all, it is time for affectionate good-byes, forgiveness, and letting go of negative attitudes, fears, disappointments, and actions with yourself and others.

As you are considering your preparation for death as well as when you are in your dying process, there is a wonderful meditation practice that comes from the Tibetan Buddhist tradition for self-caring and self-compassion.

Exercise: *Sending and Receiving Love and Kindness for Self*

This meditation, a practice called Tonglen, is a preparation for death while you are alive. It is a Tibetan Buddhist practice to develop compassion for yourself and for others. The Tibetan word *tonglen* means "sending and receiving." This meditation is designed to eliminate the source of pain and identification with your constricted self. It is done by learning to send and receive loving kindness. You do this practice so that you can come to love yourself as well as cherish all other people and beings more than yourself. Tonglen is a training to develop limitless, fearless, unbiased compassion toward all creations. It is a compassion practice designed to unravel the selfish patterning of the constricted self and gradually reinforce your confidence in the radiant wisdom and compassion of your expanded self.

Step
2

The main purposes of Tonglen are:

- To heal the difficulties and illness on your physical and spiritual self
- To heal your past suffering
- To release your constricted self and its conditionings
- To transform your relationships with others

Step 2

The importance of this practice is to shift your perspective to viewing life from your expanded self, or what I call discovering your "home base." As you begin this practice, spend time settling and relaxing your mind and body in a meditative state. If either your physical environment or the atmosphere inside your mind is uncomfortable or tense, transform it with the simple practice of breathing and relaxing that you've done in previous exercises.

Following are the practice instructions. Record them or have a friend or family member read them so you can listen to the instructions with your eyes closed. Be sure to pause between the individual instruction phrases when indicated with *(pause)*. The instructions are divided into two practices. The first is for yourself and the second is for the caring of others. The two practices are modeled after teachings I have received over the years.

- Sit quietly and allow your body and mind to relax by breathing slowly and deeply for several breaths. *(pause)*
- Now that you are centered, move your attention to your heart, feel its warmth, and focus on a deep appreciation for yourself. *(pause)*
- Take a breath in and deepen your attention on your heart. As you exhale, notice from your heart a clear compassion and love beginning to radiate outward as a warm light. Keep your breath moving in and out as the radiation of light builds in your heart. *(pause)*
- When you are ready, take in the atmosphere and feelings of negativity from your external world as well as your internal world. Notice the negativity appears over your heart as a dark cloud. This dark cloud is the band of fear that hardens your heart. *(pause)* As you exhale, notice the negativity is

transformed at your heart center. You are now to dissolve this cloud and open your heart to light, love, kindness, and spaciousness. You can dissolve this cloud of negativity by visualizing the cloud breaking apart when your in-breath touches the cloud. *(pause)*

- As you exhale, permit the negativity to dissolve and be transformed at your heart center into more love and radiant light. *(pause)*

- Continue to breathe into the raw feeling of your own pain like hot air is cooled by an air conditioner. Inhale and exhale gently. *(pause)*

- Keep repeating the breaths until the dark cloud has disappeared. On the next inhalation after the dark cloud disappears, fill your inner atmosphere with calm, clarity, and joy in the form of light. *(pause)*

- As you exhale, send calm, clarity, and joy out to the world around you. Keep repeating inhale and exhale breaths until you know you have come to an inner balance and peacefulness. Sit in silence absorbing the love, caring, and compassion for yourself. *(pause)*

- When ready, move your body and open your eyes.

Exercise: *Sending Love for Others*

Record the following meditation or have a friend or family member read it so you can listen to the instructions with your eyes closed. Be sure to pause between the individual instruction phrases.

- Sitting silently, relax your body, starting with the muscles around your eyes, moving from your face and head down to your shoulders and arms, and then down to the rest of your body to the tips of your toes. Take this time to fully relax your body. Now, breathe several deep breaths and let your mind quiet and feel the relaxation, calm, and peace within you. *(pause)*

- Imagine a spacious sky in front of you. Within this spacious blue sky see before you the presence of a being for whom you feel devotion. If there is no special being you feel connected to, simply visualize the form of a Presence of Life. *(pause)*

Step
2

Step 2

- Ask for this Presence to open compassion in your heart. Visualize the form of this Presence sending powerful rays of compassion and wisdom into your heart. Notice as these rays continue to penetrate you at your heart that your cloud of selfishness and fear melt and dissolve, revealing the warmth of your heart. *(pause)*

- Imagine the hurt, brokenness, pain, and struggle of people in wars, natural disasters, hunger, and political and human intolerance as well as the destruction of the natural world. As you bring all this to your mind and inner vision, breathe in the suffering of all beings and of the pain of the world, into your heart center. See this suffering in the form of the dark cloud. Allow all the suffering to awaken your compassion. Concentrate on some particular image of suffering in the world as this dark cloud. *(pause)*

- In your heart center, visualize and dissolve any traces of the pain and suffering of the dark cloud with the brilliant light that penetrated your heart from the being of light. *(pause)*

- Breathe out as you send to others a brilliant light of love, light, warmth, energy, confidence, and joy from your heart. Continue the giving and receiving for as long as you like. *(pause)*

- At the end of the practice, affirm or pray that the compassion is dissolving the suffering and even the cause of the suffering, filling all beings with peace, happiness, and love. *(pause)*

- As you conclude the practice, bless the positive healing power to all who have benefited from your practice and to all beings who are as limitless as the vastness of space. *(pause)*

- When ready, move your body and open your eyes.

Chapter 5
Step 2:
Dying Preparation:
Spiritual Considerations

Life and death are of supreme importance.
Time passes swiftly and opportunity is lost.
Let us awaken. Do not squander your life.
—ZEN NIGHT CHANT

Dying is not the end of your life. All the major spiritual traditions indicate that death is just the doorway for a continuation of life. You surrender your physical body, but your loving awareness continues. All the religious and spiritual traditions indicate that a spiritual practice will heighten your mental and emotional freedom at the moment of death. When you have a spiritual practice, you gain clarity, a deepened awareness, and a strengthened response to each situation in life, including your suffering. Your practice may not follow a religious or spiritual tradition. It may be connected to beauty, music, nature, or some other positive consideration that brings love and peace to you. The key is to develop a personal practice in order to be open and to merge with whatever you consider represents the mystery that is beyond death.

How we prepare to die includes spiritual preparation—however you relate to "spiritual." In this chapter, we will also consider religious traditions and practical preparations as you look ahead to your time of dying. These preparations would include what kinds of music are played, books read to you, and environment that surrounds you as you are in the dying process.

At the moment of death, the relationship you have developed with God, the Cosmos, Essence, or some indescribable Presence (by whatever name you give it) can give you strength to go through this transition. As you prepare for the hour of death, ask for the mystery or Presence of Life to help you and ask for your own guidance and courage to let go into the vast mystery you are entering.

If you don't connect to some Presence but have some type of spiritual practice such as meditation, visualizations, chanting, prayers, or other spiritual practices, you can be assured that these practices will give you strength, balance, and confidence. Your spiritual practice at this stage of dying opens within you a level of trust and faith that is rooted in both your beliefs and previous inner experience.

Part of your spiritual preparation is to take the opportunity to make peace with yourself, with others, and with the larger mystery that you may call the Infinite, the Universe, Source, God, or Presence. In this preparation, it is time to forgive yourself as soon as you feel remorse for what you have done or experienced in your life. Individuals describe as they come to this stage in dying that a Presence is always there, has always been present in their lives. This is your expanded self.

Asking for forgiveness and opening consciously to this Presence can make you more aware of what has always been within you. I speak of an intimacy between you and a Presence only because many of those who have had near-death experiences describe a Presence coming to them. Most of our religious traditions and mystics also describe this intimacy.

The best way to prepare for death is to have gained through your spiritual practice a stability of mind. At the moment of death, you don't want your mind to be broken or distracted by fear or remorse. You want it to remain in an even awareness that grows into and through the doorway of your death. As the luminosity or light of reality shines in your mind, you will recognize it as the

Infinite, the Source, the Presence, the unfathomable mystery by whatever name and naturally merge into it and then rest in it.

Religious Traditions Preparation

The Swiss psychologist Carl Jung said, "What happens after death is so unspeakably glorious that our imagination and our feelings do not suffice to form even an approximate conception of it. ... The dissolution of our time-bound form in eternity brings no loss of meaning." [26] In different religious traditions, preparation for death takes on similar messages. Christ prayed that through his death he might be able to take on the suffering and purify the sins of all beings to transcend death together. The Christian traditions have prayers said at the bed of the dying offering devotion, trust, mercy, and love.

In the Jewish tradition, many prayers and psalms are said during the dying. Often these prayers are in praise of God's goodness and mercy. Also, they encourage the dying to examine their life, to acknowledge and atone for any harm they have done, and to extend forgiveness to anyone who may have harmed them.

In Islam Sufism, the prayers at death are for the person to be in the pure light and experience the way of the heart. The essence of the path to God is to know yourself. The Sufi saying is "Know yourself, Know your Lord."

In the Buddhist tradition, the path to God is to offer up from your ego state and all things you are attached to, such as your body, health, physical appearance, possessions, jobs, talents, family, friends, fears, pain of dying, feelings of responsibility, physical control, or being abandoned. His Holiness Tenzin Gyatso, fourteenth Dalai Lama, suggests that "The purpose of all major religious traditions is not to construct big temples on the outside, but to create temples of goodness and compassion inside, in our hearts." [27]

All of our religious traditions come from some form of ancient indigenous shamanism that still exists around the world. In the shamanistic worldview, only

---

26. C. G. Jung, *Selected Letters of C. G. Jung,* 1909–1961, edited by Gerhard Adler and Aniela Jaffé (Princeton, NJ: Princeton Legacy Library, 1984), 53.

27. Dalai Lama, *The Good Heart: A Buddhist Perspective on the Teachings of Jesus*, edited by Robert Kiely (Somerville, MA: Wisdom Publications, 1996, 2016), 34.

Step 2

the natural world exists. This view includes the visible and the invisible worlds as well as the world of spirits. In indigenous cultures, a person had two or more souls. One soul was to die and be buried in this world and another soul was to fly to the spirit world and travel to the ancestors and beyond into the vast mystery. In this tradition, it was important to prepare each soul for the journey of death.

It is for you and me to prepare for this journey, both physically and spiritually into the vast mystery of light. Alberto Villoldo, who was trained in the Andean shamanic tradition, describes one indigenous view of death with: "When a dying person retains his awareness after death, he enters the light easily. My mentor compared this light to the dawn breaking on a cloudless morning, a state of primordial purity—immense and vast, defying description. The blackness of death, caused by the collapse of the senses, recedes and is dispelled by the light of Spirit." [28]

Exercise: *Preparation for Letting Go*

This is a meditation to begin to prepare for releasing and letting go of your physical, mental, emotional, and relationship lives. Again, record this meditation or have a friend or family member read it to you. Be sure to pause between instructions so you can absorb each part of the meditation.

- Close your eyes. Take a moment to breathe deeply, relax your body, and remember how precious is the human life you experience.

- Remember the people who have helped you and how you have brought joy to others.

- Remember that even through the difficult times you have learned and opened to life.

- In this relaxed state, take a look at your mind. Every thought and feeling you've had over the years has changed you in one way or another. Everything in this world changes; your body is also changing and one day it will die. Impermanence is real. Let your mind and heart feel this truth.

28. Alberto Villoldo, *Shaman, Healer, Sage* (New York: Harmony Books, 2000), 209.

- In this moment of relaxation, notice what has made you happy in your life. You may have worked hard for many things, had a good relationship, a nice house, or a satisfying job; or you've had a really difficult life perhaps with illness, loss, financial challenges, or loneliness. Yet, sooner or later, you will lose all the good and bad of your life and that which caused you happiness and joy as well as pain and fear. Notice what it would be like to live without fear. Can you feel a moment in your life when there was no fear?

- Challenge yourself: Can you release your grasping of this life you've had and open to whatever arises next in your mind? Can you let go of the reference points of solidity, identity, and separateness? Can you accept this very moment no matter what you are feeling? This begins the letting go of your identity and connection to this life. Explore these letting-go feelings.

- Let yourself rest in this contemplation and know that, as in the indigenous traditions, you have two souls. One soul that will be left here to be honored and loved by those who still live and remember you, and the other soul that is moving toward a vast mystery of experience that will take you into and beyond the light of existence.

- After a time of resting in this inner awareness, begin to move your body and open your eyes.

- Record your reflections in your notebook. If in a group, share your experience.

Exercise: *Affirmations for Letting Go and Preparing for Death*

It is helpful to change your thought patterns. First, find a comfortable position, relax, and take a few deep breaths to settle your mind and body. Then, silently or out loud, say the following affirmative phrases as you read them. Use these phrases anytime you think of your dying. Select at least one to memorize.

- I open to forgiveness and to my love flowing boundlessly in me.

- I find the inner resources to be able to let go of my body.

- I find the inner resources to let go of my emotions and my mind.

- Death is not my enemy. Death is a doorway of continuing life.

- My life is changing and I am open to my death.

- I accept things as they are and I am free of fear.

Step 2

Exercise: *Practical Preparation— What to Listen to in the Dying Process*

As you move deeper into your dying, hearing becomes one of the most accessible experiences of your surroundings. Write in your notebook from the following list what you would like to hear as you move through your dying process.

- Recorded meditations and/or prayers you will do and others will do for you and with you.

- Music such as instrumentals, songs, chants, etc., playing in the background for you.

- Recorded teachings played at your bedside for inspiration.

- Books read to you.

- Friends playing music or singing for and with you.

- Friends and family telling you stories about your life and your life with them.

- Recorded nature sounds: ocean waves, birds, rain, etc.

- Other things that come to mind for you.

Chapter 6
Step 3:
Letting Go into Transcendence

Of course you don't die. Nobody dies. Death doesn't exist.
You only reach a new level of vision,
a new realm of consciousness, a new unknown world.
—HENRY MILLER

This description of "Letting Go into Transcendence" is a digestion of many traditions that I've read and some inner experiences I've had. Death is a slow-motion process of letting go. It can be a graceful exit from a life path you traveled, it is to be hoped, with good will and contribution. If you choose to let go of your constricted self now and die before you die, it will ease your transition over the threshold of death. The teachings of many traditions indicate that if you choose to let go of your constricted self and work with the process of your dying now as you live your daily life, no experience of "letting go" needs to happen at death because there will be nothing left to release. This is critically important if you have a sudden death. If you are prepared and do not interfere with the death process, it can be a very easy process. Your other option is to wait and be forced to let go at the time of your death.

To enter this phase of transcendent surrender, whether in daily life or in the death process itself, is to release the outer struggle of your life and let go into a deep relaxation of acceptance, knowing that existence—life, your life—is larger than anything you've ever experienced. The spiritual teacher Eckhart Tolle provides the secret about letting go. He says, "Death is a stripping away of all that is not you. The secret of life is to 'die before you die'—and find that there is no death."[29]

As you turn your attention to the letting go of the struggle that happens as you enter the process of your death, the experience of letting go will actually create a clarity of mind. This is what Tolle suggests is "to die before you die." This clarity of mind lets you move away from the outer world and give full attention to "find that there is no death." Letting go with clarity eases your transition in the later stages of the dying process. When this turning away from the outer world happens, it is a signal for you, your loved ones, and caregivers that physical death is near. If you do not interfere with the death process, it becomes an easy process.

This phase of surrender is releasing the outer struggle and it opens to a deep relaxation of release and acceptance. When there is a release of the outer struggle, it is obvious that there is an impending death. A shift occurs and there may be an initial vulnerable dread-like feeling of engulfment, with a feeling of no exit. You are now in the unknown territory of death. The release of the outer world ends, the fearful constricted self jumps into an unknown space so wide, so deep that it can't even be measured.

As you make this "jump," your identity—your constricted self—is stripped away. This jump is the movement into transcendence. At this point, your expanded self emerges as an infinitely expansive sky filled with passing clouds carrying knowledge of deep healing. Strangely, many spiritual teachings indicate that you will feel immensely alive. Because of this awareness of total expansion, there is no longer a fear of engulfment. Former feelings of dread of the unknown shift to awe and ecstasy in the experience of expanding inner light. You enter into a vastness, filled with feelings of joy and peace. Into this vastness, you, as a mind, will experience the virtues of grace, loving kindness, compassion,

29. Eckhart Tolle, *The Power of Now* (Novato, CA: New World Library, 1999), 38.

centeredness, spaciousness, mercy, and stability. These loving qualities are the last connection with the world of form before the moment of death.

The expanded self is now the full expression of love. As you merge, your self-development work and psychological issues melt away and dying is no longer the frightening struggle consuming your consciousness. You are liberated from the attachment of the constricted self into a level of pure presence and you are liberated from rational cognition to direct knowing and then into this illumination. This point in the process of your dying is beyond comprehension and there is a shift of your awareness into its illumined state. This transcendence occurs as your identity is surrendered and you enter into a vast new universe of reality. The world-recognized Indian poet, philosopher, and Nobel Prize winner Rabindranath Tagore eloquently speaks to the wonder of our dying. He wrote, "Death is not extinguishing the light, it is only putting out the lamp because the dawn has come." [30]

What we consider in this chapter is an important shift in our discussion of how you can begin to move from fear of dying to the illumined state of transcendence. This is the threshold of letting go of your constricted ego self and moving to your expanded self. We will consider what is happening to you from various religious and spiritual traditions at the last moment of death when your ego identity dissolves. We will then consider the inner and outer signs of the physical manifestations as death is occurring within you. In this ending process, hearing is the last sensation you will experience. I will provide some suggestion of what may be helpful to you in listening to books, music, etc., and what you might choose for yourself. Finally, I provide some examples of traditional religious prayers at death from the world's religions.

Nearing Death

Now that we have the overview of dying and beyond, let's look at each step in a little more detail. One's near death may be from an accident, a disease, or old age. Whatever brings you to this threshold as soon as it is detected that your dying process has begun and you are still conscious and aware of your surroundings, your

---

30. Rabindranath Tagore, *Vedanta Monthly: Message of the East*, Vol. 36 (1947).

family members or friends should sit at your bedside and gently and softly share with you the beauty of your life and affirm your journey beyond your physical death.

It is helpful to note that when you are dying, you want emotionally pleasant feelings and to be without pain. Remember, during your lifetime your wants and desires have sought happiness, pleasure, contentment, appreciation, and so on. But you and I have experienced that our desires are often the root of our pain and suffering. There are still strong desires as you near the death moment, and comfort from family and friends creates a helpful bridge for the desire and drive to feel emotionally pleasant and physically without pain leads to a critical issue as you near your death. Death is both a physical and a psychospiritual process; it is not a medical event. If you focus all of your attention on limiting the physical discomfort of death by being overly medicated or are kept alive through heroic procedures to prolong your life, you miss the full impact of going consciously through the spiritual transformation of death. If you are in the process of dying only to be kept alive with the intervention of drugs and machines, you probably may not die peacefully or with compassion. Tempered with just enough palliative care you can let go naturally. This is a gift you give yourself.

In this final period, there are still strong desires and longings that you can have as you near the moment of your death. The struggle and clinging to past events is part of the continuing inner dissolution of the constricted self until the moment of taking your last breath. The gift to you is that even at the last moment you still have the opportunity to heal these deeply held mental states. The Hindu teachings say that the more complete and settled you are as you leave the practical and emotional issues of your life the easier is the movement into the journey of your next life. As you die, you want to be in the position of having nothing to complete, nothing you need to return to finish. The work for you is to simply relax and be open to dying.

The body will naturally shut down to focus on this profound transformation. This deep transformation as the constricted self dies and the expanded self is uncovered opens you to the mysterious gap into the boundless expanse of the nature of your mind. To let go naturally to this gap is a gift you can give yourself. If you let the body naturally shut down, it will let you focus on a deep and profound transformation. Simply, you will enter a deep transformation as the constricted self dies and the true expanded self opens you to reveal the boundless inner reality of the true nature of your mind.

Through your death, you will know the luminous inner awareness that enfolds the whole of existence in its embrace. As you come to this moment before your actual physical death, the purpose of life on earth is revealed to you. You may reveal to yourself that your unique purpose is to achieve union with and to know and be your own enlightened essential nature. You will come to realize what Gibran says each of us knows hidden in our dreams what lies beyond our death. "For life and death are one, even as the river and the sea are one. In the depth of your hopes and desires lies your silent knowledge of the beyond; and like seeds dreaming beneath the snow your heart dreams of spring. Trust the dreams, for in them is hidden the gate to eternity." [31]

Step

3

Exercise: *Affirmations for Approaching Death*

The following are phrases you can use now as you approach your death to focus on any remaining desires in your life. Repeat them both silently and out loud. Write down your reactions to these phrases as you repeat them to yourself. Memorize at least one of the phrases.

- I am open to releasing the wanting of things to be different from what they actually are.
- I forgive myself for my mistakes and things I have left undone.
- I ask all those I have harmed to forgive me.
- I am thankful for the loving people in my life. I name them now.
- I forgive myself for those people in my life that I dislike or hate.
- I am grateful for my family and caregivers and their comfort and love for me.

---

31. Gibran, *The Prophet*, 80.

The Last Moment of Death

As you come to that last moment when your physical body dies, you will enter an experience that many traditions have described. First there will be an experience that feels like fainting and drifting into a dark void, a space of peace that is free from all your pain. Then there will be a releasing from the dark void. As the darkness recedes, there arises a dawning of luminous clear and radiant light, like an infinite sky at dawn. The traditions indicate that the key here is to recognize this light and unite with it, as that will allow you to attain the freedom and liberation you have always wanted, even if it has been unconscious in you. If you have not prepared yourself with forgiveness, surrender, and letting go to unite with this light, you will separate from the light and be drawn back into your fears and patterns of pain. Thus, your preparedness is to heal your relationships and your wounded heart and move past your suffering and pain before you enter into this moment.

At death, your physical powers gradually dissolve, but your internal process of dissolution continues. There may still be feelings of anger and desires that have a hold on you. As you come to the moment of physical death, you may experience the effects of your actions on others. This is a type of inner review of your life. It is crucial to meet yourself nakedly. This awareness of your past at the time of the inner dissolution continues until the final moment of death. At the last moment, you still have the opportunity to heal these mental states. Once again, prepare now before you face the moment of your death to heal your relationships and your wounded heart and move past your suffering and pain. In the second part of the book, we will work directly with these issues.

Exercise: *Affirmations to Change Thoughts Before Death*

The following are phrases to use in order to change your thought patterns when fear arises in you. Repeating these statements plants seeds in the mind when you most need them. Please change the words if you need to so that they fit the way you think and speak. Try to memorize at least one phrase.

- I accept my fear, anger, and sadness as I let go of my body.

- I release my constricted self and open to my expanded self.

- I leave behind all that I use to protect myself and now surrender my life.

- I am now ready to be open to the unknown.

- I welcome the light of the unknown.

- May I love myself and others and die in ease.

Exercise: *Experiencing the Moment of Death*

In the classic work of Indian literature, the Bhagavad Gita, it says, "Whatever the state of being that man may focus upon, at the end, when he leaves his body, to that state of being he will go."[32] This next exercise is to explore this idea.

Record your responses in your notebook or computer. If in a group share your thoughts.

- Describe what you want your state of mind to be at the moment of your death.

- Ask yourself: How have I worked with my conditioned habits of desire and clinging to others and things in my life? What can I do differently?

- Explore your past: How have I opened my heart to compassion toward myself and others? What is self-compassion for me?

The Dissolution

Sogyal Rinpoche, in his book *The Tibetan Book of Living and Dying*, speaks of this process of dissolution when he says, "In death all the components of our body and mind are stripped away and disintegrate. As the body dies, the senses and subtle elements dissolve, and this is followed by the death of the ordinary aspect of our mind, with all its negative emotions of anger, desire, and ignorance. Finally,

---

32. Stephen Mitchell, trans., *Bhagavad Gita: A New Translation* (New York: Harmony, 2002), 107.

nothing remains to obscure our true nature, as everything that in life has clouded the enlightened mind has fallen away." [33]

At your death, it is said that you are returning to your original state of consciousness before you were born. As you die, you will begin to experience a gap. The gap is a growing openness within you as the body solidity dissolves. In this gap of dissolution, you find your exit out of the physical form. It has been said that this is the most profound moment in the life of a human being. It is the moment of greatest spiritual opportunity in your physical life. This gap, this openness, is like a window revealing your radiant true nature or God or Divine Presence or the Ground of Being—or whatever words you might use for this incredible revelation of existence.

Your physical body has been designed to protect your Divine Presence and the dissolution is a way to create an opening for consciousness to leave the body. The exit is like a *whoosh* of energy out of the top of the head. But consciousness can exit from other areas of the body as well. In a way, the dying process is for your consciousness to find both the exit and the entrance. The body dying is your exit to the entrance into the beyond.

In his book *Shaman, Healer, Sage*, Dr. Alberto Villoldo, who trained as a medical anthropologist and served as former director of the Biological Self-Regulation Lab at San Francisco State University that investigated how energy medicine changes the chemistry of the brain, gives one description of this exit moment at death: "When the brain shuts down, the electromagnetic field created by the central nervous system dissolves, and the Luminous Energy Field (LEF) that encompasses the body grows into a translucent, egg-shaped torus that holds the other seven chakras" (the energy centers that are connected to the major glands of the body), "which continue to shimmer like points of light for the first few hours after death. This luminous orb, which is the essence or soul of the individual, then travels through the axis of the luminous body, to become one with Spirit again. This occurs very quickly once the LEF is free from the body.

33. Sogyal, *The Tibetan Book of Living and Dying*, 259.

Step 3

The LEF squeezes through the portal created by its central axis, like a doughnut squeezing through its own hole." [34]

There are many other similar descriptions of how our energy essence leaves our physical body. People who have had near-death experiences describe their energy self leaving the body.

The Basic Signs of the Physical Death Passage

Dying is a gradual process of letting go and withdrawing. It is a very complex process that moves in stages, usually spanning several days or longer. At the ending of life, the processes of your body systems are failing. At the same time, there is an experience of deepening stillness and a hush. The final moments of the activity of your brain, heart, and lungs is said to make a sound like an engine turning off.

In the transition of dying, it is important for you to know what to expect as your body goes through its dissolution. Let me help guide you in the dissolution sequence. There are two major sequences to observe. The first sequence is behavioral and easy to observe. It includes sleep, stillness, and eating habits. The second sequence consists of more specific aspects of dissolving as represented by the five elements of earth, water, fire, air, and space. These elements occur more strongly when fear is often in control. I am including both patterns of dissolution in order for you to be familiar and aware of them as a way of identifying the different stages for yourself and also so your caregivers can be observant of them.

We will first observe the practical signs associated with sleep, stillness, and eating as obvious positive indicators of you nearing your death. Your dying process may include parts of both the positive stages and the elemental physical dissolving. The caveat is that your physical condition coming to your dying may have a significant impact on what you experience.

Chris Raymond, a dying and grief expert, gives us a brief overview of what occurs physically at the moment of death before we follow the practical signs regarding sleep, stillness, and eating that lead up to this moment: "Eventually, the

---

34. Villoldo, *Shaman, Healer, Sage*, 209.

patient's breathing will cease altogether and his or her heart will stop beating. Death has occurred. At this point, the human body immediately begins a series of physical processes after death occurs. This includes:

- A dilation of the pupils

- A relaxation of the muscles and eyelids

- A growing paleness to the skin's normal color as blood drains from the smaller veins in the skin

- If the body remains undisturbed for long enough (several hours), the blood will pool in the areas of the body nearest the ground and, eventually, chemical changes in the body's cells will result in rigor mortis—a temporary stiffening of the muscles." [35]

Sleep

As you enter this final stage, sleep is often very disturbing and agitating. As the dying person, you will be awake at night and awake during the day. There may be moments of feeling very surreal. You will increasingly feel removed from your surroundings. There is often the feeling that you are not in your own home even when tucked into your own bed. Being continuously awake, there can be a deep loneliness as you wait for death to come. Sleeplessness can go on for many days, depending on your mind state and resistance. As you get closer to your death, you may start staring at the ceiling. You may be seeing other beings. Many people report seeing dead relatives and do not seem afraid or surprised. Your caregivers may see your lips move and your brow wrinkle, but your words are inaudible. As you get closer to the doorway of death, you may see where you are going while still maintaining an awareness of people around you.

Stillness

Gradually, your agitation and resistance to sleep shifts to an inner and outer silence and withdrawal from people and the environment around you. You begin

---

35. Chris Raymond, "Coping with End of Life Issues," Verywell.com. Accessed September 2016. https://www.verywell.com/end-of-life-4014730.

to push loved ones and even beloved animals away as you detach from your surroundings. The transpersonal aspects of death that I discussed earlier begin to
enter into this time of stillness. In this state of mental and physical stillness, your
mind takes the form of a witness that observes everything within and around
you non-judgmentally. This surrender into the transformation of stillness comes
as the constricted self begins slowly to dissolve and the expanded self emerges.
In this observing state, you will know a deep stillness and have an experience of
deep peace and comfort that you may call bliss.

Eating and Drinking Stops
When eating and drinking stops, the functions of the mind stop. This is the beginning of merging and being absorbed by the expanded self. At this juncture,
you gain insight into your own nature. The nature of the "food" now is spiritual
as you move beyond mental constructs, as the mind and the body begins to fast
from physical food and drink to release the last of your personality and identity.

Outer and Inner Dissolution

The dissolution of your physical body includes the dying of your flesh and
blood. This is called the outer dissolution in most traditional death systems.
Your inner dissolution comprises two "bodies." The first is your mind and emotions and the second is the elements that compose the physical body such as
earth, water, fire, air, and space as well as the subtle energy systems such as the
chakras or energy points in the body and your ego personality, the constricted
self. Next to go is the very subtle body, which is the body that does not die. It
sheds the other bodies and moves to infinity. This is the luminous energy field
that Dr. Villoldo described.

In the outer dissolution phase, the body is focusing on keeping the brain,
heart, and lungs going. The body is sacrificing other functions, as the physical
reserves are so limited. When digestion has too much strain on it, your appetite
will go away. When the kidneys can no longer function, the ability to swallow
fluids vanishes. This is all very natural. However, the tendency, particularly in
hospitals, is to keep life going by the inserting of feeding tubes, IVs, suction

Step
3

machines, and so on. As I've suggested earlier, this inhibits the natural physical dying process of the body. These "survival mechanisms" also reduce the natural inner process that is going on for the individual as he or she is dying.

In this phase of transformation, our outer elements dissolve into the next element. The elements are the outer dissolution of the body melting into subtle energies and then into the very subtle energy. Then the three stages of inner dissolution end as the energies melt into space. This is the infinite space of the awakened mind. It is fascinating how there is a sign at each stage of dying. These signs are invaluable for your caregivers to be aware of in your dying process. Each sign represents where you are in the inner and the outer dying process and where you are going. The outer and inner signs convey the loss of connection between body and mind as well as your severance from the outside world. They signal the end of who you think you are.

At the end of the dissolution, there is no more struggle and no more effort. The following is the sequence of the elements' dissolution. The Tibetan system of the elements contains a very detailed and complex description. The text here is my condensed version.

Earth Element Dissolves

The earth element begins to dissolve when the body is unable to function in a normal fashion. At this point, many people are put on life-support systems. Often there is the need for constant sleep and there is no interest in food. When earth element occurs, there is a sense of a crushing weight holding the body down. At this time, you are mostly bedridden, as your legs are too weak to hold up your body. As noted before, your arms may develop reddish-purple splotches called mottling. On the hands, lips, and feet, a bluish discoloration appears as there is less oxygen in the blood, and the skin takes on a waxy sheen. You may experience a coldness over the bony areas of the knees, elbows, and nose. Your overall energy pattern has little strength and is very low. Your mind can be dull and unclear and you become increasingly incoherent verbally.

Water Element Dissolves

When the water element begins to dissolve the body, you experience a loss of body fluids. You become incontinent, have a dry mouth, and become very thirsty. You will probably have a constantly runny nose, as well as slow movement of blood and lymph circulation. You are sometimes emotionally touchy and easily provoked to outbursts of fear. Generally you become out of balance and your nervousness and anxiety increase.

Fire Element Dissolves

The arrival of the fire element increases the intensity of your body as though you are either burning up or freezing. The temperature in your body swings between hot and cold, but increasingly stays hot. You are no longer interested in food or drink. There is an agitation like fire that makes you begin to thrash around in the bed. You may try to get out of bed and are very agitated. The mind has difficulty seeing, identifying, and remembering family members and friends. Generally you are unable to have coherent thoughts, can't hold information, and your general senses are dull and unresponsive to outside activity.

Air Element Dissolves

The air element is the last to dissolve physically. Caregivers will know you are close to passing because your breath will become inconsistent and labored to the point of long pauses, panting, and then sudden gasping for air. You are confused and feel shut off from the environment around you. You will probably have hallucinations that you mumble about, but you are very inward. You are now so inward that you are not connecting to anyone or anything outside yourself. You may appear to be in a coma. Your breath will become increasingly labored, and then the death rattle will happen and you will cease breathing.

Space Element Dissolves

This is when you take your last breath and consciousness leaves your body. You are now beginning a journey without your physical body. Those who have had a near-death experience describe being above themselves in the room looking

Step
3

down at their body. Others report immediately seeing a bright light that is at the end of a dark tunnel. In this state, you may be clear or confused due to the practices and preparation you gave yourself before you died or the lack of them, respectively.

In this physical transformation process at the final stage of dying, being able to know and observe the basic elements dissolving from one element into the next element gives the observing family, friends, and caregivers an indication of how close you are to moving from outer experience to inner awareness to beyond this physical reality.

After the dissolving of the five elements, outside observers won't be able to observe your final subtle energy stage. This final subtle energy transformation stage is experienced in you at a different level of consciousness. The five elements are the outer dissolution of the body that permits your consciousness to make a shift into very subtle energy. When the elemental stages of inner dissolution are completed, all the energies melt into space. This is called the *very subtle energy of infinite space of the awakened mind.*

It is helpful for you and others to know that there are clear signs of the movement you go through at each stage of dying. These signs are invaluable for caregivers to be aware of in your dying process. Each sign represents where you are in the inner and the outer dying process and what the next natural movement will be.

The outer and inner signs convey the loss of connection between body and mind as well as your severance from the outside world. They signal the end of who you think you are as a personality. At this stage of identity loss, there is no more struggle and no more effort by you as you physically leave your body and die.

It must be remembered that each dying person may not follow the outer and inner dissolving process in the systematic order described here. Individuals have their own path of moving through death, but the specific signs of dissolving described here help observers understand how to support the dying in their process and give an indication of what will occur next. For some individuals, de-

Step

3

pending on their inner preparation, the transition from one element to another can occur smoothly and very peacefully. Someone has said, "We die the way we have lived."

Andrew Holecek, in his book *Preparing to Die: Practical Advice and Spiritual Wisdom from the Tibetan Tradition*, states strongly that all of us need to learn these dissolutions signs well before we enter the dying process. He says, "One of the best ways to prepare for death is to acknowledge that we really are going to die." He goes on to say, "We all know that we're going to die. But we don't know it in our guts. If we did, we would practice as if our hair was on fire." [36]

Suggested Readings and Music for Dying

As hearing is the last of the five senses to go, it is considered helpful for your caregivers to speak reminders and prayers aloud so that when you are dying and just after you have died you are reassured that you are not alone in this new state. You may experience positive things but also frightening things. When you experience strange beings or states of consciousness after you die, you need not be afraid. You need to recognize that these strange or fearful beings are projections of your own mind. You need to remember that these images no longer have a hold on you so they can no longer hurt you.

As I said earlier, traditions such as the *Tibetan Book of the Dead* and *The Egyptian Book of the Dead,* which was called *The Book of Coming and Going,* as well as many other after-death rituals from various cultures seek to help the soul or essence of the being on a journey to what some have called the land of the dead, to the highest heaven. Whatever the interpretation of what we experience after we die, these traditions took very seriously the need to keep speaking to the dying and dead person in order to maintain a positive direction of awakening in that individual's journey.

The reading suggestions that follow may be read to you or recorded for the transition period when you are dying. While the readings are read, it is important for you to know how to keep your mind stabilized so that after your physical death

---

36. Andrew Holecek, *Preparing to Die: Practical Advice and Spiritual Wisdom from the Tibetan Tradition* (Boston: Snow Lion, 2013), 24.

you will recognize the true nature of your mind. This stabilization is done through committed spiritual training and practice throughout your life, as I've suggested earlier. If you have reached this stability in your meditation practice, nothing special is required when you are dying. It is much easier for you as you die to experience directly an expanded self experience as the constricted self's cloudy layers of thought and emotion will dissolve quickly at death. These documents read to you for a period of time both before and after you die help to provide an ongoing stability for you as you journey beyond this life.

Sensitives and near-death returners have observed that at the time of death the mind and heart can fill the atmosphere of the room and touch the awareness of everyone. The reports of many of those who have had a near-death experience say that at first they see themselves above their body and many see an energy of light flooding the room while their body is below them. They report feeling a tremendous flow of love moving out of them to those in the room and that is part of this energy of light.

One caution is that you may experience any strong thoughts or negative emotions that people have brought into the space surrounding you as you die. This will have a powerful effect on your state of mind, for better or worse. You might tell your caregivers before the final stages of your dying that you would like them to prepare themselves inwardly before coming into the room where you are dying. This could be meditating, calm breathing, or mindfulness to be slow and sensitive to what is happening with you. It is helpful for the key caregivers you choose to remind people of this. This calm inward dwelling energy will invoke a presence of love and caring and have a positive influence on your state of mind as you die and leave your body.

There are two significant ways that caregivers can help you as you go through the dying process. The first way is playing music that helps to reduce anxiety and fear. The other is having your caregivers read or record various texts that will help you be attuned more fully to your dying process.

Step
3

Music with Dying

Noted neurologist Oliver Sacks, in his book *Musicophilia: Tales of Music and the Brain,* demonstrated that music affects many areas of the brain and can awaken positive memories even in people with Alzheimer's disease. Instrumental music is free of language or explicit ideas. As we move more deeply into the dying process, we enter more and more into our right brain. Music is more right-brain oriented and can help you open your heart, create a feeling of peace, and draw you deeper and more easily into the moment of death. Even though music is ephemeral, it can touch a deep chord of awareness and feeling in you. At its deepest level, music has the power to create a wonderful pleasurable stimulus that can make the dying process much easier. Talk with your caregivers about the type of music you would like played as you move through your process of dying.

There are ongoing studies of death, dying, and bereavement using the performing of prescriptive music in the dying process. Harpist Therese Schroeder-Sheker and her Chalice of Repose Project have brought music to the bedsides of dying people. She plays and sings music that entrains with the breathing of the person moment to moment as they move toward death. The music is improvised to match the process and physiology of the patient.

Schroeder-Sheker created music-thanatology, a new discipline used with the actively dying or those who have received a life expectancy of less than six months. The goals of music-thanatology are to reduce physical as well as emotional pain and to create a supportive environment for the dying person, thus allowing the person to become more conscious of his or her own death process. Schroeder-Sheker has numerous recordings that you might choose to use (see chaliceofrepose.org). Also consider friends that could play live music of your choosing as you are dying.

Selected Readings at the Time of Dying

You can create your own text readings the way you would like them spoken as you are in the dying transition phase. It is important to keep in mind some key concepts as you prepare a text to be read to you. Some of the key concepts to

Step
3

include are statements to relax, not be afraid, and feel loved. When you are in the dying transition and listen to the text read to you, it is important to remember that whatever comes to you visually or aurally is a manifestation of your own mind.

The following is a suggested text I created that you can have read to you. Use it, modify it, change words to fit your beliefs, make it your own. Add your own readings to your journal for your caregivers. Explain why you want them to read the passages to you. You can record your own voice reading or that of a close partner, friend, or family member, and it can be played continuously to you.

Step
3

Exercise: *A Reading to Be Spoken While Dying and After Death*

This reading can be spoken by caregivers and/or recorded and played repeatedly both while in the dying process and after the person has died. Read slowly and pause after each statement.

My dear (name),

You are safe as your body dissolves into the evolutionary process of dying. Know that you are also held by the presence of love.

Whatever appears before you is only a projection in your mind; it is like a dream.

There is nothing to fear. Relax and rest as your body can no longer be hurt.

When a white light appears, don't be afraid or turn away. Open your heart, go toward it, and merge with it.

You are now experiencing a smooth transition as you pass into a new life. It is just like a change of clothes. You let go of the old and take on a new awareness that is opening you into an abundance of beauty and unconditional love.

You are surrounded by total acceptance and comforted in warmth and a deep compassion for you. There is caring, support, and kindness around you. This unconditional love you are experiencing is who you are.

You see yourself with familiar souls who love you.

There is luminous light all around you.

You are feeling blessed in gratitude and in profound joy.

Rest now in natural great peace as you open deeply and receptively into the healing place of awe and ecstasy.

You are floating in a field of joy and peace that passes all understanding.

You are now being transformed into the virtues of grace, loving kindness, and compassion that is you.

Love is the last connection with the world of form as you experience your true Self becoming overwhelmingly loving of who you are.

Dying is no longer the frightening enemy. You are liberated into the level of pure essence. You are now more than a body, emotions, or mind. You are everything.

Now with the absorption into the true Self you are pure light shifting into awareness. This experience is unity consciousness. This means you have no boundaries. You are infinite space.

Go deeply into this expanded enveloping state of integration and into the most subtle and sacred dimensions of being.

As you dwell in your light of infinite awareness, focus on being one with this awareness.

The Divine Presence of unconditional, infinite, and incomprehensible love is what you now are.

As you dwell in this luminous light, you feel yourself surrounded by Divine Masters. Trust them. Be open to their guidance.

Peace passes all understanding as you keep expanding and going deeper beyond all dimensions of experience.

You are entering into your true Self, the eternal self, the expanded self that you have longed for and worked for your entire life.

All is forgiven and released into the light. This is who you are. You are at home in this light. Thank you for being who you are. Thank you for what you have given and shared in this life. Thank you for opening your heart and soul as you go home to what you really are.

You are free to go now at your own pace and your own rhythm. Go gently, effortlessly, deeply, and gratefully right into your Spirit.

Everything is okay as you move into love, gratitude, kindness, and light.

Step
3

You are in perfect rhythm with this new state of being; trust in your open spacious awareness that is like the clear, spacious sky.

You are going home to love, light, and eternal magnificence. Be at peace, be at peace, and be in oneness.

Traditional Religious Prayers at Death

Step 3

From the three major monotheistic religions—Christianity, Judaism, Islam—as well as in Hinduism and Tibetan Buddhism there are prayers and meditations for the dying and at the moment of death. Of course, there are many other spiritual traditions for prayers and rituals when one is dying. I include the last few lines of a Native American oration from Chief Tecumseh of the Shawnee Nation from the 1800s that has become a Native American prayer.

Christian Prayers

Both Catholic and Protestant Christians have similar prayers from the Bible that are prayed both as a person is dying and when dead. Find in the bibliography two books, one for Catholics[37] and one for Protestants[38] if you want to explore other prayers. One title you may be interested in is *Midwife for Souls: Spiritual Care for the Dying,*[39] where Kathy Kalina, a Christian hospice nurse, provides prayers for family members, caregivers, and friends as a person is dying as well as at death and afterward.

Below are passages from the Christian Bible.

The Lord is my shepherd;
I have everything I need.
He lets me rest in green meadows;
he leads me beside peaceful streams.
He renews my strength.
He guides me along right paths,

---

37. Bishops' Committee on the Liturgy, *Catholic Household Blessings and Prayer*, edited by United States Conference of Catholic Bishops (Washington, DC: USCCB Publishing; Revised edition, 2007).

38. Church Publishing, *Book of Common Prayer* (New York: Church Publishing, 1979).

39. Kathy Kalina, *Midwife for Souls: Spiritual Care for the Dying* (Boston: Pauline Books and Media, 1993).

bringing honor to his name.
Even when I walk
through the dark valley of death,
I will not be afraid,
for you are close beside me.
Your rod and your staff protect and comfort me.
You prepare a feast for me
in the presence of my enemies.
You welcome me as a guest,
anointing my head with oil.
My cup overflows with blessings.
Surely your goodness and unfailing love
will pursue me all the days of my life,
and I will live in the house of the Lord forever. Amen
—The Bible, Psalm 23 [40]

"In my Father's house are many rooms. If it were not so, would I have told you that I go to prepare a place for you? And if I go and prepare a place for you, I will come again and will take you to myself, that where I am you may be also."
—The Bible, John 14:2–3 [41]

Jewish Prayers

Jewish prayers come mainly from the book of Psalms in the Old Testament Torah as well as other spiritual writings. In the Jewish Kabbalah teaching for the moment of death, all thoughts, deeds, and speeches are concentrated into a pure spiritual light. It is believed that this light has an effect on everyone and everything in the world. In the book of Ecclesiastes, it is stated, "Greater is the day of death than the day of birth." Death in the Jewish tradition represents a completion of one's purpose and meaning in life.

---

40. *New Revised Standard Version of the Bible*, (Nashville, TN: HarperCollins, 1989), 662.
41. *New Revised Standard Version of the Bible*, 1304.

Among many of the Psalms, number 130 is typical of these prayers at the moment of death.

> Out of the depths I call to you, O Lord.
> My Lord, hearken to my voice; let Your ears be attentive to the voice of my pleas. God, if you were to preserve iniquities, my Lord, who could survive?
> But forgiveness is with You, that You may be feared.
> I hope in the Lord; my soul hopes, and I long for His word.
> My soul yearns for the Lord more than (night) watchmen (waiting) for the morning, wait for the morning.
> Israel, put your hope in the Lord, for with the Lord there is kindness; with Him there is abounding deliverance.
> And He will redeem Israel from all its iniquities.
> —*Prayer at the Moment of Death* (Psalm 130)[42]

> He is my God and my ever-living Redeemer,
> the strength of my lot in time of distress. He is my banner and my refuge, my portion on the day I call.
> Into His hand I entrust my spirit, when I sleep and when I wake.
> And with my soul, my body too, the Lord is with me; I shall not fear.
> —From the *Adon Olam (The Last Eight Verses of the Jewish Liturgy)* [43]

Islamic Prayers

The Islamic prayers for the dying are to remember Allah and his power to be merciful and forgiving. The dying person's last words before the moment of death are instructed to be: "There is no God but Allah." A Sufi prayer for the dying comes from a poem by Mevlana Jalaluddin Rumi, the thirteenth-century mystic. I follow it with a selection on death from traditional Islamic prayers.

> On the day I die, when I'm being carried
> toward the grave, don't weep. Don't say,

---

42. *New Revised Standard Version of the Bible*, 741.
43. Macy Nulman, *Encyclopedia of Jewish Prayers* (New Jersey: Jason Aronson, 1993).

He's gone! He's gone! Death has
nothing to do with going away.

The sun sets and the moon sets,
but they're not gone.
Death is coming together.

The tomb looks like a prison,
but it's really release into union.

The human seed goes down in the ground
like a bucket into the well where Joseph is.

It grows and comes up full
of some unimagined beauty.

Your mouth closes here
and immediately opens
with a shout of joy there."
—Jalaluddin Rumi (thirteenth-century Sufi mystic) [44]

"O Allah, forgive [name of the person] and elevate his station among those who are guided. Send him along the path of those who came before, and forgive us and him, O Lord of the worlds. Enlarge for him his grave and shed light upon him in it."

—Dua Prayers for the Dying (*Dua* means to "call out" or "summon") [45]

Hindu Prayers

The famous Vedic prayer of the dying that Hindus repeat is: "Lead me from darkness to light, from death to immortality." At his assassination, after being shot, Gandhi began immediately to repeat the name of the god Ram over and

---

44. Jalaluddin Rumi, *The Soul of Rumi,* translated by Coleman Barks (New York: HarperCollins, 2001), 94.
45. Mufti Afzal Hoosen Elias, *Qur'an Made Easy* (Lenasia, South Africa: Electronic Dawah Institute, 2012). Muslim 2/634.

Step
3

over so that he would be conscious as he died. From the Bhagavad Gita is a traditional prayer for those remembering the dead person, and from the Rig Veda the Vedic Funeral Hymn.

"Those who take refuge in me, striving for release from old age and death, know absolute freedom, and the Self, and the nature of action. Those who know me, and the nature of beings, of gods, and of worship are always with me in spirit, even at the hours of their death."
    —Bhagavad Gita [46]

"Where eternal luster glows, the realm in which the light divine is set, place me, Purifier, in that deathless, imperishable world. Make me immortal in that realm where movement is accordant to wish, in the third region, the third heaven of heavens, where the worlds are resplendent."
    —Rig Veda Funeral Hymn Intones [47]

A Native American Prayer

Tecumseh of the Shawnee Nation was a warrior and leader during the Indian wars of the late 1700s in the United States. He fought against white frontiersmen coming into native lands. After the Indians' defeat and a destructive period of alcoholism, Tecumseh became a spiritual prophet for his people. The following verse about death is from a longer oration he gave to his people:

"So live your life that the fear of death can never enter your heart. Trouble no one about their religion; respect others in their view, and demand that they respect yours. Love your life, perfect your life, beautify all things in your life. Seek to make your life long and its purpose in the service of your people. Prepare a noble death song for the day when you go over the great divide. ... When it comes your time to die, be not like those whose hearts are filled with the fear of death, so that when their time comes they weep and pray for a little more time

---

46. Mitchell, *Bhagavad Gita: A New Translation*, 104.
47. Ralph Griffith, *The Complete Rig Veda,* Unabridged, English Translation (Classic Century Works, 2012), Aitareya Aranyaka 6–11.

to live their lives over again in a different way. Sing your death song and die like a hero going home."

—*Tecumseh's Prayer for His People* [48]

Tibetan Prayer

The following is a reading from the Tibetan teachings to be read while a person is dying and forty-nine days after death. As hearing is the last sense to go, it is considered helpful to repeat this and other prayers aloud so that the dying or deceased one is reassured. In the afterdeath state, the teaching says that one may experience positive things but also frightening things. One needs to recognize these experiences as projections of one's mind. One is to be aware that they no longer have a body so they can no longer hurt the person. The teachings have family members and friends light a candle and send blessings and positive thoughts to the dying and dead person as they pray.

"Now when this moment of death dawns upon me I will abandon all grasping, yearning, and attachment and enter undistracted into clear awareness of the teaching, and eject my consciousness into the space of the unborn mind as I leave this body of flesh and blood I will know it to be a transitory illusion. Now when the light dawns upon me, I will abandon all thoughts of fear and terror. I will recognize whatever appears is a projection or vision of my mind. When I have reached this critical point, I will not fear the peaceful or negative projections of my mind."

—From *The Tibetan Book of the Dead* [49]

Exercise: *Purification for Death—Essential Phowa*

As you approach death and others are praying or meditating for you, there are spiritual practices for purifying and liberating your consciousness now and when

---

48. Ernest Thompson Seton, *The Gospel of the Red Man: An Indian Bible* (San Diego: The Book Tree, 2006), 60.

49. Chogyam Trungpa, Francesca Fremantle, *The Tibetan Book of the Dead: The Great Liberation Through Hearing in the Bardo* (Boston: Shambhala, 2000), 151.

you have exhaled your last breath. This particular practice can also be read to you after you have died. Called *Essential Phowa*, this practice is from the Tibetan Buddhist tradition and is considered in that tradition to be the most valuable and effective practice at death.

Essential Phowa means a transference or ejection of consciousness into a state of truth. This practice helps assist in emotional or physical healing at death and after death. This is a practice to prepare for your own death and the death of others who are suffering. This is a practice you may want your caregivers to do for you after you have died. If so, have this practice as part of the materials you give to your caregivers along with the prayers and other readings if you chose to use them.

It is helpful to lie down to do this visualization practice. Have a partner, family member, friend, or caregiver read it to you or record it so you can listen. Pause after each statement.

- Sit quietly and relax your body. Close your eyes and breathe slowly. Begin to open your mind and affirm that you are moving into an expanding awareness that fills you and the room and ripples outward. Open more to this awareness and rest in a state of mind that is loving, caring, and compassionate. *(pause)*

- As your mind expands, feel the space and openness all around you expand. *(pause)*

- With all my heart, I (insert name), invoke a Divine Presence above my head. *(pause)*

- I see a Presence pouring down rays of light into me, purifying and transforming my whole being. *(pause)*

- I now affirm that I am fully purified, and dissolving into light. I am now light. *(pause)*

- I am now indistinguishably merged with the enlightened Presence. *(pause)*

- I rest in this great light and Presence. *(pause)*

- When you are ready, move your body and open your eyes.

Step 3

Chapter 7
Step 3:
After-Death Experience
and Instructions

*For any culture which is primarily concerned with meaning,
the study of death—the only certainty that life holds for us—must be central,
for an understanding of death is the key to liberation in life.*
—DR. STANISLAV GROF

As I've described earlier, when physical respiration ceases, the subtle energetic body ceases to exist and your physical body is dead. As this happens, your essence or soul and your life experiences become connected and there is no separation. At your death, your senses dissolve from the top down. The experience of the dissolving starts at the eyes and then the ears, nose, tongue, and touch. You go from the most dualistic perceptions of a variety of inner and outer physical sensory experiences to a non-sensory unity with luminosity and enlightenment as the emerging possibility. You no longer have sensory awareness of your outer world or any sensory stimulus from your body to distract you. The only awareness left is your inner experience.

For caregivers and family members observing the dying person, when all the signs of physical death have occurred, the person no longer has any outer signs or clues of life, but there is still activity in the gamma brain waves. This brain-wave activity lasts for about twenty minutes as the dead person is absorbed in a state of union. This is a critical moment for the deceased. *It is important not to disrupt the person's inner state by moving, touching, or speaking loudly.* Caregivers and family members need to sit quietly and consider the dead person meditatively in love and deep caring.

We shall explore in this chapter the question of what happens after we physically die. It is a question most of us ask, particularly as we approach our death. It is our beliefs that win out generally, whether it is from a religious/spiritual tradition, as an agnostic or atheist. Investigations over the past forty or fifty years into so-called near-death experiences are shedding some light on the question. From something approaching 70,000 years ago to today anthropologists reveal that shamanic cultures around the world have traditions that describe physical death as not the end of the life journey. From both religious and shamanic traditions we explore what to expect beyond your death. From these traditions we'll consider some ways to gain inner guidance for after you die. There are some classic ways spiritual traditions help you recognize that you are dead, and then some exercises for you to explore these after-death questions for yourself.

What Happens After Physical Death?

We do not ultimately know what occurs after physical death. What happens after death is a matter of your belief, but the research into near-death experience may provide some insights for you, and many of our religious traditions explain what lies beyond death. You will find it in the descriptions of early Christian mystics who have seemingly gone through a near-death experience. They describe moving into a brilliant light, confronting beings of light, and journeying into other dimensions of reality.

According to more traditional Christian beliefs, the dead person stays in the ego state they had when alive. Then there is some form of life review and a judgment of their life, the potential of the resurrection of their body in heaven, as well as the mythic journey through hell and into heaven as described in Dante's *Inferno*, which reflects the Catholic view of a type of purgatory.

Step 3

Muslims believe that the spirit of the dead person remains in a timeless sleep until the judgment of the soul, and then there is a kind of purgatory before entering Paradise.

In Hindu tradition, death is a break in the transmigration of the soul from life to life, where one's previous life determines the karmic actions for what will be given as the next life experience, as a god, human, animal, or some other form.

Buddhism, in general, follows the Hindu beliefs of rebirth and karmic actions determining whether one goes to various heavens or lower hells before being liberated from continuous birth or returning to a human body or some other form.

Jewish scriptures or traditions do not comment about an afterlife and affirm instead living a good, moral life here on earth.

Atheists and agnostics take this one step further by asserting that one can never know what is beyond death. Or the atheist asserts that there is nothing at the end of life, saying, "I cease to exist." However, all the religious views hold that there is a continuation of your existence through some form of transformation at your death.

Near-Death Experiences

Beyond these traditional beliefs and views about after-death experience, the studies of near-death experience by pioneering researchers Raymond Moody, Bruce Greyson, Kenneth Ring, and Sharon Cooper, among others, suggest a clearer possibility of what lies beyond death. Over the past forty years, there has been a vast number of near-death reports, from blind people to those attempting suicide. In most cases of individuals who were declared clinically dead, they described a common set of themes when they "returned to life." They first describe being out of their body. They generally experience themselves above their body and looking down at it. The next common element is moving through a tunnel toward a light. For some individuals, they then meet departed friends and relatives who seem to be welcoming them.

The most notable experience for most individuals is the feeling of being completely loved and comforted, but then being told they must return to their bodies. When they do return to their bodies, many indicate that their life has been changed in positive ways. In fact, follow-up studies indicate that those who have had a near-death experience often change the direction, work, and purpose of their lives. Overall, what is interesting in the research is that, whether they are religious or an atheist, the people have similar experiences. One of the hallmarks of near death is that people report a lack of fear about dying and a greater commitment to lead a positive life and some form of wanting to help others.

Shamanistic Near-Death Experience

As I've mentioned at the beginning of this chapter, shamanistic cultures, which anthropologists have found to go back as far as 70,000 years, all describe afterlife states that can be accessed through the shamanic journey that follows the same pattern as a near-death experience. Using sonic rhythms such as dance or drumming that change the brain patterns, the shaman goes into an altered state of consciousness and travels through a tunnel into other worlds and realities. In this state, the spirit beings in these other dimensions offer healing to cure illness, guidance to where game for food will appear in the next few days, and other types of information needed by the tribe for their survival.

Kenneth Ring has studied the similarity between near-death experience and shamanistic experience. What this work suggests to me is that for thousands of years we humans have been exploring the realms beyond death in countless ways. It is apparent that only in this modern age have we lost the connection between life and what is beyond death.

From my own years of deep states of meditation practice, research into dying, and study with a Tibetan teacher, I have come to follow the shamanic, mystic, and meditative traditions that have explored the dimensions beyond our normal cognition and belief structures and have inhabited the states that go way beyond our cultural mind conditioning. Whatever beliefs you hold, being willing to explore these deeper states of mind will ready you for the journey beyond physical life. For me, this journey is particularly detailed in the Tibetan cosmology tradition, as I've been pointing out. Understand, as I present the following process of what occurs after physical death, that this is my viewpoint, but it is validated by near-death experience, the mystical traditions of our world religions, and classic shamanism.

Beyond Your Death

The teachings indicate that immediately after the cessation of the physical body is the best chance of the dead person attaining enlightenment. Several Buddhist traditions hold that it takes only about twenty minutes to confront the possibility of enlightenment because there are no external distractions for the dead person. The soul being or essence emerges literally into a new reality. In metaphysical terms, the dead person is now a surviving energy being with a new awareness.

It is described in the texts that when we experience the twenty minutes after our physical death, we will be in an absorbed state like the bonding or union of a mother with her child. The mind awareness at this moment is clear (because at this point you remain conscious as an aware entity) and the mind state is surrounded, held, and is resting with a feeling of deep comfort and safety. If you are prepared, you will be very open and receptive to this experience of union.

There is also a deep stillness in this resting state, and this unity absorption state of no thought will be noticeable. This is what is called in advanced meditation practices as the awareness of the awareness.

In this first twenty minutes, caregivers will notice that the individual doesn't look dead but appears to be asleep. If you touch the dead person, there is still warmth around the heart, rigor mortis has not set in, and at this point the body hasn't started to smell from decay.

Inner Guidance for the One Who Has Died

As the one that has died, it is the time for you to rest your mind and be open to whatever arises. If you are aware in this moment after physical death, a light will arise before you. This is the light of the true nature of your own mind. Also, recognize that whatever arises will be the projection of your own mind. There

Step

3

will be peaceful qualities, images, shapes, colors, and so on displayed before you and then there will be dark and negative ones much like when you dream. If you can recognize them as projections of your mind and not get involved in them, you have the chance to be liberated, to embrace the light of your True Being and be freed from any further pain or suffering. From the shamanistic point of view, Alberto Villoldo says, "When a person retains his awareness after death, he enters the light easily. My mentor compared this light to the dawn breaking on a cloudless morning, a state of primordial purity—immense and vast, defying description. The blackness of death, caused by the collapse of the senses, recedes and is dispelled by the light of Spirit." [50]

For you to be able to recognize yourself in this after-death state, move in consciousness toward the luminous light and know how to deal with your mind projections. It is therefore important while you are still in your physical form to train your mind to not get involved in your inner and outer projections. The mind is like a sponge. While alive, you absorb the contents of your environment, your experiences, and other people's projections on you. As you die, the contents of this mind sponge are squeezed out and become your entire experience in death. In some sense, this is like a life review. This is why you want to soak your mind with love and create as much goodness as possible in your life to prepare for this after-death experience to move toward the liberating light of your own mind/heart.

At the moment of death, it is the subtle body of your awareness that fits through the oneness point to the other side of this physical experience. We can describe this in many ways. It is the indestructible body of formless awareness of your innermost nature that goes into the beyond. It is this formless awareness that does not die. It is this luminous energy of emptiness, your empty essence, that slips through to the other side. The development and practice of being aware of both your inner and outer experience is what you need to focus on every day, particularly as you enter the dying process, to prepare for your exit and the journey into another reality.

---

50. Villoldo, *Shaman, Healer, Sage,* 209.

Ways to Recognize You Are Dead

Even though the mind is without a body at the moment of death, the habit of being embodied is so strong that the feeling of being a body continues as a form of consciousness. It is this grasping mentally at being in a bodily form that keeps you from moving toward this new experience of life. Instead, in this after-death state, you might believe that you think and feel like your old self, but what often happens is that you don't know you are dead.

The Tibetans say that we stay approximately forty-nine days in this after-death state, confronting our own mind states after the opportunity of the first twenty minutes in which the luminous light appears to us. The Tibetans call this after-death period a *bardo* state, which means an in-between state. This notion of a period of time after death is expressed in many other traditions, such as the land of the dead in indigenous cultures where they experience other dead beings.

Monotheistic traditions (Judaism, Christianity, Islam) describe a purgatory or an in-between state before going to a heaven. Also, there are many levels of "worlds" to traverse, as described in shamanic traditions. In any of these traditions, there is no fixed time for how long you stay in the after-state. According to *The Tibetan Book of the Dead*, the first half of the forty-nine days is associated with confronting the life just ended and the next half is the life you will be moving into—a new life. The tradition holds that for twelve days the dead are in a phase of trying to connect with people they knew, but often not realizing they do not have a body. Often the dead become frustrated because they can't connect with people they knew. People who have had near-death experiences describe a process of being "judged" in a life review of all their positive and negative actions, attitudes, and behaviors. These individuals say that they are their own judge and this determines other after-life experiences.

The possibility of forgetting that you are dead makes it all the more important for family and friends to read to you the after death readings you have written for yourself for a number of days or weeks after your death. These readings are to remind you that you are not physically alive and that, instead of hanging around family and friends, you need to move forward to the light and your new journey.

Step
3

Signs That Verify You Are Dead

Many death teachings indicate that your mind is so strong that when you enter through death into the next realm of existence, you keep forgetting you have died. You still believe or want to believe that you are in the normal real world of the living. The following are some indicators to help you recognize that you are indeed dead. These signs come from the death traditions and near-death experience accounts.

Step

3

- You cast no shadow as you move about.

- You look in a mirror and there is no reflection of you.

- You walk on sand and there are no footprints.

- Your body makes no sound as you move.

- People do not respond to you. You talk, but they can't hear you.

- You can move unimpeded through matter. You go through walls, mountains, anything that is before you. You are able to fly, read minds, and travel quickly from place to place.

- Events become disjointed, like in a dream.

Exercise: *Practice to Prepare for After-Death Experience*

This exercise is a practice run to begin to understand and experience what it will be like after you die. The exercise involves a certain amount of pretending, although as you relax and move with the visualization, you may, in fact, have some amazing experiences. Record this exercise so you can play it back to guide you through it. Or have a partner or friend read it to you. Pause after each statement.

Lie down on a bed or on something comfortable on the floor. You need to relax your body deeply for this exercise and permit yourself to move into an alpha and then a theta brain-wave state. Close your eyes and breathe deeply from the diaphragm for several breaths to begin to relax your body. Put your attention on relaxing the muscles around your eyes and then slowly move down your body, telling your brain to relax each area of your body all the way down to your feet and toes. When you've fully relaxed, begin the exercise.

- The first step after breathing and relaxing your body is to say to yourself, "I am dead." Imagine how you died. Imagine where you died.

- Keep bringing your mind to focus on the realization that you are dead by seeing yourself dead in whatever environment you imaged and how you died. If your mind drifts, say to yourself, "I am dead." Do not be distracted by any life events, as they are only occurring in your mind. This is difficult to realize as your mind is busy conjuring images, but without a body to provide stabilization for you, you can believe these images are real. Again, keep your attention focused by saying to yourself, "I am dead." Visualize other humans that are dead and that are in this after-death state with you. Feel compassion for them as you encounter these beings in various situations. Remember, as the traditional teachings indicate, when you are dead your mind will make up all kinds of events and people, just as you are doing now.

- After death, you can have scary, if not terrifying, experiences. Breathe and remind yourself not to be afraid, as everything you see is an illusionary situation, like a dream. When anxiety, fear, anger, or uncertainty, among other negative attitudes, arise in you, stop and refocus on the positive in your mind. Practice now to put positive images in your mind. Use images of nature, people you love, and the like. In the after-death state, you need to avoid negative states of mind.

- Practice now while still alive to keep your mind open, positive, peaceful, and in equanimity or balance. Breathing and focusing on your heart keeps your mind positive. This teaches you not to get swayed mentally. Breathe deeply and slowly and feel your inner balance.

- The big challenge after death is wanting to have a body again. To meet this challenge, visualize yourself going through a wall, or instantly be in a different location. Your mind is powerful and can create images now while alive, just as it will when you are dead. You need to cut off yearning for a body by

Step

3

realizing you don't have one. Continue to visualize flying and move through buildings, mountains, and so on.

- Give up attachments to the events going through your mind. Attempt right now to let go of your thoughts and refocus on your heart. This is basically learning a meditation practice. Breathe and focus on your heart.

- Practice now in this relaxed state to focus on your heart area and feel devotion for yourself as well as appreciation and gratitude for your life. As you focus on your heart, repeat to yourself, "Love is my essence. What I am is love. I am grateful for my life and all that has been given to me whether good or bad."

- A challenge after death is to not be attracted to soft lights but rather to focus only on bright lights. The bright light is what leads to your awakening. Practice imagining soft lights and then bright lights. Move in your imagination toward the bright light. Keep focused on this bright light until you are ready to open your eyes and get up.

- Record your experience in your notebook.

Step 3

Exercise: *Affirmation for Caregivers After a Person's Death*

This is a good exercise to give to your caregivers as part of the materials you will give them to assist you when you are dying. Also, you may use this before your death as you assist family or friends as they are dying.

I stated previously that the first twenty minutes after dying is one of the most critical times for the dead person passing through to the beyond. As part of the after-death preparation for an individual, many traditions urge people not to touch the individual during this twenty-minute time period if possible. The reason they suggest this is that time is the "gateway" passage of the soul out of the body into the next realm. From the scientific research I mentioned in an earlier chapter, this immediate period after the breath and heart stops the brain is still producing high levels of gamma brain waves that may support this sensitive time for the dead person. However, if it is not possible to leave the body untouched during this time know that the intent to be respectful of the body and whatever experience the dying person may be having is the important issue, whether one leaves the body untouched or is touching it. The mystery of what we will go through when our heart and breath stops is the amazing journey each of us will discover. Below are some suggestions for how to be with the deceased.

- As a caregiver, family member, or friend, sit quietly near the body, breathe slowly, and relax your own body.

- Imagine the body and consciousness of the person who has died take the form of a small light moving up their spine and then quickly flying out from their body at the top of the head like a shooting star and dissolving into the image of the heart of a divine or luminous Presence.

- Affirm, visualize, and even pray that the dead person be freed from all mental and emotional suffering as they are in this Presence.

- Imagine a light or star released from the deceased into the luminosity of the expanding light of the true nature of their mind. Then speak the affirmation, "May your freedom be for the benefit of all beings, especially those you are leaving behind." Sit in the presence of this person's body and trust that you are helping to release the individual into another phase of their existence and honor and appreciate them for their courage and the beauty of their journey.

Step 3

Chapter 8
Practical Preparations for Death

*It is one of the most beautiful compensations in life
that no man can sincerely try to help another without helping himself.*
—RALPH WALDO EMERSON

In previous chapters, we've discussed and explored various dimensions of the dying process. You've investigated your own experience and understanding of your beliefs about death and a number of speculations of what happens internally as well as physically as you move through the dying process and then what experience you may have after your breath and heart stop. All of this has been about you and what happens as you die and the potential of your journey after dying. In this chapter, I want to turn your attention to how you would want to be cared for as you go through your dying process.

The first question is, what kind of caregivers do you want and how do you want them to care for you at the various stages of your dying? While living, you can prepare your choice of caregivers and help them to understand the process of active dying. Also, if your dying process extends for long periods of time it adds stress and tension to your caregivers. There are some suggestions in this section as to how your caregivers can work with this situation. One critical area we will explore in this chapter is how you want caregivers to prepare your body after dying. Also, one thing you can plan for now is what kind of recognition, memorial, or funeral service you would like to have for family and friends. And, finally, at the end of the chapter, I want to raise the issue of physician-assisted suicide that is gaining legality in the United States.

Preparation for Caregivers

Depending on your physical condition at the end of your life, you will possibly have among your "caregivers" family, friends, doctors, nurses, and hospice workers. For the process of your dying, you have the possibility now of choosing who you would like to have as caregivers when you enter your dying process. You will want to consider their caring relationship to you, their ability, and how they might care for you, and discuss with them how they feel about caring for you.

Sometimes it is not possible for you to choose your caregivers, but you can express to family and close friends what quality of care you want at this most significant experience of your life. Just as adequate care is important for you in your dying process, it is also helpful to find a working structure that provides support for your caregivers. Below are some considerations of who you would want as caregivers for you.

Who Do You Want as Caregivers?

Choose caregivers who will love and nourish you and who will create an environment that will establish for you a peaceful state of mind as you go through the process of your death.

Professional caregivers can help you, but they can also hinder you with pushy behavior and attitudes about how you are to be treated. Many of your caregivers (family, friends, professionals) may exhibit a negative mind state and create undue tension at your dying. Your caregivers need to match you as you move into a peaceful, loving, and opening state of your being in the last moments of your life. Be willing to say no to caregivers, instruct them on how you want to be treated and on the environment you want them to establish, and be willing to ask individuals to leave if you do not feel comfortable with them. It is very important to have a key caregiver who you trust absolutely to fulfill and manage your desires for the kind of care, environment, and people you want with you as you die.

Take the view now before the ending time of your life to create the perspective that it is a privilege for caregivers to be with you in this once-in-a-lifetime passage. You are the one to take the lead in your own death process. Others may think there is a particular way to do things, but it is your process, not theirs. You are the guide; only let them guide you based on what you want them to do for you.

Determining the Care You Want

Here are some ideas of how you can guide your own process. Be sure to write in your notebook the kind of care you want from these and other ideas you may have about your caregivers and the environment. If you are in a group, both share and listen to others about what each of you wants in the dying process. It may give you further ideas for your process.

- Let both family and professional caregivers know you would like to have encouragement and comforting about not being afraid as you die and also to support you by creating a feeling of a safe environment where you are dying. For example, the room you are in can be sunny, shaded, filled with flowers, with music playing, quiet whispering, and perhaps only one or two people at a time with you.

- Your hearing is one of the last senses to dissolve, so let your caregivers know if they are talking too much or too loud. Your caregivers must be willing to hold a peaceful and quiet attitude when they are in the room with you and have an understanding of what you will be going through in the stages. Heartfelt listening to your needs, rhythm, and changing dynamics as you go through the various stages of dying is an ability that caregivers must have.

- Touching is also one of the last senses to dissolve, so being held or holding your hands gently may bring vital reassurance to you.

- Having caregivers breathing with each of your breaths is another connection that could be precious to you.

- The key understanding to communicate to your caregivers is to make sure throughout the dying process that their role is to enable you to relax and let go as you depart in a positive state of mind filled with the awareness of love.

- Your caregivers need to make you as comfortable as possible because you will go through several different states of response to your dying.

- Your dying is a delicate dance for both you and your caregivers. It is of great importance that you be able to give your full attention to your dying process as you move toward full awareness of your expanded self.

- Share your life story when you are able with your caregivers. This helps you release the past and be in gratitude for all aspects of your life. Let your caregivers help you through any forgiveness process that may arise from memories of people or situations.

- Have your caregivers help you remember your best human qualities, allowing you to feel uplifted as you recall memories of loving times in your life.

- One simple step that can help prepare caregivers for your ensuing death is to initiate a conversation with them about how you would like your body cared for after death. This can initiate an intimate conversation with family and friends about their own feelings about your dying and what they want at their own dying process. This is a wonderful place to explore what might be possible both for you and them.

- Intimate conversations with family and friends about their life with you can also be a time of remembrance for you. Memories can be of times when you had compassion for yourself and others, times when you had courage, times when you opened your heart to others, times of fun and adventure, and more.

- Finally, make available to your caregivers the journal or notebook that you used for the exercises in this book, including the list of readings you selected and any other material you want your caregivers to have, so they have a full understanding of what you want from them as they care for you on this final journey of your life.

Exercise: *How Do You Want to Be Treated in Your Dying Process?*

Place a yes or no beside each statement. Make appropriate comments in your notebook as to why you give each statement the yes or no. If in a group, share with the group your thoughts.

- I want to have my caregivers with me continually as death may come at any moment for me.
- I would like my hand held and be talked to by caregivers even if I do not respond.
- I want others praying or meditating in the room for me as much as possible.
- I wish to have friends told that I am sick and dying and to pray for me.
- I want kindness and joy, not sadness or crying, near my bed.
- I want quiet music and whispering when I am dying.
- I want one person from my family or a friend guiding other family members, friends, and professionals at my dying process.
- I want family and friends to sit with me, talk to me, and tell stories about our life together.
- I want my clothes to be cleaned if my bowels and bladder fail.
- I would like to die at home.
- I want family around me when I die. Who else besides family?
- I would like professional caregivers to keep my life going as long as possible.
- I want appropriate drugs to reduce my pain.
- I want drugs to remove me from being conscious of my dying.
- I don't believe there is anything beyond death, so I want to stay conscious of my surroundings as long as possible.

Information for Caregivers About the Signs and Symptoms of Active Dying
Whether a caregiver is a professional or a family member, they need to know the signals of how you are changing outwardly and physically with the dying process and what is appropriate to do to assist your dying. The many physical and practical signs and symptoms can be observed and need specific responses from a caregiver.

Caregivers will notice that, as you are dying, you digest each dying phase you go through before you enter the next stage in the physical dying process. Depending on the physical issues you face, each phase with its particular signs will be shorter or longer in duration.

The best support that a caregiver can give to you is to create a positive way for you to go through each dying phase without too much trauma or discomfort. Here are a variety of signs and symptoms for the caregiver to pay attention to as the dying process progresses. Any of these signs and symptoms can come in any order for a particular person. It is helpful to have your caregivers know what these signs are. Have your caregivers:

- Notice when you do not talk much as you begin to turn inward due to feeling the pull of images, voices, etc., that you may be experiencing. They need to watch your breathing, listen to you if you make comments as they sit with you, but generally not engage in conversation with you.

- Notice when your body gets hot. At times there is an increase in heat in the head and the heart area. They need to gently wipe your brow to keep you cool. They need to wet your dry lips periodically with a wet sponge.

- Notice when you have a decrease in food and water intake. They are not to force food or water on you, as you are letting go of physical needs as you turn inward for "spiritual food."

- Notice as you become weak and sleep a lot due to apoptosis, which is the process of programmed cell death.

- Know that your request is that caregivers be quiet and gentle at this point and create an atmosphere of meditative peace. Have the focus be on soft music, whispering, and only gentle physical movement if you need attention.

• Notice when you become unable to move or urinate and when your breathing pattern changes due to less oxygen and to metabolic changes as your body shuts down.

• Understand that any assistance with bodily needs should be done with gentleness of movement. You are in a highly sensitive condition in your dying at this point.

• Notice any restless movement. This movement can range from gentle to extreme agitation with tossing and turning, kicking off blankets, attempts to get up out of bed, etc. This restlessness is due to decreased circulation in your brain and blood acidity, which creates erratic responses in you.

• Help to reduce the agitation with a calm, soft, and reassuring voice. Placing a hand under your hand, doing energy work like Reiki if they know how, repeating verbal prayers softly, playing theta brain-wave music, etc., will be reassuring to you. The purpose is to create a calm, peaceful environment for you as much as possible.

• Know that what caregivers do at this point is not the most critical, but their state of presence that will be reassuring to you.

• Notice when you become physically and emotionally disorientated. One moment you may seem lucid and present, and the next disjointed in speech and you cannot recognize people and the situation happening to you. This is due to integrating into a new structure of time and place, and the falling away of your identity. The caregiver's role is to be gentle and reassuring, with a calming voice and comforting manner toward you. Soft and gentle touching is reassuring to you.

• Notice that your skin is becoming transparent. This is a sign that you are progressing toward physical death.

• Breathe with you. Caregivers may increase a presence of love and a meditative atmosphere with a gentle focus on the breathing and movement of you. This puts the caregiver into rhythm with you as you are dying and helps them attune more emotionally and spiritually to you.

- Notice when your breathing pattern changes. The breath can become fast, slow, shallow, strong, or struggling. This is due to changing brain patterns as the chemical structure changes in the brain and is part of the dying of your brain. Given your medical instructions forcing oxygen on you or trying to apply more drugs, etc., may not serve you at this stage of dying. The change of breathing patterns is a natural phase of your dying process.

- Notice when your legs and arms become discolored due to circulation slowing down. Caregivers need to be careful not to attempt to rub or put ice or heat on the arms or legs. Once again, this is the natural progression of your dying process.

- Notice when there is a rattling of your breathing and when the breath stops. The brain is still functioning, so you are not technically dead yet.

- Know that you have materials you would like read to you after the breathing stops. A significant challenge for caregivers is to continue to sit with you after you have died both reading or speaking to you as I've suggested above. It is important to be prepared at this stage to have material written out that you want caregivers to read and speak aloud to you. If possible, caregivers remain in a meditative and intuitive space on behalf of you as the "dead" person for several hours.

What Caregivers Can Do When Dying Drags On

Reverend Jerry Farrell, of the church Unity of the Gold Country Spiritual Center in California, is a former Catholic priest and former spiritual director of Hospice of the Foothills for Nevada County, California. He provides some insightful observations for caregivers from his years of being with the dying.

- One of the important things Reverend Farrell urges caregivers to watch for is fear arising in the dying person. What is needed, he suggests, is to speak softly in the ear of the dying person and tell them that they are loved and forgiven and should simply relax and let go.

- He also notes that if the dying process is dragging on for many, many days, be patient. Even if you can't figure out what or why things are happening, know there is important work taking place in the dying person. Everyone has their own internal timing and rhythm.

- When the person is peaceful and all the physical signs of dying are present, but dying is prolonged, it may be the family's refusal to let the person go. Over the years, observing how families resist letting go of the dying person, he developed the following "release formula" for family members or friends to say to the dying person.

- Release Formula: The family or friends either singularly or together talk softly and gently saying the suggestive release statements to the dying person. Not all the statements need to be said, but those giving the dying person permission to let go and that friends and family will be okay when they die should be emphasized. These statements can be said in a person's own words to the dying person:

    * Know you have led a complete life and are dearly loved.
    * Know that we love you and want you to be in peace.
    * We know that the time has come for you to choose what is best for you.
    * None of us are angry with you and we release you from our care and concern. Know that you have our love and permission to go.
    * Know that there is no more that we can do for you.
    * We know that your pain and suffering will soon be relieved.
    * We love you and hope to see you in the next life.
    * We will do fine. We will be okay after you leave us.

Exercise: *What Do You Want from Your Caregivers?*

Describe the things that you want your caregivers to do to keep you comfortable. Use this list as a starting point. In your journal, modify and explain in detail what you specifically want or don't want from your caregivers. Add to this list as things come to mind. This is a list to give to caregivers. If in a group, share your lists with each other for further ideas.

- I do not want to be in pain. Give me appropriate drugs but don't make me unconscious of what I need to experience in the dying process.
- If I have signs of depression, nausea, or hallucinations, do what you can to help me.
- If I have a fever, then place a cool moist cloth on my head. I want my lips and mouth kept moist to stop dryness.
- I want to be kept clean with warm baths as long as I am able.
- I want to be massaged with warm oils as often as possible.
- I want to have my favorite music continually played until I die.
- I want to have personal care like shaving, nails clipped, hair brushed, teeth brushed as long as it does not cause discomfort.
- I want to have religious readings and poems read aloud to me when I am close to death.
- I want friends beyond my family to meditate and pray for me.
- I want to have the option for hospice palliative care for physical comfort.
- I am willing to have them overdose me to speed my dying.
- Indicate other things you may want caregivers to do for you at your death.

Preparation of the Body After Death

Various death traditions tell us not to disturb the dead body for at least *three* days. This means not taken to a mortuary or cremated, but generally remaining where the person died. These three days are important for the dead person in the after-death experience. When we died at home and were celebrated and then buried, it was usually three days before the burial service. In Irish tradition, for example, the body was dressed up and often sat up while a party of music, singing, dancing, and toasting the dead person took place. In most Eastern religious traditions, the body is prepared with oils and dressed, and then candles and flowers are put around the dead person to honor them.

These three days are important for the family and friends to emotionally and spiritually integrate the loss of the dead person, as well as prepare for some community ritual of recognition of the dead person. It is also the time of the continual reading of the after-death "reminder" to the dead person that they are dead and to move toward the light. These three days are an important time of inner and outer preparation for both the caregivers and the dead person.

If caregivers had open, compassionate hearts toward the dying person, the grief process has already begun for them and continues in deep awareness through these three days of caring for the body. Often it is not possible to wait for the three days, given preferences of the deceased or other circumstances such as shipping the body across country. Again, the intent by caregivers is to continue to honor and provide prayers, affirmations, or readings that affirm the person's passage whether in the three-day period or not.

Immediate Care of the Body at Death

There are many traditions about preparing the body by washing it, rubbing the body with oils, dressing the person, and having people come and meditate and pray for the deceased person. After the first hour, including the period of twenty minutes during which the dead person is facing the possibility of moving into the light, caregivers will observe continuing changes in the body. There will be a stiffening of the body after about three hours that will continue to maximum rigor mortis up to twelve hours. The heart will progressively grow colder. The body will appear tight and tense. Caregivers need to shut the eyelids after the twenty-minute period of not touching the body, as rigor mortis affects the eyes and face first.

After about twelve hours, the maximum state of stiffness will begin to loosen due to chemical and tissue decay. This process occurs gradually over three days. The rigor mortis reverses, starting with fingers and toes, up through the body to the face, resulting in the appearance of deep relaxation in the face and body.

One issue that confronts caregivers is keeping the body for three days, if those were the wishes of the deceased. Particular circumstances may cause difficulty for the caregivers to keep the body for three days. Intent is always the important issue. What matters the most is that the caregivers are doing their best and expressing their love.

If you, as the dying person, choose this three-day waiting period with the body, I will present in the legal chapter how this needs to be taken care of before your death. If, for example, your death is in a hospital, there must be arrangements in advance to keep your body for a longer time or to move the body to a home. These issues, plus disposing of the body via cremation, burial, or willing to science, are considered in the next chapter.

Traditional Three-Day Preparation of the Body

When preparation has been granted for keeping the body for three days, the next stage of the death process begins for the caregivers. It is after the body has relaxed that the washing, oiling, and other preparations to the body can take place. There are also the rituals around the body that may be instituted. This can include candles, music, and people who continuously sit with the body, meditating, praying, and reading to the dead person in their journey beyond death.

Hopefully, you, as the dying person, will have detailed what rituals you want at this point. Most of all, these three days can be a time of sacred, quiet reflection, prayer, and focus on the person who has died. If it can be arranged to have people sitting quietly, meditating, praying, and reading to the deceased around the clock during the three days, that is optimal. Beyond the three days is then the planning and carrying out of the memorial, announcements in newspapers, death certificates, and other legal issues that need to be taken care of by family members (more on this in the legal chapter). Resources on preparing the body during the three-day period and gravesite preparation can be found in appendix A.

Exercise: *Grief Affirmation Phrases for Caregivers*

The affirmations below can be helpful to your caregivers when you die. Provide these affirmations to your caregivers so that it may help give them a sense of calm to support their grief when you die. Provide these in your notes to caregivers if it is appropriate for you.

- I accept my grief and forgive anything that did not meet my loved one's needs.
- I open to and release all sorrow and pain for my loved one.
- I accept my sadness knowing I am not my sadness.
- I will find my inner resources to be present for my sorrow.

Recognition of You After Your Death

After you die, family and friends want to honor your life. What kind of service or memorial do you want? Perhaps you don't want any public recognition. Do you want an obituary in a newspaper, an announcement on Facebook, or nothing at all? Do you want an open casket for viewing? Do you want just family at a gravesite? Do you want a memorial open to anyone who wants to come? Who do you want to arrange your after-death recognition? You have a right to resolve all these and many other questions before you die. There is also a host of legal issues that come after death that we will consider, but the question at this stage is: What recognition if any do you want after you die?

Exercise: *What Do You Want During and After Your Death?*

In your journal, respond to the following questions. These questions can help in planning both your dying process and your after-death experience the way you want it. If you like, you can create your entire memorial service should you choose to have one. You can write your own obituary. Plan what music you want played as you die and at your service. Be creative and aware of what this planning does for you in anticipation of your death.

- List who you want as your caregivers. Who do you not want to be present as you die?

- Are there particular people you want to come to you to resolve issues with you before or during the dying process?

- Who is the person that you want to manage the caregivers and the process of your dying?

- When you are dead, do you want your body to be buried in the ground or at sea, cremated, or given to science for research or your organs donated?

- What kind of ceremony or memorial would you like after you die? Do you want a standard funeral-home service or something you design, or no memorial at all?

- Who do you want to attend your service or memorial if you have one?

- If you have a service or memorial, what kind of structure, minister, leader, music, speakers, ceremony, food, or celebration do you want?

- Do you want your death published in the newspaper?

- List any other things you want attended to after you die.

A Word About Physician-Assisted Suicide

Laws are being passed in various parts of the United States to permit individuals to take their own lives through the legality of physician-assisted suicide. This "death with dignity" movement raises a number of issues and options for a person's dying process. In the assisted-suicide process, a medical doctor provides the knowledge and means for the person to commit suicide. The important thing to note is the doctor is not present at the time of death. Most of the laws governing physician-assisted suicide require that the individual has a physical condition from which he or she will die within six months. Euthanasia is similar. With euthanasia, however, a medical doctor is present and provides and administers a lethal drug to the patient. Euthanasia is legal in the Netherlands.

There are pros and cons about assisted suicide based on beliefs, suffering, and long-term pain and terminal illness. With the physician-assisted suicide movement growing in the United States, it is raising moral, ethical, and religious questions regarding suicide within the discussion of end-of-life issues. Each person's physical condition and beliefs will determine one's choice on this end-of-life issue. It is helpful to become informed about this topic as you consider your own end-of-life options.

Chapter 9
Legal Document Planning

Before everything else, getting ready is the secret of success.
—HENRY FORD

In preparation for death, we know that we can soften our dying by making amends with others, settling scores, doing everything to tie up loose ends, seek the forgiveness of those harmed, and work through all the mental/emotional matters of this life. What is also important is to complete all the legal issues involved. This section is to assist you ahead of the time of your death in handling your legal, health, and funeral affairs.

To have everything organized is a gift you give your loved ones, others, and yourself. When the needed legal work is finished, you will know you are complete on this side of the "grave" and your caregivers will be able to step in and expedite your wishes with minimal difficulty. However, if an accident happens or sudden death and you haven't been able to get everything in order don't despair or feel guilty. My encouragement is to simply consider and act on these matters as you can now.

There are a number of key documents that need to be filled out and filed before you die. This before-death preparation helps family members, partners, or close friends take care of your health wishes and your estate. You will need to name individuals to take control of health care as well as legal and financial matters when you are not able to do so. These include signed legal papers and directives before you die. You will need to appoint a medical care person and a power of attorney to represent your desires as you die. After death, there will be a need for a key person to implement wills and trusts.

There are legal firms that provide services for all the various legal issues and documents I will describe. You may have already met with legal help and created these documents. However, if you have not considered these legal issues, in each section that follows is a list of legal forms and documents needed to be completed before, during, and after you die.

To view the type of legal forms I describe, refer to appendix B, where online links to the main forms for the state you reside within are provided. The websites in appendix B link to the various legal topics I present. These websites are directed at US readers. If you are from Canada or another country, please do an Internet search on these topics that apply to your country or region. I will be giving exercises in this section to help you think or rethink the various issues these documents raise for you. I have found that as we age our considerations and wishes change. You may already have many of these forms, but it is good to review them on an annual basis.

We must consider the primary legal documents that would be critical for you to have before you die suddenly or of sickness or old age. The most important documents to consider for yourself is a will, a living trust, and an ethical will.

Medical decisions will include an advance health care directive that covers your wishes for medical treatment at end of life. Most important is to designate a person to act in your behalf when you can't for yourself. This is the durable power of attorney. The medical power of attorney is a bit different as you designate a person or a relative that will help with your medical decisions and wishes when you are unable to do so yourself.

Other medical directives that you may decide you want include a do not resuscitate directive and the physician's orders for life-sustaining treatment, known as POLST. Finally, in this chapter you can consider whether you want to provide organ donations or medical school donations. Be sure to put all your responses to the exercises in your notebook as a reference for your caregivers.

Your Will

A will is a legal document that spells out who gets what from your estate. A will can be written or audio or video recorded. The will includes such areas as estate planning, legal contract documents, assets, marriage licensees, and loans, among others. A last will and testament is important in order to make sure that your final wishes are respected. The only way to ensure that the proper heirs or organizations inherit the right property from your estate in the probate process or living trust process is through the will. Taking the time now to prepare a will can prevent unintended consequences that often occur if you avoid creating a will. Again, if you have a will it is useful to reevaluate whether it still reflects your wishes and intentions.

Living Trust

A living trust form is used to prepare your estate. A living trust is a trust established during a person's lifetime in which a person's assets and property are placed within the trust, usually for the purpose of estate planning. The trust then owns and manages the property held by the trust through a trustee for the benefit of the named beneficiary, usually the creator of the trust. A trust is a legal and financial arrangement between the creator of the trust and the person or persons that the trust represents. A trust designates by whom and how it will be controlled and managed for any and all of your assets. States can have different forms for your trust, so if you choose to consider a trust, check appendix B for a website to investigate what would be involved for you having a trust.

Why Do You Need a Living Trust?

When a person dies, there are a set of "intestate succession rules" if the individual does not have a will or a trust. When a person dies without a will, she or he is said to die "intestate," and if a person dies with a valid will, she or he is said to die "testate."

What this means is that if you die without a will, a court of law will distribute your property according to the laws of your state. How it is distributed may not fulfill your wishes. According to these rules, your property, insurance, money, and even minor-age children go to your closest relatives. If the prescribed sequence reveals no relatives, it all goes to the state. If you have a will, after your death, your property, investments, and so on will go through the probate courts of your state for taxing purposes before being distributed according to the instructions in your will. If you have a living trust, all assets go directly to the beneficiaries named in the trust. In the absence of a will, the court system decides where any minor children will go and who their guardians will be. For further information on these issues consult appendix B for a website.

Ethical Will

An ethical will is a personal legacy. It is a philosophical portrait of you. The portrait is a chance to leave wisdom you have gathered that may inspire others or transmit to others what is in your heart. You may want to share your values and traditions, what you want continued after you die, things you have done in your lifetime, lessons earned, and lessons learned.

There are many ways to provide an ethical will. There are wonderful stories of a grandchild who sits by the bedside listening to a grandfather tell his life story. A recorder captures his words, preserves his history, and gives dignity to his life. Or a family helps make a scrapbook reflecting the mother's life with photos spread out on the bed as they adore the treasures of a life well lived. One suggestion is to write out your portrait or, as an alternative, develop an audio or video recording.

Many people choose to have such recordings played or handed out at their funeral or celebration. This ethical will can be available just to family or close friends. In appendix B, there is a website that provides a template and worksheets to give you an idea of how to do your ethical will.

Exercise: *Evaluate Your Documents*

If you have not yet created a will or a trust, consider setting a date to take care of creating such a document. Determine if you want to create an ethical will and the form it will take. If you want to do an ethical will set a date to begin the process.

Remember you can do a little bit over time. It doesn't have to be a burdensome project for you.

Advance Health Care Directive

An advance health care directive is a form of living will that allows you to document your wishes concerning medical treatments at the end of life. Your living will guides medical decision-making and requires two physicians to certify the actions you want doctors to take in different medical conditions you may confront. This document is also called the "Living Will Registry" form. When filled out it is available in every state and available at every hospital. When you fill out the form, you will be contacted annually if you want to make changes or if you want to update any part of your directive.

This directive is required when:

- You are unable to make medical decisions.
- You are in the medical condition specified in the state's living will law (such as "terminal illness" or "permanent unconsciousness").
- Other requirements may also apply, depending on the state and your wishes.

Durable Power of Attorney

A power of attorney directive names someone that you trust to act as your agent if you are unable to speak for yourself. The power of attorney will manage your assets when you are no longer able to do so. You may want to choose one person to speak for you to make financial decisions. You can do separate financial and health care powers of attorney. A link to a sample form is in appendix B.

Medical Power of Attorney

A medical power of attorney is a legal instrument that allows you to select the person that you want to make health-care decisions for you if and when you become unable to make them for yourself. The person you pick is your representative for purposes of health-care decision-making. The purpose is to enable the representative to make decisions regarding the type of medical responses you want. You can limit your representative to certain types of decisions, for example, the decision to put you on life support or not when there is no hope of you getting better. On the other hand, you could allow your representative to make any health-care decision that may arise, based on their own judgment of the situation. This includes decisions to give, withhold, or withdraw informed consent of any type of health care, including but not limited to medical and surgical treatments. Other decisions that may be included are psychiatric treatment, nursing care, hospitalization, treatments given in a nursing home, home health care, and organ donation.

The medical power of attorney provides directions for the medical doctor and the medical team or hospice personnel supporting you as the dying person. It is telling your physician, for example, that you want life-sustaining medical intervention discontinued in a specific or extreme circumstance. Another example is that the document can tell your physician to pull the plug to artificial nourishment after seven days if it is the only thing sustaining your life. This document is for you to write your own wishes and give the power to your representative to make all the medical decisions.

An example of a medical power of attorney statement is: "I direct my agent to make decisions concerning life-sustaining medical treatment with the knowledge that I do not want my life to be prolonged artificially nor do I want life-sustaining medical treatment to be provided or continued if such means are the sole source of my continued living."

It is important to travel with this advance directive so your wishes will be known if you need life-sustaining treatment when away from home. Also place this document with your medical records at home and let your partner, family, and any other caregivers know where you keep your documents. It is important to review yearly to see if any changes are needed. In appendix B, there are two websites for the legal form and answers to questions you may have about this document.

Exercise: *Choices for Individuals to Fulfill Roles*

In your journal, respond to the following questions:

- Who is the person you will appoint to be your medical power of attorney?

- If you haven't obtained certain documents above, when will you download the forms on the computer and begin to fill them out? Give yourself specific dates and put them on your calendar.

- If you don't have this document, write your own medical power of attorney or go online to get a form from the link in appendix B under this section title.

- What medical directives do you want your medical power of attorney representative to carry out for you? Read some of the downloadable documents for ideas.

Other Medical Directives You Can Choose

The basic directives above are recommended for each person to have, particularly as you get older, but all adults should have them. The following documents are critical if you are in an accident or in an unconscious condition so that emergency personnel, medical doctors, and others know your wishes.

Cardiopulmonary Resuscitation (CPR) Directive

Currently, the advance health care directive is not enough if you do not want any resuscitation. The "Do Not Resuscitate" directive allows for a natural death. A cardiopulmonary resuscitation (CPR) directive allows you to refuse in advance any attempts to resuscitate you by chest compressions, medications, defibrillation (electric shock), or intubation (artificial breathing machine) if your heart or breathing malfunctions or stops.

CPR directives are almost always used by people who are severely or terminally ill or elderly. For them, the trauma involved in CPR is likely to do more harm than good (only about 3 percent of these individuals will survive CPR), but emergency personnel are required to perform CPR unless a directive tells them not to.

CPR directives must be immediately visible to emergency personnel. At home, it's a good idea to post it on the refrigerator, near the front door, or near the patient's bed. For more active folks with CPR directives, a wallet card or special CPR directive bracelet or necklace can be used. A CPR directive form does *not* have to be original nor do the signatures have to be original. Photocopies, scans, and faxes are just as valid as the original.

A note about the DNR and CPR directives: Joseph Gallo, MD, who is a professor at Johns Hopkins University in Baltimore, Maryland, took part in a decades-long project called the Johns Hopkins Precursors Study.[51] Gallo's part was studying both doctors' and patients' answers to questions about end-of-life medical treatments. Gallo's study looked at the preferences of these doctors and patients for treatment. The study showed there is a huge gap between what patients want and what doctors want in their end-of-life treatment. The study covered questions on CPR, ventilation, dialysis, chemotherapy, surgery, invasive testing, feeding tube, blood, antibiotics, IV hydration, and pain medication. They used a 0-to-100 scale chart to gives responses from "Yes, I would want," "No, I would not want," "Undecided," and "Trial, but stop if no clear improvement." Here is a summary of the results:

For doctors' preferences in all the categories (CPR, antibiotics and IV hydration), on a scale of 0 to 100 the range of "no" responses was from 90 to mid-80 that they did not want the various treatments at the end of their life. Without going into further detail about the study, the implication for us as patients is that while we may want to prolong our lives medically, doctors would not seek to have the same treatments for themselves because of the side effects of these treatments. If you are interested in learning more about this study, see the article by Dr. Gallo.

---

51. Joseph J. Gallo, "Life-sustaining treatments: What do physicians want and do they express their wishes to others?" *Journal of the American Geriatrics Society* 51, no. 7 (July 2003): 961–969.

Exercise: *Resuscitation Choices*

In your journal, respond to the following questions:

- Is it an important issue for you not to be resuscitated? Describe why.
- Do you want to be resuscitated if your heart stops?
- Do you want aggressive treatments such as intubation and mechanical ventilation?
- Do you want antibiotics?
- Do you want tube or intravenous feeding if you can't eat on your own?

Do Not Intubate (ADNI)

This is another advanced directive if your wish is to not use a breathing machine. For more information go to appendix B under this title.

Physician's Orders for Life-Sustaining Treatment (POLST)

This is a document to improve end-of-life care in the United States. The document encourages doctors to speak with patients and create specific medical orders to be honored by health-care workers during a medical crisis. The POLST document is a standardized, portable, single-page form that documents a conversation between a doctor and a seriously ill patient or the patient's surrogate decision-maker.

This document is a medical order. The POLST form is always signed by a doctor and, depending on the state, the patient. One difference between a POLST form and an advance health care directive is that the POLST form is designed to be actionable throughout an entire community. It is immediately recognizable and can be used by doctors and first responders (including paramedics, fire departments, police, emergency rooms, hospitals, and nursing homes).

POLST forms are recommended for all patients with life-limiting illnesses or progressive frailty. A pragmatic rule for initiating a POLST can be if the clinician would not be surprised if the patient were to die within one year. The link to the forms are in appendix B.

Exercise: *What Type of Support Do You Want?*

In your journal, respond to the following questions:

- Do you want to contact your physician and discuss the POLST form?
- When close to death, do you want life-support treatment or do you want it stopped?
- If you are in a coma and not expected to wake up, do you want life support or not?
- Do you want life-support treatment if you have brain damage?
- Is there any other condition under which you do not want to be kept alive?
- Are there other medical conditions you want addressed?

Organ Donation Directive

Donated organs and tissues are in great demand, as medical technology has made successful organ and tissue transplants safer, easier, and less expensive. Currently, common organ and tissue transplants are: kidney, liver, heart, lung, cornea, bone and bone marrow, tendon, ligament, connective tissue, skin, and pancreas.

Organ, tissue, or body donations must be carried out immediately after death, so if you want to be a donor, you should make arrangements in advance, usually with a local university medical teaching hospital. You should also discuss your plans and wishes with those closest to you, especially your health-care representative if you have named one in an advance health care directive or medical power of attorney document.

Even if you have expressed a desire to donate your organs, an objection from close family members could defeat your intentions. The best safeguard is to put your wishes in writing and be sure family and friends know what they are. The organ donation registry has more information and forms; its website can be found in appendix B.

Exercise: *What to Do with Your Body*

In your journal, respond to the following:

- Write the instructions for your final disposition of your body.

- Where will you put your written instructions (at home, in a safe-deposit box, or with a health-care representative, partner, or friend) for final arrangements of the disposition of your body?

- What details need to be included for a final arrangements document?

- What arrangements do I want, if any, from a mortuary, home burial, cremation, organ donation, or other means for deposing of my body?

Medical School Body Donation

Whole-body donation is a generous gift of knowledge. It provides the finest source of education for medical students—far better than any textbook or computer. For medical professionals, nothing is equivalent to the human body in providing an essential and thorough understanding of anatomy. Your gift will help advance medical training and research, and in turn, benefit your children, grandchildren, and people for many generations to come.

You and the medical school of your choice will decide the details for final disposition. Options for final disposition vary slightly between medical schools, but generally begin with cremation as soon as studies are completed. According to prior agreement with you or your next of kin, the cremated remains can be returned to the family for burial in a family plot or disposed as the family desires. Alternatively, the school can bury remains in graves owned by the institution. Some schools offer scattering of the ashes over water in the maritime tradition.

Your donation helps ensure the future of high-quality medical care and innovative research. The gratitude expressed by the medical profession to each donor cannot be overemphasized.

If you choose this method, your body needs to be kept undisturbed for as long as possible after death. If that option is not possible there is an alternative. One suggestion is for your caretakers to tap the top of your head, just before the school comes for your body. This area of the head is the most auspicious gate for your consciousness to leave the body. Your caretakers should then offer prayers, tell your consciousness to go to the light, and burn some incense in your honor.

There is a national center for whole-body donation that directs you to the research medical university nearest you that can receive the body. The link to this national center is in appendix B.

Exercise: *Should You Donate?*

If you want to donate your body, go online and contact the medical school that you are interested in receiving it. Download the application and instructions. Fill out the form. After you fill it out, copy it and send it to your medical power of attorney representative.

After-Death Decisions for Your Durable Power of Attorney Representative

There are a number of legal actions your durable power of attorney representative must do for you after you die. It is useful to have a conversation with this person so that they understand what you are asking them to do for you. These actions include death certificates, the type of burial or cremation process you want, if they've been prepaid or not, and where the institutions are that provide these services. Also, there is a general checklist for the representative of things needed to be done. Finally, in this section are some cautions for your representative of how they display your information.

Death Certificates

A death certificate contains important information about the person who has died. Details vary from state to state but often include: full name, address, birth date and birthplace, father's name and birthplace, mother's name and birthplace, complete or partial Social Security number, education, veteran's discharge or the cause of death, marital status and name of surviving spouse if there was one, the medical examiner, and the date, place, and time of death. In appendix B is a link to the US standard certificate of death.

The funeral home, cremation organization, or other person in charge of the deceased person's remains will prepare and file the death certificate. Preparing the certificate involves gathering personal information from family members and obtaining the signature of a doctor, medical examiner, or coroner. In general, the process needs to be completed within three to ten days, depending on state law.

When someone dies, the death must be registered with the local or state vital records office within a matter of days. The vital records office can then issue copies of the death certificate, which you may want for handling the deceased person's affairs.

Death certificates must be obtained for cremation, burial, and organ and body donation. The simplest way to get certified copies of a death certificate is to order them through the funeral home or mortuary, or Neptune Society at the time of the death. If you are in charge of winding up the deceased person's affairs, you should ask for at least ten copies. You will need one each time you claim property or benefits that belonged to the deceased person, including life insurance proceeds, Social Security benefits, payable on death accounts, veteran's benefits, and many others.

If the time of death has passed and you need to order death certificates, contact the county or state vital records office. For deaths that occurred within the previous few months, you should start with the county office, because it is more likely to have the certificate on file. After a few months have passed, the state office will probably have it, too.

Exercise: *Information for Death Certificates*

In your journal, record the following:

- Use the US standard certificate of death linked in the appendix and create a list of the information needed to fill out a death certificate.
- Place the information with your durable power of attorney document.

Burial at a Conventional Cemetery

Burial costs include the cost of the plot, casket, and in-ground burial with vault or grave liner. This cost does not include other funeral fees from the mortuary. You may be embalmed and then buried in the earth in a biodegradable casket or without any container. The cemetery may allow simple markers such as engraved stones or a plot using a GPS system.

For burial, you can buy a one-piece "box" called a grave liner, usually concrete, metal, or fiberglass, to prevent the casket from sinking down when buried in the ground. A grave liner is a less expensive alternative to a vault, which is an above-ground holder of the body placed in a mausoleum with a facing stone. The fee for the grave or vault may include upkeep of the gravesite, including the cemetery's fees. Without a casket, the body is wrapped in shrouds or blankets in the vault for interment.

There are several places to get information on burial costs, including a local funeral home. The Federal Trade Commission of the US government gives consumer information on costs and a pricing checklist for various funeral fees including burial through a mortuary. See appendix B for this link.

Green Cemetery Burial

There is also a new/old burial process called green burial. Green burial has re-emerged due to people becoming concerned with how cemetery burials have a negative chemical impact on the earth. These "natural" burials were the norm up until the early 1900s.

In a green burial, the body is placed in the earth to decompose naturally. This type of burial has little environmental impact by using biodegradable products such as refrigeration or dry ice instead of embalming fluid. Caskets are built with bamboo or sustainable woods or cardboard. Another option is to simply place a cloth shroud around the body before burial. The idea of this type of burial is that it reduces carbon emissions and aids in the restoration and preservation of the environment. There are certified green cemeteries or natural burial grounds in some sections of the country. See appendix B for a link to information about green burials.

Exercise: *Information on Burial Services*

In your journal, record the following:

- Get information on burial and other services from your mortuary of choice.
- List the total costs for:
    - ★ Cost of the plot
    - ★ Casket
    - ★ In-ground burial with grave liner (concrete, metal, or fiberglass)
    - ★ Above-ground burial with vault
    - ★ Other funeral fees
    - ★ Markers such as engraved stones or a plot using a GPS system
    - ★ Upkeep of the gravesite, including the cemetery's fees

---

Cremation

Cremation is a cheaper and more convenient method of disposing of a body compared to burial. Direct cremation provides a no-frill package at a cheaper cost. Funeral homes will pick up the body, file the death certificate, and give the ashes to the appropriate person. When choosing a casket for cremation, it simply requires a rigid combustible container. Rosewood, mahogany, pine, or cloth-covered caskets are all available for cremation. You will be charged for these containers. Another option is to have your own casket built that will carry your body to the cremation. If the family were to choose a non-combustible casket for viewing, the crematory would still need a simple combustible container for cremation. In this case, it is possible to rent an attractive casket for viewing.

Time of death is important for cremation. The person must be deceased for forty-eight hours prior to cremation. This is a legal precaution to ensure that there is time to complete an investigation of the cause of death should one be needed. Neptune Society is a national organization that provides information about cremation options, other services, and local funeral homes. A link to this section can be found in appendix B.

Exercise: *Information on Cremation Services*

If you believe cremation is an option for you, check on the total expense of cremation at your local mortuary including delivery of the body and box to the mortuary home, fee of the cremation, delivery of the cremains, insurance, and extra handling. Compare the local service with that of the Neptune Society, which is a national organization. Also, check to learn if there are green burial services available in your community.

Checklist for Immediate Actions to Take After Death

This checklist can be used by the individual you identified to have power of attorney for medical care and legal and financial matters of the will or estate. Remember, you can choose different people for each of these areas of power of attorney or you can have one individual as power of attorney for all of them. The following is a useful checklist to remind the person who will represent you after your death. Be sure this individual has this list:

- Notify your loved one's close family members and friends.
- Make appointments to arrange for the funeral, burial or cremation, and memorial service of your loved one.
- Notify your loved one's employer or clients.
- Notify the appropriate parties if your loved one was a member of any professional organizations, charitable organizations, or labor unions.
- Contact your loved one's financial advisor.
- Contact your loved one's estate-planning attorney.
- Locate important legal documents, such as marriage certificates and birth certificates, to retitle your loved one's assets or apply for benefits for a surviving spouse. If you open the safe-deposit box, you may want to consider having a witness to help you record the contents of the box.
- Locate insurance policies.
- Notify credit card companies.

- Contact past employers regarding pension plans, and contact individual retirement account (IRA) custodians or trustees.
- Notify your loved one's financial institutions(s) to retitle or distribute the accounts(s).
- Retitle jointly held assets, such as bank accounts, vehicles, stocks, bonds, and real estate.
- Notify utility companies.
- Contact your loved one's mortgage company.

Cautions to Consider for Immediate After-Death Actions

In our culture, criminals today watch for death announcements and attempt to use the dead person for identity theft. The following are some immediate things for the person who has durable power of attorney to do after a loved one's death to help prevent identity theft:

- Immediately send death certificate copies by certified mail to the three main credit reporting bureaus. Request that a "deceased alert" be placed on the credit report.
- Mail copies as soon as possible to banks, insurers, and other financial firms requesting account closure or change of joint ownership.
- Report the death to the Social Security Administration at 800-772-1213 and the IRS at 800-829-1040. Also notify the DMV.
- In obituaries, don't include the deceased's birth date, place of birth, or last address or job.
- Starting a month after the death, check the departed's credit report at www. annualcreditreport.com for possible suspicious activity.

Documents to Settle the Estate

There are important documents you may need for your representative to settle your estate. These documents may be in your desk, in a safe-deposit box, or with a friend or relative. Your representative needs to know where to find these documents. The following list comes from the Edward Jones Advisors pamphlet, "Steps to Take When a Loved One Dies": [52]

- Birth certificate
- Marriage certificate or divorce papers or prenuptial agreement
- Military records
- Uncashed Social Security checks
- Adoption papers for minor children
- Trust documents
- Bank account records
- Mortgages and deeds
- Partnership, operating, and shareholder agreements
- Leases
- Most recent and prior year-end brokerage/investment statements
- Stock or bond certificates
- Insurance polices
- Most recent statements or employer-sponsored retirements plans or IRAs
- Loan documents
- Income tax returns for the past three years
- Prior gifts tax
- Most recent credit card statements
- Records relating to the value of tangible assets
- Titles to automobile and other personal property

Have Everything Prepared Legally Before You Die

Hindu philosophy states that if there is confusion among your family or friends in attempting to figure out your practical affairs, personal wishes, and estate is-

---

52. Edward Jones, Inc., *Steps to Take When a Loved One Dies* (St. Louis, MO: Edward Jones Pamphlet, 2015), 1–7.

sues after your death, you will be affected as you pass through to the other side of this life. In other words, after you die, you will know and feel the confusion and try to help those left behind to fix the situation and find everything that they are seeking to discover in your affairs and estate. This potential confusion of the practical issues you didn't take care of before you died keeps you attached to the situation and people on this side. This will stop you from moving on to the next stage of your journey. This is helpful advice whether you believe in the afterlife or not.

You may have heard the stories of how families are torn apart because they could not find or figure out the deceased person's will, information, insurance, wishes for how the body was to be treated or buried or cremated, as well as clarity in who receives personal possessions and important individuals to contact such as estate lawyers, financial advisors, whether they had bought prepaid burial or cremation contracts, and so on.

There is one more thing you need to do to get your affairs in order and give yourself total peace of mind. If you complete this next process, you will be confident that your affairs will be in order. It will allow family or friends to have clear direction and ease to find information and make the decisions you want. I recommend a valuable book to help you put all your practical matters in order right now before you have any sense of your death approaching. The book is *A Graceful Farewell: Putting Your Affairs in Order.*[53] The book with the downloadable computer documents will help organize and guide you to be totally prepared with all the practical things you should have ready for those you leave behind. More information on this book is in appendix B.

Whether you get this book or not, the principle is to think through all of the things you take for granted and that your representative or family or friends would not know where to find, such as where you keep the key to the mail box, the key to the safe-deposit box, passwords for all your charge cards, passwords to online accounts, etc. The more you can have this information in one place the easier it is for your representatives to settle your affairs.

---

53. Maggie Watson, *A Graceful Farewell* (Fort Bragg, CA: Cypress House, 2006).

This first half of the book was created to work with the underlying fear of approaching the end of your life. Understanding and preparing at a practical level what to do for ourselves and our family and friends brings release and a sense of inner relief and freedom to live more fully now. I hope you have guided yourself into a more peaceful and practical awareness of the dying process. I also hope that you have worked with the exercises, and have made practical preparations for your eventual death. It is important to know what to expect and how to prepare your family and caregivers for this event.

When I considered and worked on all these issues for myself, I could sense that there was still something missing. I knew there was something that needed further exploration. As I pondered the whole process of dying, one piece stood out. As I considered the missing piece, it became obvious to me. When we physically die, we do not take our egos, personalities, or constricted selves with us. As you explored in this first half of the book, while in the crisis time of dying, you have to let go of everything. You let go of your attachment to people, things, memories, and situations. Most of all, you have to release yourself into a place of nothingness. It is this unknown that causes the greatest fear and pain, because you have to become no one. You are stripped of your identity, and as you are confronted with this reality, it can be terrifying.

The truth is, you and I are attached to being someone. The big struggle is the release of identity, the constricted self, at the last moment of life. It became clear to me that if I knew how this personality was developed, then I could let it go while I was still alive. If I learned how to let go, then in my final days on earth I could be at peace as I released myself into a new beginning.

I set out to explore an understanding of the development of my personality or, as I call it, the constricted self. I wanted to know what keeps me so attached to being someone and answer the question of how this self and body are structured. In the course of research and long periods of meditation, I also came to understand that the process of releasing the constricted self at death is the same process you and I can use to let it go now and awaken to a fully alive life before we die.

The second part of the book is to take the journey now of awakening to the expanded self and to true and vital freedom in your life. This exploration will follow the steps of how we created the constricted self and how we take the return journey home to awaken to our true self. Let us begin the next stage of the journey from fear to freedom.

Part II
The Journey to Freedom:
A Guide to Life

In an unusual Internet circulation that was attributed to the Dalai Lama, James J. Lachard wrote in an unpublished essay the following: "Man, sacrifices his health in order to make money. Then he sacrifices money to recuperate his health. And then he is so anxious about the future that he does not enjoy the present; the result being that he does not live in the present or the future; he lives as if he is never going to die, and then dies having never really lived." [54]

The Dalai Lama points out that one's life is too frequently unlived. We can assume that there must be another way to live. To some degree, we have all been caught up in our own version of an unlived life. This next section of the book begins by exploring how your body, mind, and emotions make up this constricted self we've talked about. This is the self that sacrifices itself for money, security, pleasure, being important, and trying to survive. The core question that we will be examining is "What is the prime motivation in the structure of the constricted self that snatches us away from living a fulfilling and meaningful life?"

In this part of the book, we will start taking a journey of eight steps that will continue on in part 3. These journeys will take you step by step through

---

54. James L. Lachard, *An Interview with God*, unpublished work.

the birthing process of your constricted self and the process to awaken to your expanded true self. It is key for you to know how you are structured and developed so that you can become conscious and make changes in your life that give you more inner freedom. The changes you make will build a new foundation to live your life more in the present and not die having never lived. To build a new foundation, I utilize an energy structure called the chakra energy system. This system explores how your energy is developed and how it builds and decreases in strength. The constricted self blocks this energy system and restricts its natural flow. I also use the Enneagram structure to deepen your journey by identifying your personality type. You will take assessments and do exercises to find your personality type and begin to understand how you have constructed the patterning of your life. After going through how you've created "what you are not," that is, the compensation pattern of the constricted self that comes from the emotional and physical wounding we all have experienced in one form or another, we will begin the journey back to our essential nature that I've called our expanded self.

Let me review the eight steps before we begin. *The Journey to Freedom: A Guide to Life* has eight steps to discover how you created your ego personality, or constricted self and how you can awaken to your expanded true self. In the first four steps in part 2, I explore how your fear of death was created. Knowing that the ego is filled with fear, the first four steps describe how your ego was born and created this death phobia. There are a variety of exercises, practices, and meditations to provide you tools for this journey.

Here are the first four steps:

1. *The Journey of Separation* describes how fear begins to be a central part of your life. It explores the effect on your body and how it separates you from others.

2. *The Journey of Emotions* describes how you use your emotions to hold on to and to resist people and situations in your life. The ego uses your emotions to generate pain and suffering in your life.

3. *The Journey of the Mind* investigates your personal thinking process and how it can become a very powerful force dividing you from your physical body.

4. *The Journey of Self-Identity* delves into the process of how you identify yourself as a separate person from the world around you. This step explores at how you define yourself as a person and are caught in the subject/object dilemma of perception.

Steps five through eight in part 3 are the steps to help you unwind your ego-created journey. Each step includes exercises and meditations to help you explore your own personal journey.

5. *Freedom from Personal Identity* is the beginning place to detach from your constricted ego and identify.

6. *Freedom from the Mental Self* is releasing the mental patterns that have bound you to your inner pain and suffering.

7. *Freedom from the Emotional Self* is when unwinding your emotional impulses helps you gain the possibility of inner expansion and release from fear.

8. *Freedom from Separation* is the final step and recognizes the illusion of your false inner home and the awareness of the truth of the separation you lived with all your life. The last part of this eighth step is the *Process of Integration*. Of all the eight steps the process of integration opens the possibility for your awakening to your true self.

Each of these eight steps will take you into and then out of your contracted awareness into the freedom of expansion to experience a vital and full life as you complete this journey of your existence.

Chapter 10
The Development
and Structure of the Self

Growth does not come from either obeying or disobeying rules,
from either doing as you are told or rebelling against it.
Growth comes from allowing your ego's story to drop away.

—DON RISO

We must each have a reason to look honestly and fully into the face of the constricted self. As described in the first part of the book, when you die, you do not die in your constricted self. The need to let go of this constricted self when you die is a compelling reason to awake to your expanded self now and live your life out in joy and inner peace before you die. I hope you have come to realize from the first half of the book that your dying is a necessary part of life. You and I know that we cannot run away from death. Hopefully, that fact alone will motivate you to learn to live well now because you can die at any time.

In my view, one of the most important actions you can take for yourself is to learn to open and live now with your expanded self.

As described in the first half of the book, the expanded self is the self in which you would want to die because it gives you a quality of mind that is aware, loving, relaxed, spacious, peaceful, and balanced. I describe this expanded self's structure and development in chapter 2. Where we need to begin, however, is to explore how you and I created our constricted self. There are three parts to the constricted self: the body, the mind, and the brain. We will follow the construct of how these three elements develop your ego constricted self.

The Constricted Self

The constricted self follows a pattern of development that includes the body, mind/brain/emotions, and beliefs and behaviors. The body becomes the foundational identification point of our ego identity. We will note that the body is made up of information, energy, and space. Out of this content we sense and experience an energy field, which some call an aura. The mind functions to tell the brain what to do and the brain directs the body. Out of the body mind/brain function there arises in us senses and emotions and perceptions that create our beliefs and behaviors. From this sequence, self-identity arises in which we see our constricted self reflected like a mirror in the world around us governed by "me, my, and mine." All this leads to a disconnect of reality and generates the source of our fear and suffering.

The Body

In my investigation into the constricted self, I began by asking the obvious question: Is the body the constricted self? I asked this question because most of us believe and identify that our body is who we are. What I ultimately discovered was that the body does not contain or hold self-identity. I may try to identify with my body as my "self," but, as I explored both in meditation and biological study, I learned that this flesh we call our self is just made up of energy, information, and space.

What you and I know from our education is that the body at its most basic component is made up of the physical atom. The atoms that make up your body are the most basic units of human matter. Consider what an atom is. The atom is the size a ten-billionth of a meter. Each atom has an electron that moves around the atom. To give some perspective on the size of the atom, the nucleus of the atom is like an SUV and the electron is the size of a chickpea. There is a lot of space between them, but that space is full of energy frequencies and information. When two atoms bond together, they form a molecule, connecting energy information through the space around them. When more molecules bond together, it creates chemicals and the chemicals share a field of informational energy. When the chemicals form together, in their field they create cells and the cells organize to form tissues within the field of energy around them. The tissues move together to organize into an organ. There is also a field around them that creates systems such as the digestive system or the cardiovascular system. These systems function as a collective consciousness in a field of energy to create a body. *This body matter we call our self is an interconnecting set of energies, information, and, most of all, space!* Buddhists would say that our body is simply an interdependent web of causes and effects and there is no Self present.

This interdependent set of cause-and-effect energies within our body seeks coherence. Coherence means that the pulsating frequencies will align with each other. They fall into rhythm, much like a group of clocks will eventually start ticking at the same rhythm or drummers will naturally come into mutual drumming to each other's rhythm. Physics describes coherence as energy waves that align in perfect phase and balance.

When this happens, they have a constant oscillating or repeated frequency pattern. *What we call our body identity is this oscillating frequency pattern.*

When we apply this idea to the body's energy, if our energy is low, there is an imbalance or incoherence. When the frequency gets low enough, the body becomes incoherent, that is, it moves out of balance, order, and rhythm. Disease is created when the energy is low and there is incoherence. The body is made up of oscillating energy frequencies that affect this body matter and information that is communicated throughout the body in healthy or unhealthy body symptoms. When you have a disease, the energy frequency is lowered. You are out of coherence and the chance for the body to "die" becomes possible. The body is an amazing mechanism, but it is not yourself!

From a metaphysical viewpoint, we can add one more aspect to the body matter. Most spiritual traditions claim that around the body is a field of information energy that radiates from the physical form. This is called the auric field or personal field of informational energy. An aura is a field of subtle, luminous radiation surrounding a person or object like a halo. The aura is the manifestation of the electromagnetic field believed to come from the minute electrical impulses running through the body. This view holds that there is a rhythm or pulsation to our physical matter that extends out approximately four feet from the body. This invisible field of information gives life, order, or coherence to matter. You will discover later how you can begin to experience your expanded self as related to this aura.

Let's stop and explore in a simple exercise a coherence pattern of our auric field. Remember that this field of personal informational energy is the result of charged microcurrents of electricity that are being given off by the nerves in your body. To begin to become aware of this energy field is to sense and feel it before the possibility of seeing it.

Exercise: *Sensing the Energy Field of the Body*

Become still in silence and breathe deeply so that your mind and heart settle and you can listen to the deepest part of yourself. Then follow these steps:

- One of the easiest ways of experiencing this energy field of your body is to first rub your hands together rapidly.

- After rubbing for a few seconds, hold your hands opposite each other and apart about six inches and slightly move your hands back and forth. As you move your hands back and forth, you will feel a slight magnetic pull between your hands.

- As you continue to move your hands back and forth, spread your hands farther apart. As you focus your attention on the space between your hands, you can begin to feel a "ball" of energy building between your hands.

- This feeling of "energy" between your hands is what is experienced in martial arts, tai chi ch'uan, and Qigong energy practices. There are other practices that one can learn to train one's eyes to see this energy.

The Mind

Let me come back to the idea of energy coherence in your body. How is the rhythmic and balanced frequency lowered in your body? What causes the frequency to become out of balance or not in coherence? From the research I covered in my previous book, it is clear that imbalance coherence has to do with the functioning of your mind/brain.

The brain is the command center for your nervous system. However, your mind is not located in any specific place in the body or the brain. Yet your mind is intimately involved in all the brain's activities. Neuroscientists' definition of the mind is that *the mind is what the brain does*. To use a computer metaphor, your mind acts like software in a computer. The brain is the hardware that allows a variety of different software programs to run. Because you and I have different brain functions and different types of "software" as a mind, this can account for the different reactions we may have to the same stimulus. Our brain/mind hardware and software are each a little different to match the differences between us. The mind, the brain, and the body all interact like a perfect computer. *The mind's function is to tell the brain what to do and the brain directs the body.*

When the brain directs the body, then the body responds and behaviors are acted out. You identify with the actions and behaviors as being you—the person doing the action or behavior. You believe these behaviors must be who you are, as they are behaviors your mind is guiding in the actions of your body. You believe repeated actions and behaviors that your brain and mind make up define your personality—your identity as an individual. However, all your actions and behaviors ultimately come from the evolution of that simple atom to make up this illusive and complex construct we call the personality or ego. But there is still more to this construct.

The Senses and Emotions

As your biological organism grows and ages, the perception of yourself as a personality grows through the increasing development of your sensations. When your mind's attention is on an object, such as a tree in the environment, it records a variety of sensations registered in your brain. Your senses (hearing, sight, smell, taste, and touch) register the physicality of the tree. Your brain/mind receives this information as it travels through the body, where there is some type of reaction or response. It sees or touches or smells or feels or hears the wind in the tree. Through this experience of the sensations, there is a response in your mind/brain/body to the tree. The response has an emotional feeling reaction as to whether the tree is enjoyable or not enjoyable, pretty or not pretty, or no response at all to the tree. What we know from research is that this emotion or "feeling tone" function is part of every sensation and the resulting perception you have.

What happens next is that this sensation/perception generates thought. Your thought formulates a belief or judgment about the tree in the environment given the awareness of your sensations. This quality of your mind's feelings and thoughts has a direct effect on the energy of the brain and on the body. The judgment also has a direct influence on the energy and frequency of your entire biological system. The judgment of negative reaction can lower your energy balance or the judgment of positive enjoyment can raise your energy coherence frequency.

Beliefs and Behaviors

But wait, there is more to be constructed in this pattern of your identity. Here is more familiar ground, as it is where you become aware of yourself as a personality with particular beliefs and behaviors. When your thoughts are spoken and feelings experienced, such as when you say or feel "I like that sunset" or "I hate hot weather" or "Weather doesn't bother me at all," these beliefs and behaviors create a personification that is called "me" because all the sensations, emotions, thoughts, and judgments are happening within and to you. As your personality gets stronger in its beliefs, values, and assumptions of the "me," you become attached to them and assume they are "mine." Your inner dialogue could go something like: "I must be a real person because this is me. It is happening to me and this experience is mine because I can feel it inside. Therefore, this is now my identity because everything I see, feel, or think is me."

Me, My, and Mine

The habit of me, my, and mine are continually repeated until your personality gets stronger to resist any outside doubt of who you are. The more the repetitive behavior of the inner and outer experience of "me" the more real you feel you are "you." What we know is that the mind, brain, and body helps concoct the "me." You are, in fact, an evolutionary and biological learning machine that constructs the "me and mine" called your personality or ego self.

Two Minds: Constricted and Expanded

To make things a little more complex, you and I live in two states of mind. It all depends on which mind you chose and how that mind is directed. One mind is the mind of survival or the constricted self. This mind lives in fear, anger, shame, and stress and experiences all the survival issues that define your reality. When your body lives in survival mode, it lowers the frequency and your body health by consuming a lot of your energy. In the short term, the negative emotions and stress affect your body by contracting and lowering the mental and emotional frequencies of the brain. The good news is that in the short term your energy can be restored. But if the stress goes on and on for a longer period of time, it affects your energy levels, draws from the energy reserves of your body, and becomes chronic.

When this happens, you begin to lose the sense of your energy coherence, balance, and inner and outer rhythm. You struggle to maintain your material body to survive.

Mentally and emotionally, your personality wants the "constricted you" to survive and not die. What is real to you then is the physical, material reality that your senses can verify as "you." When this survival component happens, you begin unconsciously to fortify the belief that you are more material body than you are energy or a frequency wave. However, deep in your personality is the hidden fear that "you" are only a construct, an illusion, and that "you" does not really exist. You may experience this when you have waves of anxiety that seem to come from nowhere.

Don't fear, you also have the other mind available to you. This mind is the creative self or the expanded self. This self creates energy and utilizes energy to extend compassion for all beings. This expanded self is still connected to the constricted self of survival, but it has the potential to be free. The quality of your expanded mind has a higher frequency such as love, appreciation, intuition, and gratitude, rather than fear, anger, and shame. The expanded self does not need the material world to exist. Awareness of space, energy, and expansiveness are qualities of the expanded self. You can wake up now before you die and align with what Jesus said, "Be in the world but not of it." [55]

Before you die, your expanded self can release your constricted attachment to the material world of survival, problems, and suffering. The creative mind of this expanded self creates energy and utilizes energy to express compassion for your life and for all beings. To be able to wake up you must confront the fact that your "I" personality of me, my, and mine does not exist. You made it up as a strategy for survival in your particular circumstance. We will now look at the impact that the "I" constricted personality has on your life in terms of pain and suffering. This is what is called the "pain body."

The Pain Body

This expanded mind is not oriented as the "I" personality, rather, the "I" personality does not really exist. It has been made up. When you move from the constricted personality self to the expanded self, it doesn't mean you no longer have a personality. When you become free and expanded, the focal point of your senses, perception, actions, and behavior naturally change toward a positive, more fluid, and open expression of your unique nature. You will look the same, speak the same, do many of the same things you always have done. You will still confront what Eckhart Tolle calls the "pain body." [56]

The pain body represents the patterns of genes, environment, and personal experiences (particularly emotional ones) that shape you and me. The pain body is what you experience in the constricted self. Tolle calls the pain body "an ac-

---

55. *Holy Bible: 1308.*
56. Eckhart Tolle, *The Power of Now.*

cumulation of painful life experience that was not fully faced and accepted in the moment it arose ... [it is] an energy entity consisting of old emotion."[57] It is out of your lifelong struggle that you created your own pain and emotional suffering.

As your expanded personality becomes healed and free through your conscious presence and awareness, the pain body will still be there, but you will no longer experience the suffering when situations activate it. As I've described, the body/mind/brain is a creator of your ego identity for good or ill. As we continue our exploration, you will be exploring the way you used all three to construct your constricted self, starting as a young child and how you can come to experience your expanded self.

After the following exercise, I will describe brain frequencies a little more, how two systems in your brain are part of constructing and keeping you hooked into the constricted self, and then the system that can move you into your expanded self.

Exercise: *Impact of the Body, Mind, and Emotions*

The intent of the exercise is for you to observe your conscious awareness of emotional impact or lack of it on your sensations. In your notebook, describe your observations.

- What is the type of emotion, feeling tone, or non-emotions you experience as you contact or observe something in the room or outside via your senses (sight, smell, touch, taste, hearing)? Just notice what sensations are the strongest for you and what sensations generate emotions, if any.

- What happens to your body energy and attitude toward yourself or others when you are angry or disturbed by someone or something? Or when something brings you joy? Or when something has no response and is just neutral for you? Think of a situation in which anger or disturbance occurred recently. Describe the differences in your notebook.

---

57. Eckhart Tolle, "Living in Presence with Your Emotional Pain Body," *Huffington Post* (blog), March 10, 2014, http://www.huffingtonpost.com/eckhart-tolle/living-in-presence-with-y_b_753114.html.

The Two Brain Systems

The two brain systems consist of four major brain frequencies, the default mode network, and the task positive network. These frequencies and networks determine the movement from constricted self to expanded self.

Within the brain are a variety of frequencies that function to maintain your body and mind systems. There are four main brain frequencies to which you have easy access, and these four will be the ones you will work with when using the videos. These four frequencies are beta (13–38 Hz), alpha (7.8–13 Hz), theta (4–7.8 Hz), and delta (0.5–4 Hz). These four frequencies are active in you from when you wake up in the morning, when concentrating on work, relaxing, daydreaming, and at the end of the day entering deep sleep.

The brain research over the past fifteen years has demonstrated that if you know how to consciously use these brain frequencies, you can make fundamental changes in your life. The great understanding from these years of research is that your brain is "plastic." The meaning of the brain being plastic is that, by using simple repeatable patterns both consciously and unconsciously, you can change and shape, grow and develop the actual tissue of your brain.

Default Mode Network (DMN)

One remarkable discovery in the brain research is a system in the brain that makes up the constricted self structure. This system is called the default mode network (DMN). This network of brain neurons is activated in your external conscious life to recall past experiences, to plan the future, and to navigate social interactions. It is also used in your internal awareness and conscious thought when not engaged in the external world. The DMN operates as low as 0.1 hertz and is activated when you are internally focused, such as when dreaming, when you are retrieving memories, and when your mind drifts unfocused on past and future perspectives and social interactions.

The DMN consists of the medial temporal lobe (visual memories), the medial prefrontal lobe (the personality), posterior cingulate (integrates with the internal cingulate cortex), ventral precuneius (imagery of self), and the inferior parietal cortex (interprets and senses body image). The DMN is activated between the ages of nine and twelve. It is also strongly active in people with long-term trauma, childhood abuse, and other constrictive emotional patterns and experiences. The importance of you understanding that you have a default mode network is the knowledge that you can change the structure of your DMN brain. Earlier, I presented the notion that meditation has a powerful impact on daily life, emotions, and behavior. Even more important, brain research on meditation practice demonstrates that it changes brain structure and activates another network in the brain.

Task-Positive Network (TPN)

This other brain network is called a task-positive network (TPN). The TPN is activated when the mind is in focused attention and consciously aware. The brain areas of activation when focused and aware are the prefrontal cortex and parietal structures of the brain. Thus, when there is an increased mental focus, as with meditation, it decreases the DMN and decreases the personality of the constricted self. It allows for the expanded self to be constructed.

This is amazing research that supports the practice of meditation as a positive tool to release your constricted self. These TPN frequency patterns can shift both your brain and your mind in your work of awakening to your essential nature by releasing your constricted DMN patterns and open the expanded nature of your being.

Right and Left Hemisphere Brain Functions

There are other brain functions that also affect the constricted self and the expanded self, particularly when we are dying. The brain has a right and a left hemisphere connected by a network of nerve fibers called the corpus callosum. The left hemisphere is dominant in language. It processes both what you speak and what you hear. It is also the dominant logical part of the brain and has the ability to do mathematical computations as well as retrieve facts from your memory.

The right hemisphere is mainly in charge of visual spatial abilities, face recognition, and processing music. It performs some math but not difficult problems.

The brain's right side also helps us to comprehend visual imagery and make sense of what we see. The right brain's use of language is primarily in interpreting form, the big picture, context, and verbal tones.

Each side has its dominant characteristics, but there are elements of both hemispheres in either side. It is important to note that the left brain houses your personality, which is your constricted self. This is the self that is gradually released when you die. The right brain is the last to be dissolved when you die. The detaching of the constricted self from the left brain allows the right brain to be active until you die. This is why I call dying of the constricted self before we die the waking-up process. You can do this consciously before you die and live in the peace, love, and freedom in the right brain today.

In summary, brain research tells you that your left-brain houses the survival personality. This dissolves when you leave your body. Then your body is free of verbal language, judgments, and figuring things out. This leaves the right brain, which primarily houses the expanded self, as the functioning brain. This self is aware, with expression of positive emotions, light, and color.

In my view, the quality of mind you are in when you die will determine the most important spiritual experience of your life. Some people say, as they are in the transformation process of dying, "This is what I have been searching for all my life." Your opportunity is to prepare your mind to slip into that quality of mind now before you physically die. This is the purpose of this awakening work. If you are aware in the transformation process of both living and dying you will be able to raise your energy frequencies or consciousness to a high level of releasing your old patterns and your "pain body." This energy release of tension from thoughts, memories, beliefs, emotions, and sensations by your trained brain/mind will raise your consciousness to perceive life around you very differently from what you currently experience. Your higher energy frequency will increase mind awareness and will expand and dissolve the left-brain's tightness and your constricted self.

Exercise: *Right/Left Brain Assessment*

The following are forced-choice questions. People will do both at times. Choose the response that is *most characteristic of your natural tendency or behavior,* not what you think you should do, or how you've trained yourself to do something. Do not analyze the questions, but simply put down your first response. Circle either *a* or *b.*

1. In solving a problem:

   a. I will stay at my desk and write out possible solutions, arrange them in order of priority, then pick out the best one.

   b. I will take a walk, mull things over, discuss it with someone, and then digest the problem while doing something else before arriving at a decision.

2. When making decisions:

   a. I occasionally have hunches but don't place much faith in them.

   b. I frequently have strong hunches and follow them.

3. If I have a project to complete:

   a. I file the materials in folders and put them away when I am not working on the project.

   b. I leave the materials in piles on my desk, floor, etc., and generally prefer not to put them away where I can't see them.

4. I learn athletics and dancing better by:

   a. Memorizing the sequence and repeating the steps mentally.

   b. Imitating someone and getting the feel of the game or music by simply trying to do it.

5. In communicating with others:

    a. I more easily express myself verbally.

    b. I more easily express myself in written or graphic form.

6. When I take notes:

    a. I rarely print.

    b. I frequently print.

7. When situations require that I take a risk:

    a. I become anxious in making the risk.

    b. I enjoy the adventure of the risk.

8. We all become moody from time to time:

    a. I have almost no mood changes.

    b. I have frequent mood swings.

9. In school, I preferred:

    a. Algebra.

    b. Geometry.

10. When I sit in a relaxed position with my hands clasped comfortably in my lap, the thumb on top is:

    a. My right thumb.

    b. My left thumb.

11. All of us have some type of written or unwritten goals for our life:

    a. I am very strongly goal oriented, and try to fulfill them.

    b. I have some general goals but don't focus my life on them.

12. When wanting to know what time it is:

    a. I need to look at a clock to get the accurate time.

    b. I have an inner sense of how much time has passed without looking at my watch.

Scoring

Add up all the As and all the Bs you circled.

a = _____

b = _____

a represents your left brain score

b represents your right brain score

The higher the number in the left or right score, the greater the tendency toward that perspective. The following gives some information on the use of left- and right-brain hemisphere function in your thinking style.

    The human brain consists of two hemispheres that are mirror images of each other. The hemispheres are connected by the corpus callosum, a series of nerve fiber bundles that transmit information from one brain hemisphere to the other. Each hemisphere controls the movements and sensations of the opposite side of the body; that is, the left hemisphere controls the right side of the body, and the right hemisphere controls the left side of the body. Study of the hemispheres indicate that the left brain controls a significant portion of the analytical mental functions such as language (both speech and comprehension) and logical and rational capabilities, whereas the right brain controls much of the intuitive capabilities—the ability to produce and appreciate music and art—as well as spatial skills. The hemispheres also differ in their methods of processing information. The left brain processes in a sequential manner, dealing with details and features, whereas the right brain tends to deal with simultaneous relationships and global patterns. Although the two hemispheres have these separate characteristics, they are more integrated than is fully understood in current brain research.

Comparison of Left-Mode and Right-Mode Characteristics

Left	Right
Verbal	Nonverbal
Symbolic	Synthetic
Abstract	Analogic
Temporal	Nontemporal
Rational	Nonrational
Digital	Spatial
Logical	Intuitive
Linear	Holistic

Exercise: *Convergent/Divergent Thinking Assessment*

The following are forced-choice questions. People will do both at times. Choose the response that is *most characteristic of your natural tendency or behavior,* not what you think you should do, or how you've trained yourself to do something. Do not analyze the questions, but simply put down your first response to them. Circle either *A* or *B*.

1. When studying an unfamiliar subject, I:

    a. Gather information by exploring many areas relating to the topic.

    b. Stay focused with the information on the central topic.

2. Given the time and opportunity, I prefer:

    a. To know a little about a great many subjects.

    b. Become an expert in one subject area.

3. When studying from a textbook or manual, I:

    a. Skip ahead and read chapters out of sequence that have special interest to me.

    b. Work systematically from one chapter to the next, not moving on to the next chapter until I've understood what I've read.

4. When asking other people for information about some subject of interest, I:

   a. Tend to ask broad questions that call for rather general answers.

   b. Tend to ask narrowly focused questions that require specific answers.

5. When browsing in a bookstore or library, I:

   a. Roam around looking at books on many different subjects.

   b. Stay more or less in one place looking at books on just a few subjects that interest me.

6. I am better at remembering:

   a. General principles.

   b. Specific facts.

7. When given an assignment or task, I:

   a. Prefer to have background information that's not directly related to the task but may give a context for the work.

   b. Prefer to only concentrate on having strictly relevant information for performing the work.

8. In training people for new jobs, I would have the training program:

   a. Expose the person to a wide variety of skills and information about the company and its programs as well as the new job.

   b. Focus the training on just the skills the person needs to perform at a high level in their new job.

9. When I go on vacation, I prefer to:

   a. Spend a short amount of time in several different places.

   b. Stay in just one place the whole time and really get to know it.

10. When driving to a location in a new city from my hotel, I prefer:

   a. Looking at a map and getting a general overview of where I am going.

   b. Have someone give me detailed instructions on how to get from my hotel to the destination.

11. When working on a project, I prefer:

  a. Valuing the importance of the details but having someone else manage them as I focus on broader issues.

  b. Controlling the details of the reports and other data that will determine the success or failure of the project.

12. Given that both are important, in managing within an organization I prefer:

  a. Developing strategy.

  b. Developing operational plans.

Scoring

Add up all the As and all the Bs you circled.

A = _____

B = _____

A represents your divergent score.
B represents your convergent score.

The higher the number in the divergent or convergent score, the greater the tendency toward that perspective. The following gives some information on the use of convergent and divergent in your thinking style.

The convergent/divergent questionnaire gives information on the approach that individuals take when they are confronted with a problem or situation that needs to be contextualized or framed before one begins to "think" it through. The concepts of divergent and convergent give the framework in which the thinking takes place. These two are the screen or filter for how one's thought pattern will proceed.

Convergent is a narrow band approach to problem-solving. Like induction, the convergent approach moves from an individual point, set of facts, or cases and builds toward a generalized conclusion or answer.

Divergent is a wide band approach to problem-solving. Like deduction, it moves from the general to specific by finding specific solutions or results from conclusions, concepts, theories, or broad empirical observations. Most people have a mix of the two approaches. The number ratio on the assessment gives an indication of which of the two is emphasized or not for you as an individual. The convergent/divergent pattern has a significant influence on the sequence pattern of our thinking process, decision-making, and conflict resolution. The convergent/divergent pattern creates the context for how we analyze, synthesize, implement, and question the people and situations we face daily.

Chapter 11
The Energy Template of the Self

Although the existence of the Chakras is accepted in the east
it is not so readily recognized in the west. In fact, it is not so uncommon
to be greeted with a look of bewilderment at the very mention of the word,
followed by utter skepticism and scorn when attempting to explain their purpose.

—ALBERT EINSTEIN

As we've discussed, we are not just our body/mind/brain and emotions. We are also a complex energy system that in the Eastern traditions are described as nonvisible lines of energy throughout the body called meridians and centers of energy called chakras. In this chapter, we will consider the history of how the various energy systems have come to the West. We will examine what chakras are, how they can be activated and balanced in your body, and how the five elements of earth, water, fire, air, and space relate to the five key chakras that we will work with in this process of energetically identifying your ego personality. Also, in this chapter we will explore your personality type through an ancient system called the Enneagram, a nine-point system of different personality types that will help you reveal more clearly the construct of your unique constricted self. You have the opportunity to take an Enneagram assessment to determine your particular type.

The Chakras

Chakras are an ancient system that originated in India and moved and changed in description to different cultures. They reveal a system of understanding that provides tools and experiences that can heal, rebalance, and energize your life. According to the Vedas and the Upanishads—the oldest of the Indian spiritual texts—the chakra system originated between 1500 and 500 BC. A similar energy system can be found in Chinese medicine based on the meridians that is still used today. There are also energy systems like the chakras in Tibetan Buddhism, the Jewish Kabbalah, and Islamic Sufism. For our purposes, we will focus on the Hindu chakra system.

Chakra means "wheel" or "wheel of life." The chakras are spinning energy wheels at seven major points along the spine from the base of the spine to the top of the head. Each of the seven spinning wheels of energy is connected to the nervous system through the endocrine system. For example, the crown chakra at the top of the head is related to the pituitary gland. The forehead chakra is linked to the pineal gland, the throat chakra is connected to the thyroid gland, the heart chakra to the thymus, the solar plexus chakra to the spleen/pancreas glands, and the groin chakra to the testicles or the ovaries. The base or root chakra at the adrenal glands is where the "kundalini" or serpent energy that activates the chakras is coiled (the core energy of the body) and where physical survival for a person is protected.

You may be aware of the energy system of the meridians in Chinese acupuncture. These meridians, or channels of energy, are connected to the "hubs" called the chakras. Neuroscientists have demonstrated with an electrocardiogram (EKG or ECG) and electroencephalograph (EEG) that there is a constant electromagnetic energy exchange between cells and there is continuous electrical magnetic activity of the heart and brain as well as other parts of the body. There is much more information about electrical magnetic fields of the body, but all I want to do at this point is to indicate that chakras and meridians have been the physical-spiritual methods of ancient teachings and current neuroscientists, as they both have explored and mapped the electrical magnetic energy of the body.

This remarkable chakra system is an energy template that has helped me understand how the personality develops and how it can detach itself. The chakra system is also a helpful guide to show when the chakras are in balance and out of balance. Each chakra has an energy force that vibrates at a particular frequency. The chakra system can be compared to computer hardware with software and a power cord connected to an energy source. The body is the hardware and the mind is the software. If there are energy problems with the power cord, it will shut down the computer system.

Similarly, if your internal energy system represented by the chakras and the physical electromagnetic forces begins to get out of balance or shut down, it can dramatically affect your physical body, your clarity of mind, and your emotional state as well as your overall physical, mental, and emotional balance. Even if there are minor disruptions in the various elements of your chakra/electromagnetic system, your energy flow goes down and that will affect your mood, difficulty in problem-solving, and susceptibility to colds, as well as other mental and physical imbalances.

The seven wheels of energy currents maintain your physical, emotional, and mental health. Each chakra carries a different level of mind consciousness. The lower three chakras (root, sacral, and solar plexus) link you to the dense material energies of your body. Through these three energy wheels you experience how to perceive the physicality of your body and environment. These three centers of energy focus on your experience in the material world. The upper four energy centers (heart, throat, brow or third eye, and crown) express your heart of compassion, joy, freedom, and, eventually, liberation.

There is a color and sound unique to each chakra frequency. As frequencies increase up your spinal cord, these chakras are like a rainbow bridge of color vibrations. As the frequency in the wheels move faster, the color and sound change. When you are vibrating at a particular frequency, you will receive information at these different chakras in the form of images, emotions, sensations, thoughts, or perceptions of that chakra. You then can assimilate what you receive from this information and use it to inform your life. Learning how to unblock energy imbalance in the chakras and to keep the frequency of each center vibrant and strong is part of maintaining your physical, emotional, and mental health.

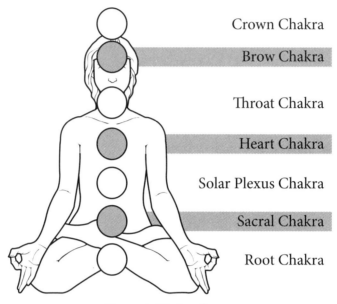

Figure 1: Chakra figure

Exercise: *Chakra Balancing Practice*

As you practice this meditation, you will discover the placement of each energy center. With practice, you will also notice which center has less energy and what in your body or mind may be creating the imbalance. Again, either record the exercise or have a partner or friend read it to you. Pause between each instruction. After the exercise, record in your notebook your sensations and experience in each chakra. You may want to do this exercise several times to become familiar with what sensations each chakra has for you. As you practice, they will become more differentiated for you. Let's begin.

• Find a quiet place and sit with your body comfortable, with your back straight, or lie flat on a bed or the floor. Close your eyes.

- Take three deep abdominal breaths through the nose, focusing on relaxing your entire body. Feel your body relaxed and centered in either your sitting or lying position. In this relaxed state, visualize a root growing from the base of your spine into the earth and feel your connection to the solidness of the earth.

- As you visualize and feel the root go deeper into the earth, experience even more relaxation in your body.

- Imagine a spinning wheel at the very base of your spine. It is a red color.

- Tighten the muscles in this area for a moment as you visualize the wheel and the red color. Then let go, relaxing your body. Notice the sensation of energy at this point.

- Slowly move your attention to each of the chakra centers up your spine, tightening muscles in each chakra area, then relaxing, and then observing the different sensations of energy at each chakra.

- Move first from your root chakra to your pelvic area. Here the color is orange. Note the sensation.

- Next is the solar plexus where the color is yellow. Note the sensation.

- Move to the heart where the color is green. Note the sensation.

- Move to the throat where the color is blue. Note the sensation.

- At this point before moving up the spine, take a few more deep breaths and feel your body relax more deeply.

- Move now to your forehead chakra, where the color is purple. Note the sensation.

- Finally, move to the top of your head, where the color is violet. Note the sensation.

- As you reach the top of your head, also notice if your entire body is vibrating.

- Review and then recall what chakras seem to spin or vibrate more than others.

- Which of the chakra centers seemed stronger or weaker in their sensations?

• Finally, be aware of your body and the room you are in. Move your body and open your eyes. Please record your experience in your notebook. The writing will bring your inner experience more consciousness and increase your learning about your chakra system.

Ways to Activate Each Chakra

In both the Indian and Chinese systems, everything in nature is made up of five basic elements: earth, water, fire, air, and space (ether). Each chakra is made up of a different element as well. The qualities of each chakra include the elements, physical functions, emotional, and psychological states. Knowledge of these states and functions in each chakra allows you to experience the chakra and to give you a sense of whether there exists balance or imbalance at a particular chakra. As you become more familiar with your own chakra's characteristics, you will be able to balance the energy within the chakras. Experience of this balance will then give you an awareness of the development of the constricted self and ways to detach from it.

Another reason it is valuable to gain a perspective of your own particular chakra characteristics is that the five basic elements are also the same nature elements that are prominent in the dying process, as described in the first half of the book. Here is a brief overview of the characteristics of the elements related to the chakras.

The first chakra, the root, is energized by the earth element, located at the base of the spine. This element represents stability. You will notice when the root chakra is not in balance, you may feel unstable, worried, and fearful. What is needed to bring the energy into balance is to seek ways to be connected, nurtured, and grounded in the earth element, which will create stability for you. One of the easiest things to do when feeling unstable is to go outside to a safe place and lie on the ground. The earth has a natural balancing frequency called the Schumann Resonance, which is the earth's electromagnetic field spectrum. What you will experience from the earth is a frequency of approximately 5 to 7 hertz as you lie and absorb its healing power. This is a basic repairing and rejuvenating energy frequency for your body and mind.

The water element is the energy characteristic of the second chakra, located in the pelvic or sacral area of the body. The water element represents the flow in life. If this chakra is obstructed, you will not be able to move your lower spine appropriately. When you are out of balance, you may feel stuck and rigid, as well as emotionally and sexually drained. Without the appropriate water element, there is little to no pleasure or feelings of sensuality in you. There is also no release of built-up toxins in your body when you feel sluggish or stuck in some part of your life. There are many ways to reestablish the water element. Taking a bath or a shower, being in a hot tub or a sauna, walking in the rain or snow, or just sitting by a pond, lake, river, or ocean. All these water conditions will provide negative ions that neutralize stress, charge the energy cycle of the body, remove negative bacteria from the air, and create a sense of well-being by reducing the production of serotonin, which creates the breakdown of positive flow in our body and emotions. In general, any type of hydrotherapy rebalances and smooths the energetic flow of your body, mind, and emotions.

The fire element is the energy characteristic of the third chakra, located in the solar plexus area of the body. This chakra has to do with producing action in your life. It is the kind of action that you need to make your life a success. When this chakra is in balance, you develop your own power and passion in your life. When this chakra is strong and balanced, you have inspirational goals, courage, strength, and follow-through to fulfill your dreams.

When you can't put your passion and dreams into action, there is an imbalance and an energetic block in this chakra. If blocked, you may feel heavy, limited, restricted, closed down, or depressed and need inspiration. When the fire element has cooled, research indicates that one of the fastest ways to recharge is to exercise and to stimulate the brain's neurotransmitter dopamine. Meditation, certain foods such as avocados and leafy vegetables, and green tea can revitalize your fire element.

The air element is the energetic characteristic of the fourth chakra, located in the heart region of the body. The air embodies lightness and the freeing quality of love. When you are open to loving yourself and loving others, you are living in balance. When you are balanced in your body, mind, and emotions, you accept love and give love. You feel worthy and, like air, your awareness holds love all around you. When there are challenges in this chakra or blockages, you will have an inability to offer love and be very self-contained and unsure of your own self-identities. When this chakra is blocked in some way, it is also hard to know that you are worthwhile and have meaning in life. The most obvious way to respond to a closed heart feeling is breathing. Conscious breathing charges the body, warms the heart area, and recenters you by changing mood and mental conditions.

The space element characteristics are energy, spirit, love, emptiness, freedom, and being everywhere. This embodies the upper three chakras of the throat, brow, and crown. Each of these three chakras has individual characteristics, but for our purpose of understanding the elemental forces, I include them in the space element. When our four elements of air, earth, water, and fire are balanced, we connect to the Universal Life Force element of space. This element is at a very high frequency, and the three upper chakras are activated together to move your energetic awareness to experience the power and grace of this element. Continuing to be present with the space element is fundamentally maintained in various forms of meditation, tai chi, Qigong, prayer, and contemplation practices. At a body/mind/emotion level, these practices open you to a continued state and development of balanced energy, calmness, and openness to life, which are the conditions that nurture the space element.

Exercise: *Element Sensations*

Find a quiet place and sit with your back straight but your body comfortable, or lie on a bed or the floor. Again, either record the exercise or have a partner or friend read it to you. Pause between each instruction. After the exercise, record in your notebook your experience.

- Close your eyes and take three deep abdominal breaths through the nose, focusing on relaxing your entire body. Take time to move through your body and relax each area, starting from your head and moving down to your toes.

- Move your attention to the base of your spine. Feel the solidness of your root chakra connected to the earth as you sit in your chair or lie on the floor. Notice the growing heaviness in your hands and arms resting on your lap or beside you. There is a heaviness to your entire body as it becomes more relaxed.

- This perceived weight is the heaviness of gravity and the earth energy. As you feel the solidness, notice if you feel supported, connected, and stable within yourself. Also notice what keeps you from this awareness if you are unable to sense the heaviness.

- As you stay aware of your connection to the earth through the root chakra, notice if you have any tingling pressure sensations in your body.

- Now turn your attention to the pelvic area of your body and notice a sense of pleasurable warmth enveloping this area of your body. Let go to this flow of warmth. When you let go, it will be like a flow of moving water. Follow the moving water and drop your body and mind into the ebb and flow, like waves moving in and out of your body. Let your body physically move with this warm flowing energy. Feel the undulation of your spine as you slowly move your body parts.

- Consider in your emotional life where you may not be in this easy flow of energy. If you are aware of this possibility, let your body relax even more and say. "I let go of this … and I release myself into the flow of my life."

- Move your awareness upward and into your solar plexus as you open to this center of your body. Either with your inner visual or your sense feeling, notice a brilliant fire burning in your belly.

- Feel the heat coming off the fire and notice your energy increase as you put your attention there.

- This energy of power brings a burning self-confidence and passion inside of you. What is the source of this power in you? Notice the strength of this power, confidence, and passion you are feeling.

- Take a moment to consider what puts out the fire in you and reduces your power, passion, and confidence.

- Now move your awareness to your heart area and experience your breath flowing in and out of your heart. This air is the element that moves you out of the material world into the domain of spirit, energy, and presence.

- Follow your breath and notice the air as it goes in and out at your heart area.

- Let your mind and body move into and become the air. Let yourself become as light as the air. Feel yourself floating.

- Notice how free and aware you are and of the rest of your body floating as the spirit of air holds you and passes through you.

- Notice how your identity shifts being in this quality of freedom in the air. Can you perceive yourself as loving others and being an expression of love in your life? What difference would it make for your life if this love was always moving in you and through you?

- Finally, be aware of your body and the room you are in. Move your body and open your eyes. Please record your experience in your notebook. The writing will bring your inner experience up into your conscious mind and increase your learning about your own element system.

The Enneagram

The energy template we are exploring also includes the work of the Enneagram. The Enneagram is a model of the human personality and has nine interconnected personality types. These nine personality types are described as *who we are not*. It is a description of our constricted self. The Enneagram will help you identify your constricted self, and you can use your personality type as a reference as we go through the awakening process. Here I give an overview of the Enneagram. I encourage you to go to the Enneagram Institute website for further information.

The symbol of the Enneagram is ancient and has been found in Egyptian ruins that date back ten thousand years. The Enneagram appears in Pythagorean philosophy, the work of Plato, Judaism, Sufism, and early mystic Christianity. The reemergence of the Enneagram in modern times came through the

Russian mystic George Gurdjieff in the early 1900s and then emerged in more modern spiritual form in the late 1970s with Oscar Ichazo in Chile. It then came into broader culture through Claudio Naranjo, a pyschologist, who learned the concepts and practices from Ichazo. Naranjo framed the material in psychological concepts and brought them to the United States, where he began to teach groups. This psychospiritual process of understanding and working with personality structure has spread throughout the world, and the nine types are recognized in different world cultures as the universal nature and functioning of human beings.

Figure 2: The Enneagram

Following are the four-word trait sets for each type. Keep in mind that these are merely highlights and do not represent the full spectrum of each type.

Type One is principled, purposeful, self-controlled, and perfectionistic.

Type Two is generous, demonstrative, people-pleasing, and possessive.

Type Three is adaptable, excelling, driven, and image-conscious.

Type Four is expressive, dramatic, self-absorbed, and temperamental.

Type Five is perceptive, innovative, secretive, and isolated.

Type Six is engaging, responsible, anxious, and suspicious.

Type Seven is spontaneous, versatile, acquisitive, and scattered.

Type Eight is self-confident, decisive, willful, and confrontational.

Type Nine is receptive, reassuring, complacent, and resigned.

Besides learning to identify which of the nine types fit you, there are other ways to use the nine points. The first is with "centers." Each one of the nine types is related to three basic centers: the thinking center, the feeling center, and the instinctive or body-oriented center. For example, you can note that the feeling center represents types two, three, and four.

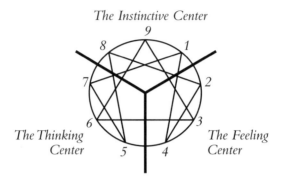

Figure 3: The Structural Centers

The centers give you an orientation of your type to how your personality basically functions in each of the three centers. For example, my type is a six, so my challenge, growth, and development come from my thinking. Thinking for me has both positive and negative issues I need to work with in my development. My husband is a one, so his issues are around being a body type which is described as the instinctive center. Our son is a three and our daughter is a two, so they confront their types around the issues of feelings and emotions.

There is also the dominant negative emotion of each of the three centers. These center emotions reveal how we tend to cope emotionally. These negative emotions tend to be unconscious for us, so the method of the Enneagram system helps to bring these to conscious awareness for our healing.

Figure 4: The Emotional Centers

The work with the Enneagram to transform our lives and to awaken to our true nature covers a wide breadth of insights and understanding. Beyond what I've mentioned, there is the understanding of your type's "wings," meaning the types on either side of your primary type that influence your personality pattern. Most important, the major contribution that Don Riso and Russ Hudson of the Enneagram Institute made to modern Enneagram understanding is the work with your nine levels of development ranging from unhealthy to average to healthy. Levels give you a measure of where you are in your own type development and what challenges of growth are the next steps in your life cycle development. Beyond all of this material, there is the work of direction of integration and of disintegration in your personality structure, the work with subtypes, and many other factors such as complementary types in relationships.

What I have found most useful in understanding the patterns of personality is how my Enneagram type affects my different emotional conditions. Your type will also demonstrate what you become fixated on and therefore where your resistance is to life's flow. The Enneagram points to the patterns that reveal your fundamental self-identification, with the way you create your "me, my, and mine" projections into the world around you. The unique structure of your Enneagram template reveals the compensatory patterns you developed from your family conditioning and onward through life. It will teach you what generates your pattern of stress and what conditions you need to create, integrate, and grow in your life.

Please take a short assessment below. This assessment will help you identity your Enneagram type. You will need to know your type to do many Enneagram exercises that are in the next four chapters. I strongly recommend you explore the many facets of the Enneagram in your life as you continue to explore your own awakening. You can also find further resources on the Enneagram in Appendix C.

Overview of the Enneagram Triad Assessment

The Enneagram is a word that refers to nine personality types. *Ennea* is a Greek word for "nine." Within the nine types are three centers that are called the triads. There are three Enneagram types in each triad. The triad centers are called: the thinking center, the feeling center, and the instinctual center. They are sometimes called the head, the heart, and the body or "gut." Each person tends to have their primary Enneagram type in one of these three triads.

- Thinking triad has the Enneagrams five, six, and seven
- Feeling triad has the Enneagrams two, three, and four
- Body triad has the Enneagrams one, nine, and eight

Note the graphic of the triads in figure 4. Each of the three triads is dominated by a particular negative emotion.

- The thinking center's negative emotion is fear.
- The feeling center's negative emotion is shame
- The body center's negative emotion is anger.

The underlying principle of the Enneagram is a pathway to discover our true nature. The Enneagram is then a very helpful model to work with our constricted self and discover our expanded self. Each triad center responds to all types of emotions but is significantly affected by one of the particular negative emotions above. The negative emotions of the triads represent the constricted self's main issues of self-worth, emotional reactions, mental anxiety, and our means of self-protection. These triads with their particular Enneagram types can assist us in uncovering aspects of our constricted self that we will identify as we proceed through the next four chapters of the book.

One of the clues to your primary Enneagram type is how you identify with one of the three triads and one of these three negative emotions. It is these two aspects that are the basis of the following assessment.

Exercise: *Taking the Enneagram Assessment*

This short assessment uses the triads as a way of helping you identify your primary Enneagram type. This assessment is a general indicator of your Enneagram type. The process of fully understanding your type may need a more comprehensive review. You can find additional information on other Enneagram assessments in appendix C.

Step 1: Review the Three Groups

There are three statements in each group below that describe behaviors, identity, emotions, and beliefs representing that triad. Read through all three groups. After reading each group, select *one group* with the three statements that seems *most* like you (either when you were younger or the way you are now). Within your chosen group *select the one statement* that is *most* like you.

GROUP I

1. I like to be organized, but I can be strongly critical of myself. My drive is that I am never good enough.

2. I am self-reliant and strong, and I don't like being weak or dependent.

3. I can seem peaceful and placid, but I am critical of myself for not taking initiative and being disciplined enough.

GROUP 2

1. I am loyal and supportive of others, but tend to be sensitive, hypervigilant, and nervous.

2. I have a deep need to know and understand everything, but have trouble expressing succinctly what I know.

3. I am restless when not having fun, being spontaneous, or contributing to the world. But I also tend to avoid my inner pain and any physical or emotional suffering.

GROUP 3

1. I don't want to be ordinary, as I am motivated by my strong feelings, by my drive to be creative, and time alone to be introspective.

2. I am very busy and productive in order to be successful. I avoid failure and want to be recognized.

3. I need to be valued and to be loved by others, but I also can be manipulative with my generous and often possessive love to get people to support my self-esteem.

Step 2: Finding Your Enneagram Description

The nine Enneagram descriptions are below. Go to the group and the statement you've chosen and read that Enneagram description. This will represent your primary Enneagram type. If you are not fully satisfied that the Enneagram represents you, read the other two descriptions within that same group to find the one that best represents you.

GROUP 1: The Instinctual or Body Group

1. This is *Personality Type One* and is often referred to as the reformer or the perfectionist. They tend to have a hard time making mistakes and become disappointed when their expectations are not met. This type can become obsessed with taking things too seriously and overtly concerned by not doing things perfectly. Type ones tend to be serious, inflexible, and resistant,

and they believe that they are not good enough. They are hard on themselves and judge themselves about their thoughts, actions, and behaviors with others. At their best they are ethical, reliable, idealistic, and live their life the right way as they improve their life and the world. They are organized, orderly, self-disciplined, and able to accomplish a great deal. They are responsible in everything they do. When they put facts together they figure out wise solutions and take their anger and criticism of the world by turning it in on themselves.

2. This is *Personality Type Eight* and is referred to as the asserter or the challenger. They are direct, powerful, and authoritarian. They are assertive, strong and aggressive when they need to be and can overwhelm people. They tend to be restless and impatient with other's incompetence. They put a lot of pressure on themselves and express anger toward people who don't obey the rules or when things don't go the right way. At their best type eight supports the underdog, fights for what is right, and respects people who stand up for themselves. They take their anger and project it out into the world.

3. This is *Personality Type Nine* and is referred to as the peacemaker or the compliant. This type tries to keep the peace, be gentle, and appear mild mannered. They don't like expectations or pressure. If they do not have a structure, they procrastinate and have difficulty getting things done. This type would rather walk away from a disagreement rather than confronting someone. At their best they are kind, reassuring, supportive, and nonjudgmental. They focus on being positive and supportive and comforting others. Personality type nines are often unaware of their anger and suppress it. However, they can be outwardly judgmental, which is a cover-up for their anger.

GROUP 2: Thinking Type

1. This is *Personality Type Six* and is referred to as the loyalist or the committed. This type is often in a constant push and pull trying to make up their mind. Procrastination is due to their fear of failure, which can lead

to low confidence in themselves. They are continually scanning for danger, protecting their need for security and support. Their rigidness and self-defeating attitude can make them controlling and defensive. At their best sixes are loyal and committed to their family and friends. They are hard-working, witty, warm, compassionate, and very responsible. This type is outwardly fearful in their environment and seeks approval.

2. This is *Personality Type Five* and is referred to as the investigator or the in-novator. This type can be defensive and can become arrogant, believing that they know it all at all times. However, they are deep thinkers and very intelligent. Also, they are not attached to having a lot of material posses-sions and status. They are not influenced by social pressure and can remain distant while being critical of others. Type five at their best are able to concentrate on complex ideas and are very sensible, persevering, wise, ana-lytical, and self-contained. The five Enneagram type can be moody, high-strung, and experience ongoing anxiety and tension.

3. This is *Personality Type Seven* and is referred to as the enthusiast or the ad-venturer. This type never has enough time and can't even count the many "happy" things they want to do. They have the tendency to be scattered with a host of activities that often feel overextended both in work and play. With their many interests and abilities, they have difficulty keeping focused on their priorities. They are restless and have problems with impa-tience and impulsiveness. At their best, they are spontaneous, quick men-tally, charming, fun loving, and they can focus their talents on worthwhile projects. They often struggle with exhaustion from all the activities. This struggle drives them to hide the anxious uncertainty and fear that is often the driver of their emotional pain.

GROUP 3: *Heart Type*

1. This is *Personality Type Four* and is referred to as the individualist or the cre-ative. This type tends to feel defective and will tend to focus on feelings of shame and self-hatred when things are difficult in their life. This may lead to crying with dark melancholy moods and becoming nonfunctional for

days. They are highly sensitive to criticism and becoming hurt, but long to be understood and not disappoint others. At their best, they are sensitive, creative, introspective, and self-aware, as well as being warm and caring with an independent and individualist nature. The dark side of the four Enneagram type is that in being so self-aware it also can cause them to renew their sense of shame and guilt about their lives.

2. This is *Personality Type Three* and is referred to as the achiever or driver. This type keeps busy working to achieve success and seeking appreciation for their accomplishments. They have difficulty with inefficiency and incompetence as they have a strong push to get things done quickly and thoroughly. They are overly concerned with their image to impress others. As a result of this inner pressure to achieve, they can become exhausted from keeping up the image and facade of success. At their best, Enneagram type threes are pragmatic, optimistic, energetic, and confident. Their challenge is to become overly competitive, and to deal with the fear of failure.

3. This is *Personality Type Two* and is referred to as the helper or pleaser. This type is driven to be close to others sometimes being overly accommodating as a manipulated way to be needed. This type also has trouble saying no and then begins to feel drained from not taking care of themselves. With their low self-esteem they sacrifice themselves to care for others often becoming possessive of loved ones. At their best, they are knowledgeable in determining how others feel so they can take care of others in a loving, caring, insightful, and generous manner.

In your notebook write down what your Enneagram type is, as we will be doing Enneagram exercises related to your type.

Chapter 12
Step 1:
Journey of Separation

Teach me how to trust my heart, my mind, my intuition,
my inner knowing, the senses of my body, the blessing of my spirit.
Teach me to trust these things that I may enter my sacred space and love beyond my
fear; and thus walk in balance with the passing of each glorious sun.

—LAKOTA PRAYER

As you take this journey of separation to understand the development of your constricted self, you will utilize the information of the structure of the self, the energy template, the elements, and the Enneagram to guide you on the journey. This section starts with examining the foundation of how the constricted self is born, then examines how the constricted self is a shadow of the expanded self, how the physical senses animate the constricted self, and, finally, how your sense of subject vs. object separates yourself from your expanded self. We conclude the information of this chapter by describing what I call the "age activations." At different times or ages in your life, certain aspects of your constricted self becomes more activated, dominating and separating you from yourself than at other times. At the end of this chapter, we begin using the tools with exercises that I've been describing.

How the Constricted Self Is Born

At the very beginning of life, you experienced a fundamental fear and anxiety when removed and separated from your mother's womb into the outer world. Physical birth is the first step when human consciousness arises. Right from your birth your consciousness begins a process of confronting aloneness that is rooted in fear. This consciousness at birth vibrates and correlates with the frequency of delta brain waves of 0.5–4 hertz. These brain waves mark the first unfolding of consciousness of the newborn. Consciousness vibrates in this frequency at the unconscious level and is primarily located in the reptilian part of the brain. The reptilian brain is the survival mechanism in you. These brain waves of survival form your physical foundation to maintain and protect your existence. Delta brain frequency gives you your sense of grounding and solidity. These slow frequencies support your growth as a baby, allowing for deep sleep, need for nourishment, and total support from your caregivers.

It is through the intimate relationship of being fed and cared for that you as an infant are anchored on this earth and to others. This close relationship also allows you as an infant to belong or be connected to other objects (people, things, etc.) and to begin to configure a self separate from the "other." Thus the unconscious drive of survival of your physical body gives the first sense perception of being or having a self. At this first phase of building the ego self, there begins a false experience of inseparability and security as your constricted self attempts to connect to people and the world.

The Shadow of the Expanded Self

At this early stage of emergence from the womb, however, there is still connection to what I've described as the expanded self. Imagine holding an infant in your lap with its radiance, wholeness, and absorbed presence. One can see and feel that presence. But then, one year later, notice the infant exploring the world. Recall in your imagination the shift from the being of presence to a child perceiving the world as "me" as separated from everything else. The child begins to find a new separate universe of body, space, and other. The space is a gap between the subject and an object. The body as the self (the subject) becomes surrounded by the environment (the object). The child may still know there is an inner world but lacks the rational distinction.

At this first phase of building the constricted self, there begins an experience of inseparability and security as the ego attempts to connect outside of self in order to belong and have a self-identification. Now your body-boundary self is constructed with space between yourself and other objects. If you didn't have a body, you would be space. But space is now constructed as the means of separation between the subject and object. The contact of the senses (hearing, sight, taste, touch, smell) with others and with space gives a dimension that you are separated from all others and things. As you as the child grows and matures, your self-definition becomes more separated from the space of the "other." In this beginning state of life, the sensations of your body emerge as your primary form of the constricted self.

Physical Senses and the Constricted Self

Imagine trying to hold a squirming three-year-old as she investigates her environment with all her physical senses, but is held back from doing so. This struggle by the child to reach out and explore what is going on around her is the natural drive for separation in the newborn. It is the physical senses that create a sense of boundary between you and others. As a child, what you sense with your eyes and what you hear, taste, touch, and smell tells you that the "out there" is to be discovered by these sensate mechanisms that interpret your "out there" world. With the power of your senses, there is now a boundary, which makes up your reality.

Space Equals Subject and Object

Space is constructed as the separation between the subject and object. To protect and defend your boundary, the reptilian part of your brain produces anxiety and fear if your senses pick up a threat to your boundary. At this first phase of building the constricted self, there begins a false experience of both a sense boundary and a drive for security as the self attempts to connect outside of self to belong and have a recognized identification as distinct from others. The body-boundary self is constructed with space between it and other objects. The contact of the senses to others by the ability to hear, see, taste, touch, smell, and space between gives a dimension that there is an "other," thus solidifying a growing perception and separation from the inner and outer world of experience. This is the beginning of creating your reality structure outside yourself.

The Age Activations

There are other stages in your life at which activation and development of the separation from the "other" increases through the intensity of your physical sensations. These stages increase awareness and the space between you and other people in particular as objects outside yourself.

The first activation of special separation, as I've described, continues from birth until ages three to five years. The next stage of basic separation occurs between the ages of thirty and thirty-four, again between sixty and sixty-four, and again at ninety to ninety-four. At these ages, you reassess your grounding roots and focus on security, safety, self-confidence, physical aspects, self-worth, survival, support, and a sense of belonging. You will explore these different age stages experimentally as you work with the bonus videos in each journey session.

Physical protection systems begin to occur when there is separation from your expanded self. They develop because of your growing perception of the need for physical survival, particularly as you become aware of your death. In these various age stages, physical symptoms will occur as the mode of the constricted self becomes more dominant. You may notice problems with your feet, legs, hips, eating disorders, addictions, and adrenals that govern the fight-or-flight response to danger. Psychological issues may occur such as depression, loss of inner security, negativity, cynicism, people pleasing, and black-and-white thinking. These symptoms illustrate blocks in the energy frequency in this root energy center of the body. If you later begin to detach from the constricted self, these physical and psychological issues will have less of an impact on your life.

Journey of Separation Exercises

In the Journey of Separation, you begin to assess your roots of separation and your basic needs for connection. These needs of connection are the instinctual tendencies of how you are grounded to your body sensations and to your environment. The degree of your constriction will depend on whether you feel you belong and feel that people include you. To be included also raises questions like "Where do I want to live and with whom?" When you feel you do not belong in your family, community, workplace, or region, there is a continual experience of being abandoned or betrayed until you finally make a connection to a place, which connects you to the element of earth.

Feeling grounded in your physical body is essential to this journey of releasing the power of separation over your life. The lack of being grounded in your body can show up, especially in a weakness of strength and flexibility, in your lower limbs. These physical symptoms can occur in your feet, legs, hips, hemorrhoids, fissures, musculoskeletal problems, and more.

The big issue of separation is feeling insecure. With insecurity you may feel anxious, fearful, terrified, and even panicky. Fear will be manifested in your body as the fight response. This response comes when you perceived a harmful event, an attack, or threat to your survival. These insecure responses will affect your day-to-day living pattern and activity, your vitality, and your sleep, and, ultimately, they will keep you from living a life of harmony and equanimity.

These reaction tendencies at the various age stages will let you know when you are confronting and increasing process of separation and tightening your constrictions on your self. The following exercises will help you on the Journey of Separation.

Exercise: *Age Separation Development*

Become still in silence and breathe deeply so that your mind and heart settle and you can listen to the deepest part of yourself. Then answer these questions:

- Take a moment and ask yourself how the Journey of Separation affected your life between birth and four years old, and between the ages thirty to thirty-four and sixty to sixty-four as they apply to you. What were key events during these age periods? Record in your notebook.

- Make a list of fears and keep questioning yourself and your feelings until you get to what has been your basic source of fear throughout your life. Freely and spontaneously describe that fear in your notebook.

Exercise: *Brain Frequency Patterns*

Become still in silence and breathe deeply so that your mind and heart settle and you can listen to the deepest part of yourself. Then answer these questions:

- Recall your energy pattern vibration imbalance experiences, especially at any of the three developmental ages in the Age Separation Development exercise when functioning in this delta brain wave frequency (0.5–4 Hz), the slowest brain wave. Here are some examples of frequency imbalance to stimulate your thinking.

Frequency Imbalance: Brain injuries, learning problems, inability to think, severe ADHD, overeating, depression, material fixation, work, alcoholism, excessive spending, slow revitalization of the body, poor sleep, fear, underweight, disconnected to body, difficulty manifesting, and patterns of avoidance and resistance to structure.

- Write in your notebook about an age when one or more of these were dominant in your life. How did you cope? How did you deal with it?

Exercise: *Enneagram Patterns*

If you haven't determined your Enneagram type, please do so, as we will be working with this information. These exercises are to stimulate both your thinking and feelings about how your particular form of ego separation developed throughout your life and formed a unique pattern of constriction.

Step
1

Your Enneatype Unconscious Childhood Message

Check your Enneagram type in relation to your unconscious childhood message and your basic fear. Which message patterns fits in your life? Give an example and write in your notebook.

Type One: It is not okay to make mistakes.

Type Two: It is not okay to have your own needs.

Type Three: It is not okay to have your own needs and identity.

Type Four: It is not okay to be functional or happy.

Type Five: It is not okay to be functional in the world.

Type Six: It is not okay to trust yourself.

Type Seven: It is not okay to depend on anyone for anything.

Type Eight: It is not okay to be vulnerable or trust anyone.

Type Nine: It is not okay to assert yourself.

Your Enneatype Basic Fear

From the following list, what basic fear fits your life? Give an example and write it in your notebook.

Type One: Of being bad, imbalanced, defective, and corrupt

Type Two: Of being unloved

Type Three: Of being worthless

Type Four: Of not having identity or significance

Type Five: Of being helpless, incompetent, and incapable

Type Six: Of being without support and guidance

Type Seven: Of being trapped in pain and deprivation

Type Eight: Of being harmed, controlled, or violated

Type Nine: Of loss of separation and fragmentation

Meditation Practices to Explore the Journey to Freedom

In the remaining chapters, I will be using guided meditations along with a variety of exercises to help you discover your unique patterns of personality structure. Each meditation is written in the text, but I suggest that you either pre-record or have a friend or family member read the text to you. The reason for pre-recording or having it read to you is I will be first guiding you into a relaxed state with your eyes closed and taking you down into the appropriate brain-wave frequency to access your unconscious mind state. Each meditation will also give you the option to go to the appendix and access the video that has my voice guiding you along with music and binaural beats that entrains the mind to a specific brain frequency. Let me give you an overview of the different parts of the meditation practices.

The four chapters: Journey of Separation, Journey of Emotions, Journey of the Mind, and Journey of Self-Identity include guided meditations that explore how you began to separate from your essential nature and created your constricted self. The purpose of each of the meditations is for you to experience different aspects of the birth and creation of your ego identity. The intention of these guided meditations is for you to relax into and recall the experiences and conditions that formed your constricted self's birth and development. These guided meditations will help you to open and gain awareness of the foundation on which your personality has been built by teaching you how to access your inner world. I truly encourage you to try the guided meditations and let them open a place of insight, understanding, and healing within you.

As we go through these next four constricted self development chapters, you will focus on different ages of your life. Some of these periods may not apply to you, as you may not have reached a particular physical age. Only do those age meditations that apply to you at the current ages and time in your life. For example, the first set of three meditations relating to the Journey of Separation presents the first meditation focused from birth to four years old. The second meditation is focused on ages thirty to thirty-four and the third meditation is ages sixty to sixty-four in your life. Obviously, if you have not reached thirty years old that meditation doesn't apply to you. If, for example, you are forty years old, you would just focus on exploring in the meditations birth to four and the thirty to thirty-four year ranges. If you are seventy years or older you would do all three of the guided meditations for all three age periods.

In each of the four chapters, you will be doing various preparation assessments and exercises like the ones above. These exercises will help you remember particular issues and events in your life before and during the meditations. Each guided meditation begins with a relaxation process and then a guided journey in to each particular age group. When you come out of the meditation, it is useful to record what you experienced or talk with the person who guided you or others if you are in a group.

It is helpful to do these meditations two or three times if you can, as you will go deeper and access more insight about these ages and experiences of your life. In preparation for the guided meditation, I will give you several questions to consider before doing the meditation. These questions are to help you reflect on the potential issues of the age meditation that will "prime the pump," so to speak, for deeper memory access while doing the meditation.

Let me emphasize from what I said above, please either pre-record the meditations in order to listen to them, or have a partner or friend read and guide you through it. Where there is a *(pause)* indicated, give yourself time to experience the instructions at that point. Also, once again, if you are interested you can access bonus videos for these meditations that I will guide you through. Besides my guiding in words, these meditations have specific brain frequencies, colors, and music. It's not necessary to watch the videos, but it is a bonus for this second part of the book. You can access these videos through your computer or mobile device. You can find video information for each meditation in appendix D.

The following meditation practices are a way you can explore this process of separation in your life more deeply. These first two guided meditations in the Journey of Separation will help you to begin to explore the birth of your constricted ego self. These are the first of what I call a "deep" meditation process. You will be guided into a deep state of relaxation and given a way to quickly put yourself into a deeply relaxed physical and emotional state whenever you want. This deep relaxed state will enable you to explore many aspects of both the development of your ego structure and as well as the next stage of your journey to inner freedom and happiness.

The relaxation process in this first guided meditation is longer than the ones you will have as we progress through the various journeys. In this relaxation process you will give yourself a marker—a symbol, an image, or a word—that is used to anchor in your body/mind to the direct physical experience of your relaxation state so that when you want to relax you can recall this marker and it will more quickly move your body/mind into a relaxed feeling.

Exercise: *Meditation Ages Birth to Four Years Old*

Please either pre-record this meditation in order to listen to it or have a partner or friend read and guide you through it. Where there is a *(pause)* indicated, give yourself time to experience the instructions at that point. (If you want to use the bonus video for this meditation go to appendix D.)

Before beginning the meditation, I want you to focus on several questions in order to help you clarify your early pattern of developing your constricted self. Much of what occurs in us at this stage impacts us at a more unconscious level. Reflecting on these questions is preparation for going deeper into the guided meditation. Write your results in your notebook after doing the meditations.

Questions on Ages Birth to Four Years Old

- What is the result of being separated at birth in your life? Did you feel lonely and have connection needs, or did your environment and family seem okay and supportive to you?

- What did you need from your parents that you did or did not get, such as security and feeling grounded and at home in yourself and with others?

- When did you have an unstable time of feeling ungrounded and fearful?

- Throughout your life, did you feel safe and did you trust your environment? Were there perceived times when you did not feel safe?

Let's begin the meditation:

- Find a safe, quite, comfortable place with your back straight but not rigid or if you prefer to lie down. *(pause)*

- Close your eyes and inwardly visualize a red color.

- As you settle in to listening to the instructions, keep visualizing the color as well as any other sounds in the environment. *(pause)*

- Sensations arise in the body just as thoughts arise in the mind. They come and go like bubbles.

- Let each mind/body/moment arise and pass away of its own momentum.

- Just be aware now of what you feel. *(pause)*

- Bring your attention to your eyes and allow the tiny ligaments around your eyes and the muscles behind your eyes to soften. Shift your attention from the outside environment you are in to turning inward. Be aware and feel this inward space within you. *(pause)*

- Let the growing softening behind your eyes flow into the brain cavity and into your scalp. It can feel like warmth flowing into your head.

- From your scalp, move the softening quality to your face. Experience your forehead being spacious, open, and relaxed.

- Notice your cheeks softening and drop their tightness.

- Drop any tension around your lips to allow your tongue to soften and rest in the mouth cavity.

- The softening of the jaws will free the neck, back of the neck, and shoulders to begin to drop and relax as well.

- Feel the multiple sensations arising and dissolving in the body. There may be tingling here and there as you focus on different parts of your body. *(pause)*

- Now allow the soft flow of energy to move down your arm, hand, and fingers.

- Notice the heaviness of your body as it becomes more relaxed. *(pause)*

- Put your attention now on your upper torso, chest, and diaphragm. Notice your breath slows as the heartbeat slows. *(pause)*

- Move to the top of your spine at the base of your neck and gradually allow the softening of the muscles down your spine to the bottom of your spinal cord.

- Feel the pressure of the buttocks on the chair (or where you are lying).

- Move through to the belly, pelvis, and hips, letting them gently relax as you put your attention on them. Let any tension release.

- Let the flow of relaxation move to the area where the legs meet.

- Gently be aware of receiving sensation arising in this very tender, very powerful life-giving area of sexuality and birth.

- Notice whatever feelings and emotions arise from focusing on this sacred area. *(pause)*

- Now move your attention and let the gentle relaxation move into the thighs, calf, feet, and toes.

- Let yourself feel this deep relaxed experience and let yourself open to being fully in your body. Be present and aware of your body from the soles of your feet to the crown of your head.

- Take a few moments now to reflect on your experience of this deep relaxation. I want you to remember what it feels like to be so deeply relaxed and connect this relaxation feeling to a symbol, an image, or a word. *(pause)*

- Now anchor this relaxation marker (the symbol, image, or word) somewhere in your body. Notice that this marker is deeply connected to this state of relaxation you are now in. *(pause)*

- Each time you want to relax, go to your anchor and recall your marker. Your brain will reenter into the state of relaxation more quickly.

- Move now to your belly. Take in three slow, deep breaths. On the last exhale, release any other tensions in your body. *(pause)*

- Once again take a deep inhale and notice the volume of openness and space inside you. On your exhale, merge with the space all around you in the room you are in. Do several more inhales and exhales as you expand into the space inside and outside of you. *(pause)*

- Gently and slowly move your awareness down into the center of your body right below your belly button.

- Rest your mind into this soft, warm space as a place of refuge, of quiet, of letting go, and as a place of healing. Let yourself feel the appreciation of being held within yourself. *(pause)*

- Imagine now that there is a television screen in front of you that is showing you your birth. Notice how you were emotionally held and how you were nurtured? Were you breastfed or bottle-fed? How did that type of holding and nourishing make you feel? Did you feel connected or loved? *(pause)*

- Now allow your inner remembering to show you yourself from ages one to five years old. *(pause)*

- Where were you living or what were you doing when you became aware that there was someone other than yourself?

- Recall also when you did not feel connected either to yourself or others. When was it when you sensed a space between you and others at this early age?

- Was there a time when you did not feel safe with parents or caregivers? At any time in this young age were you disgraced or shamed by adults?

- Who gave you the assurance that you belonged, were included, and were not left out from family or friends?

- What frightened you and where did you feel it in your body?

- Observe your thoughts about these questions. Just be present with them and let any memories or images arise on their own.

- Observe any emotions or feelings arising as you remember any of these events. *(pause)*

- If you lose awareness or get spaced out, come back to your remembering movie of yourself and allow the movie of your memories to continue.

Step

1

- Continue exploring in this deep, relaxed place and then, when you are ready, open your eyes and be conscious of your body. Move your hands and feet and other parts of your body to come back to this waking consciousness. *(pause)*

- Now is the time to write in your notebook. Reflect on what you remembered about the beginning structure of the experiences and conditions that began to create your ego or what I've called the constricted self personality structure.

Exercise: *Meditation Ages Thirty to Thirty-Four and Sixty to Sixty-Four*

Use this meditation for both age periods. Please either pre-record this meditation in order to listen to it or have a partner or friend read and guide you through it. Where there is a *(pause)* indicated, give yourself time to experience the instructions at that point. (If you want to use the bonus video for this meditation go to appendix D.)

Here again, I want you to focus on several questions in order to help you access and clarify your separation pattern at a deeper, and perhaps from a more unconscious, level. Write your results in your notebook after doing the meditations.

Questions on Ages Thirty to Thirty-Four and Sixty to Sixty-Four

- Did you feel alone and separate at this time in your life?
- What is your behavior like when feeling separate?
- What triggers your anxiety and fear?
- What is it like for you when you try to connect to others and the world around you?
- What is it like not to be safe or trusting?
- What does separation or loneliness feel like for you?
- What gives you security?

Let's begin the meditation:

- Relax into a safe, quiet environment and in a comfortable chair with your back straight but not rigid or lie comfortably on a mat or a bed.

- Close your eyes and then focus inwardly on the image of the color red for a few moments at the base of your spine.

- Notice any sounds in your environment as you focus your attention on the color red. *(pause)*

- Now recall the depth of your last meditation. Your brain/body remembers that relaxation state. As you remember the feeling, continue to release all your body and mental tensions.

- Whatever you now feel, simply notice where you may have any tension and consciously let go.

- Remember now your marker (see it or say it to yourself) and let your body/brain take you to that deep place of relaxation you experienced before. *(pause)*

- As you move deeper into relaxation, notice how your marker continues to release the tensions of your body. Experience yourself letting go to relaxation.

- Now take three long, deep breaths slowly.

- Allow thoughts, feelings, or outside disturbances to float through you without holding on to them.

- Using the symbol, image, or word of your marker, feel yourself inwardly move down into a deeper and deeper state of relaxation. As you move into that deeper state, experience yourself deeply at ease, content, and open to yourself. *(pause)*

- Now move into the belly, pelvis, and hips, relaxing and dropping tension.

- Let the flow of relaxation move to the area where the legs meet.

- Gently be aware of receiving sensation arising in this very tender, very powerful life-giving sacred area of being born and emerging into the world. Hold the color red at this place for a few moments.

Step 1

Step 1

- Be completely at rest, open, and without tension. *(pause)*
- Imagine now you are in a time machine going toward your age (either thirty to thirty-four or sixty to sixty-four.)
- Let your memories arise in you and notice what was going on in your life that involved a sense of you being separated from yourself, family, job, friends, health, or whatever naturally arises in you. *(pause)*
- Here are some questions to explore about this time period. Pause for a moment after each one to let any awareness arise.
- Do you feel alone and separate at this time in your life? *(pause)*
- What is your behavior like when feeling separate? *(pause)*
- What triggers anxiety and fear? *(pause)*
- What in you or about you is trying to connect to the world around you? *(pause)*
- Do you feel safe or trusting? What situations create an unsafe or untrusting feeling? *(pause)*
- What is it like for you to feel lonely and separated from yourself or others? *(pause)*
- Did you feel like you belonged in your family? Why or why not? *(pause)*
- After considering these questions and what has arose in memory, just observe your thoughts in this moment. Don't judge yourself. Just notice and be present with your experience. *(pause)*
- Observe any emotions or feelings that arise in you.
- Continue exploring in silence until you are ready to open your eyes and move your body.
- Now is the time you can write in your workbook. What did you find about the beginning structure of your constricted self personality at this age?

Chapter 13
Step 2:
Journey of Emotions

But human beings are like that, she thought.
We've replaced nearly all our emotions with fear.
—PAULO COELHO

As you grow older, step by step you are separated from your expanded self reality. It is similar to a plant in the earth—as it gets a little water, it sends its roots into the earth to try to get more connection and to be more earthbound. Your emotions, like water, are part of the step-by-step process of becoming more bound and constricted as you grow older. In this Journey of Emotions, there are two major additions to constructing the constricted self. The first is an emotional tension between desire and resistance and the second is between space and time. We then, as we will do in each chapter, describe the age activations, brain frequencies, and the emotion exercises leading to the guided meditation.

The Push and Pull of Emotions: Desire and Resistance

The next addition in developing your constricted self is the push and pull between desire and resistance. The more you experience likes and dislikes in the form of wanting and not wanting or simply resisting everything before you, the more emotional tension and reaction builds within you. You can feel the desire and opposition in your body and it creates emotional reactions that continue to build and reinforce the framework of your identity. If you are basically happy, that is who you are. If you are fundamentally sad, that is who you are. But being happy, you tend to want more. If you are unhappy, you resist people and situations around you. *This desire and resistance is the way you build more structure in your constricted identity through emotional response and reaction.* These emotional structures create boundaries that keep you in a life separated from yourself and others. As you are held more solidly by these emotional boundaries, you protect the continued developmental structure of your constricted self.

Space and Time

Space is another way you add on to your separate constricted self. This is accomplished by automatically placing an awareness of separation between you and other people and objects. The result is it makes other people and objects appear to be outside of you. This space of separation also uses a sense of time by employing the past, present, and future. You will tend to avoid the present by focusing your attention on time and space primarily of the past and future. For example, you were with your friend yesterday and plan to be with the friend again next week. This past/future structure provides the known condition for the constricted self to operate. There are circumstances and references available in that time and space to be able to tell what happened in the past and what will possibly happen in the future. However, there also may be fear related to what happened in the past and what may happen in the future. This fear increases and builds tension, tightness, and constriction in you.

The fear of the future is ultimately the unconscious unexplored boundary between life and death. You know what life is, but you want to avoid death. Death is the unknown that is the unconscious fear in us all. This is the huge emotional driver for the protection of the self and the justification we have to be constricted and try to maintain inner and outer protection of our lives.

The Age Activations

The activation and development of the feeling drive of desire and resistance, space and time, and life and death begins to be experienced between the ages of four and eight. This emotional development brings another form of unconscious protection from the uncertainty of your death. Very early in your life, you were told things like "Don't touch the fire," "Be careful crossing the street," "Watch out for the neighbor dog as it may bite you," and so on. These types of statements planted in you the unconscious fear that any one of these situations could cause you to die. These and other statements generate the emotions that generate the fight-flight-freeze pattern that is part of survival. When you are in some form of fear, you don't trust yourself or others. This fear and lack of trust deepens your constriction. This fearful response can affect your relationships, your confidence, and how you go forward in life or not.

Blocks in Life Flow

Your ongoing emotional journey builds and develops more constricted patterns again from ages thirty-four to thirty-eight and sixty-four to sixty-eight. For example, at these age stages of your life, you may find yourself wanting to have more of everything, better relationships, or more passion and creativity. These strong desires build and create tension, restrictions, or blocks in the flow of your life. If it seems like you are stuck being blocked by a person or situation. Resistance will grow both outwardly and inwardly and nothing will seem to move for you. Generally, this resistance will come in the form of judging, negating, doubting, or belittling yourself—or the opposite, projecting these same qualities onto others and situations. These emotional reactions strongly reduce the flow of your life and add emotional tightness, strain, worry, and apprehension. For example, you may want to have a more meaningful relationship, but it is not happening fast enough for you, so you judge yourself as not acceptable or not good enough or criticize prospective partners. Being impatient is time driven, which means you are pushing against the flow. Notice how you get frustrated, wanting time to move quickly and achieve some desire you have. Consider whether impatience is part of the driven quality of your constricted self.

Your constricted self learns to react in fear and push away in anger to protect your perceived vulnerability. This is another way separation works for survival. This continued fear and anger response eventually creates an inflexible tightness and an imbalance that blocks the flow of energy from moving naturally through you. The constricted self refuses to look inside itself at its feelings and because of that it is more and more focused on the outside world's activity of separation for protection. To bring unconscious feelings and emotions into conscious awareness, it is helpful to ask the question "Is this feeling pleasant/strong or unpleasant/weak for me?" This answer gives you an awareness of the flavor of the feeling. The feeling can be a strong desire of "I want" or a reaction of pushing away "I don't want." The more you become aware of this dance of your emotions trying to go forward and then pushing back, you will realize how it stops the flow of your life energy.

Another block to your life flow is when a feeling of fear arises and there suddenly occurs an innate response of a variety of self-protective emotions. Some of these reactive emotions may be anxiety, worry, anger, shame, panic, guilt, and doubt. This pulling and pushing away from yourself and outer situations creates tension, which keeps you far away from the flow and the source of the actual reality of the situation.

As the constricted self builds its structure, it takes on other people's feelings or emotions as its own. This happens more when you are highly sensitive or out of emotional balance. The more separated you are from an inner connection to yourself the easier it is to be influenced by other people's emotional field. Taking on their emotions can deeply negatively impact your mind and body, as well as your own emotions.

Knowing how to have a conscious protective emotional shield is helpful, especially in relationships where you become too sympathetic or empathic to others' feelings. When caught in the negative sympathy and empathy pattern of others, you cut yourself off from your essential energy and inwardly seal off the pure power of your expanded self.

The Brain Frequency Patterns

The frequencies for this emotional stage correlate with the theta brain waves of 4 to 7.8 hertz. These brain waves are predominantly activated in the limbic brain. Feelings and emotions as well as memories are accessed in the limbic brain and are subconscious.

Given that emotions are activated in the subconscious, you may push them down when they arise to be experienced because you don't want to feel them or because they may be too painful for you as they activate negative memories. Because many of us push our emotions down into the unconscious, we become unaware of what we really feel at any given moment. The tragedy is that these feelings or emotions can run your life or ruin your life as they pop out of the subconscious and spontaneously react without your control.

Journey of Emotion Exercises

The Journey of Emotions as it increases the constricted self has to do with your inflexibility, lack of inner balance, longing for all types of pleasure, sexual experience, relationships, success, meaning, and other emotional drives. When the sacral chakra energy frequency is negatively affected by constrictive emotional conditions, the physical body can react with kidney stones, lymph problems, urinary inflammation, lack of blood circulation, physical inflexibility, fluid retention, sexual dysfunction, stiffness in joints, sore ankles, lower back issues, as well as trauma or physical injury or disease to stomach, intestines, and sexual organs. The power of your emotions can have huge negative as well as positive impacts on your mental, physical, and behavioral life.

Exercise: *Age Development*

- Take a moment and ask yourself how the Journey of Emotions affected your life during the ages of four to eight, thirty-four to thirty-eight, and

Step
2

sixty-four to sixty-eight. Record in your notebook. What were the challenges, conflicts, and successes you had?

- Make a list of key emotions that run your life.
- How does the idea of space/time affect your life?
- How have negative emotions affected you physically and mentally throughout your life?

Exercise: *Brain Frequency Patterns*

- Recall your energy pattern, especially at one of your three developmental ages when functioning in an imbalanced emotional theta brain-wave frequency (4–7.8 Hz). Here are some examples of frequency imbalance to stimulate your thinking.

Imbalanced Frequency: Rigidity/inflexibility in physical movement, unable to deeply feel or enjoy physical or emotional sensations, inappropriate sexual drive, scarcity of creative ideas, feeling dull, lack of passion, poor social skills, excessive boundaries, and a focus on sexuality, acting out, and addictions.

- Write in your notebook about an age stage when one or more of these were dominant in your life.

Exercise: *Enneagram Patterns*

In the following two lists, check your Enneagram type in relation to how your type focuses on feelings and how you have learned to defend yourself. Where does this pattern operate in your life today? Give an example. Write them in your notebook.

Enneatype: Feeling Fixations
> *Type One:* Resentment (judging)
> *Type Two:* Flattery (ingratiation)
> *Type Three:* Vanity (deceit)

Type Four: Melancholy (fantasizing)

Type Five: Stinginess (resentment)

Type Six: Cowardice (worrying)

Type Seven: Planning (anticipation)

Type Eight: Vengeance (objectification)

Type Nine: Indolence (daydreaming)

Step

2

Enneatype Defense Mechanisms

Reflect on how your type creates defensiveness in you and with others.

Type One: Repression, reaction form is displacement

Type Two: Identification, reaction form denial

Type Three: Repression, projection, displacement

Type Four: Introjection, displacement, splitting

Type Five: Displacement, projection, isolation

Type Six: Identification, displacement, projection

Type Seven: Repression, externalization, acting out

Type Eight: Repression, displacement, denial

Type Nine: Repression, dissociation, denial

Journey of Emotions Meditations

The previous exercises were to stimulate both your thinking and feelings about how your particular form of emotional patterns developed throughout your life. Your reflection is in preparation for the following guided meditations. These meditations are a way you can explore how you used your emotional structure to create constriction in your life.

These three guided meditations in the Journey of Emotions will help you to continue to explore the development of your constricted ego self. You will be guided into a deep state of relaxation and given a way to quickly put yourself into a deeply relaxed physical and emotional state whenever you want to use the "marker" you created in the first set of meditations. Recall that this "marker"—a symbol, an image, or a word—is used to anchor in your body/mind the direct physical experience of your relaxation state so that when you want to relax you can recall this marker and it will more quickly move your body/mind into a relaxed feeling. This deeply relaxed state will enable you to explore many aspects of both the development of your constricted ego structure as well as the next stage of your journey to your inner freedom and happiness.

You will now examine patterns of the Journey of Emotions and how your constricted self developed through the ages four to eight, thirty-four to thirty-eight, and sixty-four to sixty-eight. The patterns identified emotionally in these time periods are the effect of worry, denial, desire, and judging in our experience.

Step 2

Exercise: *Meditation Ages Four to Eight*

Again, as with other exercises you've done before, please either pre-record this guided meditation in order to listen to it or have a partner or friend read and guide you through it. Where there is a *(pause)* indicated, give yourself time to experience the instructions at that point. (If you want to use the bonus video for this meditation go to appendix D.)

The intention of this meditation is to go back to the early part of your life to recall the emotional conditions that began to shape your constricted self development.

This early period of ages four to eight is a powerful shaper of our emotional life and identity. Consider the following questions as access points to explore what your emotions in this time period were like in preparation for the guided meditation. Write your results in your notebook after doing the meditations.

Questions on Ages Four to Eight

- What kinds of moods or emotional reactions did you have to people and situations?

- What were the interests that you were excited or even passionate about?

- How did you resist change in your life? For example, did you move a lot? Were you forced to eat things you didn't like?

- Do you remember having pleasant/strong or unpleasant/weak feelings about yourself, friends, teachers, parents, activities, etc.?

- How did you protect yourself from bad or unpleasant feelings?

- Do you remember being scared of dying or something negative and bad happening to you?

Let's begin the meditation:

- Take three deep breaths and begin to let yourself relax into a safe, quite comfortable place with your back straight but not rigid or lie on a bed or a mat.

- Close your eyes and notice the movement of your breath and then the sounds in your environment. *(pause)*

- With your eyes closed, focus inwardly on the image of the color orange along the spine at the ovaries and gonads for a few moments.

- Notice any sounds in your environment as you focus your attention on the color orange. *(pause)*

- Recall the depth of your last meditation. Let yourself relax into that re-membered state. What does that state of relaxation feel like inside you?

- Remember your marker. It was either a symbol, an image, or a word. Use your marker to return to that deep state of relaxation. As you move deeper into your marker, feel the tensions of your body letting go. *(pause)*

- Now take three long, deep breaths slowly.

- Allow thoughts, feelings, or outside disturbances to simply float through your mind, emotions, and body without holding on to them.

- With your marker in mind, move down deeper inside yourself as though you were falling like a leaf through the air to the ground. Let yourself drift down and down and down within your body. *(pause)*

- As you move into that deeper state within you, feel yourself in a comfort-able, safe place deep within your body.

Step
2

Step 2

- Now move through your body to your belly, right to the center of your body below your belly button. This is your healing center. Let yourself drop deeply into the center of this healing circle. Feel yourself resting in the center and opening and sinking deep into this healing place. *(pause)*

- In the center of this healing center, imagine that you are in a small boat on a beautiful lake. Notice the color of the lake, the trees around the lake, the beautiful sky with white fluffy clouds, and a breeze that allows you to float easily in the boat. *(pause)*

- Let yourself relax deeply as you just float, having no worries or concerns.

- Now, as you float on this beautiful lake imagine yourself going back in time to when you were four years old to eight years old. *(pause)*

- I am going to ask you a series of questions about this period in your life. Try to respond to them with the first thought that comes to mind. Also, note any feelings that arise as well.

- Now take three long, deep breaths slowly. *(pause)*

- Where were you living when you were the ages four to eight years old? What was life like at that time for you?

- If there were changes going on where you lived how did you react to them?

- Were you moody or upbeat as a child? Were your emotions different when you were home? Or in school?

- What were good feelings like? When did you have them?

- What were bad feelings like? What people or situations triggered these feelings?

- How did you protect yourself from these feelings?

- Did anyone die that you knew at this time? Did you know about death? If so, what was your reaction? *(pause)*

- Let go of these questions. Feel your breath and the relaxation of your body. Return your imagination to the lake. Continue to float in your boat on this beautiful lake. As you float in your boat, review the answers to these memories of your past. *(pause)*

- Now allow yourself to come back to the healing circle right below your belly, having the feelings of peace, ease, and present awareness.

- Place your attention on the sensation of moving gently upward until you reach your chest. Notice your breath slowly moving in and out. Follow your breath for just a few moments. Let yourself integrate what you learned from your four- to eight-year-old time period.

- Notice your hands in your lap. Notice how heavy and relaxed they are. Begin to wiggle or stretch your fingers and hands and move your body.

- With a big inhale and exhale of breath, come back into the room.

- Please write in your journal what you learned and experienced.

Step

2

Exercise: *Meditation Ages Thirty-Four to Thirty-Eight*

Again, as with other exercises you've done before, please either pre-record this meditation in order to listen to it or have a partner or friend read and guide you through it. Where there is a *(pause)* indicated, give yourself time to experience the instructions at that point. (If you want to use the bonus video for this meditation go to appendix D.)

This meditation is to explore events or situations that generated emotional structures in part of your constricted self's development. There are a number of questions below that can clarify your emotional pattern at a deeper level during this time period. Reflect on these questions about yourself as you go into the guided meditation. Write your results in your notebook after doing the meditations.

Questions on Ages Thirty-Four to Thirty-Eight

- Are you aware of the type of dominant emotions or feelings you have or had?

- How did you react to them? How do you usually react?

- Were you aware of your sexual attractions? Did you act on them, sublimate them, or what did you do? Were you excited, worried, or resistant, etc.?

- What is your fundamental fear of not getting what you want in your life?

- How much do your past experiences influence you today? Which ones?

- What are your deep interests and passions at this age, if any?

- What causes you to be fearful of death?

Step 2

Let's begin the meditation:

- Once again take several deep breaths. Take them with a long inhale and exhale. Permit yourself to relax into a safe, comfortable place with your back straight but not rigid or lie on a bed or a mat. Imagine the color orange around the lower half of your body.

- With eyes closed, imagine the color orange and notice the sounds in your environment.

- Take three deep breaths and feel your body relaxing. *(pause)*

- Recall the depth of relaxation in your last meditation. Let the body memory relax your body right now. Notice how you feel mentally, physically, and emotionally inside yourself as you relax.

- What does that state of relaxation feel like inside you?

- Remember your marker. It was either a symbol, an image, or a word. Use your marker to return to that deep state of relaxation. As you move deeper into your marker, feel the tensions of your body letting go. *(pause)*

- Now take three deep breaths. Slowly inhale and exhale.

- Allow thoughts, feelings, or outside disturbances to float through you without holding on to them.

- With your marker in mind, move down deeper inside yourself as though you were falling like a leaf through the air to the ground. Let yourself drift down and down and down within your body. *(pause)*

- As you move into that deeper state within you, feel yourself in a comfortable, safe place deep within your body.

- Now move through your body to your belly, right to the center of your body below your belly button. This is your healing center. Let yourself drop deeply into the center of this healing circle. Feel yourself resting in the center and opening and sinking deep into this healing place. *(pause)*

- Now imagine you are in a canoe on a slow-moving, gentle mountain stream. Be aware of the colors, the sounds, the forest, the beautiful sky above with drifting clouds, and a soft breeze that allows you to float slowly in your canoe.

- Let yourself relax deeply as you just float downward with no worries or concerns. *(pause)*

- Now, as you float in your canoe imagine yourself moving back in time to ages thirty-four to thirty-eight. *(pause)*

- I am going to ask you a series of questions about this period in your life. Try to respond to them with the first thought that comes to mind. Also, note any feelings that arise as well.

- How aware are you of your emotions and feelings at this time? Can you see situations or events where you experience these emotions and feelings? How strong or disruptive were these feelings in your life and with others?

- Were you aware of your sexual attractions to others and did you respond or react to them?

- Did you emotionally act on what you wanted or did you hold back? Either way how did that feel at that time?

- What were you passionate about in your life at this time, or were you troubled or depressed?

- Did you consider yourself dying from accidents, illness, etc.? If so, how did you protect yourself from possibly dying?

- Come back to yourself floating in the canoe. As you gently float in this canoe, reflect on what your emotional life was at this time of your life.

- Now allow yourself to come back to the healing circle right below your belly, having the feelings of peace, ease, and present awareness.

- Place your attention on the sensation of moving gently upward until you reach your chest. Notice your breath slowly moving in and out. Follow your

Step 2

breath for just a few moments. Let yourself integrate what you learned from your thirty-four- to thirty-eight-year-old time period.

- Notice your hands in your lap. Notice how heavy and relaxed they are. Begin to wiggle or stretch your fingers and hands and move your body.
- With a big inhale and exhale of breath come back into the room.
- Please write in your journal what you learned and experienced.

Step 2

Exercise: *Meditation Ages Sixty-Four to Sixty-Eight*

This journey is focused during the ages of sixty-four to sixty-eight. The intention is to become more conscious of your emotion structure that is part of your constricted self's development. Again, as with other exercises you've done before, please either pre-record this meditation in order to listen to it or have a partner or friend read and guide you through it. Where there is a *(pause)* indicated, give yourself time to experience the instructions at that point. (If you want to use the bonus video for this meditation go to appendix D.)

Below are a number of questions to make you more aware of your emotional experience. Considering them can help you go deeper into the guided meditation. Write your results in your notebook after doing the meditations.

Questions on Ages Sixty-Four to Sixty-Eight

- How would you describe what it is to emotionally flow with life?
- What emotions do you respond to when you resist life?
- What pleases you in life?
- Do you have a strong interest or passion in your life at this time?
- What are the sensualities in your life? How do you express them?
- What are the routine emotions you fall back on in tense situations?
- How do you protect yourself from the feelings of fear and anger?
- What are your fears about dying?

Let's begin the meditation:

- Once again take several deep breaths and take them with a long inhale and exhale. Permit yourself to relax into a safe, comfortable place with your back straight but not rigid or lie on a bed or a mat. Imagine you are in a room that is all an orange color.

- With eyes closed, feel the orange color feel like the sun on your face and notice the sounds in your environment. Take three deep breaths and feel your body relaxing. *(pause)*

- Recall the depth of relaxation in your last meditation. Let the body memory relax your body right now. Notice how you feel mentally, physically, and emotionally inside yourself as you relax.

- What does that state of relaxation feel like inside you?

- Remember your marker. It was either a symbol, an image, or a word. Use your marker to return to that deep state of relaxation. As you move deeper into your marker, feel the tensions of your body letting go. *(pause)*

- Now take three deep breaths. Slowly inhale and exhale.

- Allow thoughts, feelings, or outside disturbances float through you without holding on to them.

- With your marker in mind, move down deeper inside yourself as though you were falling like a leaf through the air to the ground. Let yourself drift down and down and down within your body. *(pause)*

- As you move into that deeper state within you, feel yourself in a comfortable, safe place deep within your body.

- As in other meditations, now move through your body to your belly, right to the center of your body below your belly button. This is your healing center. Let yourself drop deeply into the center of this healing circle. Feel yourself resting in the center and opening and sinking deep into this healing place. *(pause)*

- Resting in the center opening, sink deeply into your healing place.

Step 2

- Imagine now that you are at the beach looking out at the waves of the ocean sliding up the sand and then back again. Notice the color and the sound of the waves, the movement of birds in the beautiful blue sky above you. Feel the breeze that caresses your body as you sit on the sand. *(pause)*

- In this beautiful and restful place you have no worries, no concerns with a feeling of safety and rest.

- As you feel this deep restful place on the beach, go back in time and remember your life at the ages of sixty-four to sixty-eight. *(pause)*

- I am now going to ask you a series of questions about this period in your life. Try to respond to them with the first thought that comes to mind. Also, note any feelings that arise as well.

- Now take three deep breaths and slowly inhale and exhale. *(pause)*

- At this period of time in your life are you flowing or struggling with life?

- What situations do you react to and emotionally close down or what situations are you open to and express yourself emotionally?

- Is sensuality a part of your life? How do you express that sensuality or cut it off?

- How do you protect yourself from fear and anger?

- Do you consider the closeness of death? Is death a part of your life? Do you avoid thinking about it? Do you resist or avoid or have you faced it? *(pause)*

- See yourself now back at the beach watching the waves come in. As you relax on the beach, reflect on what was important to you at this time of your life.

- Now allow yourself to come back to the healing circle right below your belly, having the feelings of peace, ease, and present awareness.

- Place your attention on the sensation of moving gently upward until you reach your chest. Notice your breath slowly moving in and out. Follow your breath for just a few moments. Let yourself integrate what you learned from your sixty-four- to sixty-eight-year-old time period.

- Notice your hands in your lap. Notice how heavy and relaxed they are. Begin to wiggle or stretch your fingers and hands and move your body.

- With a big inhale and exhale of breath, come back into the room.

- Please write in your journal what you learned and experienced.

Chapter 14
Step 3:
Journey of the Mind

*If the structures of the human mind remain unchanged, we will always
end up re-creating the same world, the same evils, the same dysfunction.*
—ECKHART TOLLE

In this Journey of the Mind we consider the structure of our thinking at different ages, how the body and mind get separated from each other and the intentional power of the mind to create change. You will then do the Enneagram exercises and move into the guided meditation.

Our Thinking Structure

The thinking structure of the mind leads to further construction of the separate sense of Self. The age when this development emerges is around eight through twelve years old. In this period, there is a continued focus on language as one of the important developmental functions in the school years. At this age, language is essential for encouraging your sense of constricted self. Thinking is the center of activity to open its full rational potential in school. The awesome power of speech, writing, communication is implicit in the formation of the constricted self's roles, values, status, thoughts, experienced contents in the world, and growing perception of reality. The frequencies of this age mind state are the alpha 2 brain waves (7.8–13 Hz). These frequencies stimulate the way you think and are dominant in the brain's growth at this period.

The structure of mental communication is developed further from thirty-eight to forty-two years old and sixty-eight to seventy-two years. You are able to express through language all that you see, hear, touch, and taste. Your speech, writing, conversation, and vocabulary allow you to connect to the world. It has enabled amazing advancements and achievements in all areas of human life. By this period, you have been fully conditioned by the patterns of language in which you participate. In the brain research of the past fifteen years, it is observed that where you put your attention is who you are. Attention gives language its environment, like water for a fish. Language focuses our attention to shut out a vast expanse of reality and narrow it down in scope. We only perceive reality where we place our attention.

The Mind–Body Divide

The key in building the constricted self at this stage is being enthralled with talking, figuring things out, and communicating to others. You are no longer aware of the sensations of your body or that you have a body or that you have emotions. Words become who you are and you separate more from the sense of being grounded and from your emotions and sensory awareness. James Joyce put this separation from ourselves in a stark image. One of his characters in his novel *Dubliners*, Mr. Duffy, he described as, "He lived a short distance from his body." [58]

As you grow older, increasing your focus on thinking creates a deeper degree of separation within you. You become even more contracted and unable to experience expansiveness. At this stage, you have forgotten who you are. You have not even realized this loss of the deep integrity of connection between mind and body. The loss is of the unified functioning of mind and body, which can naturally draw your attention to your feelings and grounding. Thus you are cut off from the source of your core energy.

---

58. James Joyce, *Dubliners* (New York: Penguin Classics, 1993), 57.

As the mind and body are separated, a deeper sense of self-image is created. This individuation must be developed for survival and for you to become a member of our technological society. You may not be aware of your increased tension and your scattered mind, or of the loss of the immediate sensate experience of your life. You are in your head and miss the smell of the rose, the incredible sunsets, the feel of petting a cat, or the inner building tension and emotions as you respond to life unnoticed. The psychological armoring is so strong that you can no longer be authentic.

The result is that the mind's separation from the body births the "doer" into the world. Now there is an even deeper belief that this constricted self "I" is doing everything in the world on its own. There is an additional notion that you need to defend and protect yourself to uphold your self-image. It is through this motivational drive that you identify once again with being someone who is not real or authentic. You identify with creating a self that has a purpose, which gives you a sense of power. Power can be used to control the world and others for your own claim to fame. On the other hand, the strength of your will and power may appear to be far more effective through taking action for the good in the world. But even this so-called positive good is only another creator of a false self.

The Power of the Mind

The alpha 2 brain-wave frequency allows you the thinking capability to produce changes in the world and in your life. The mind utilizes an intention or a plan of some kind of change. This energy frequency directs your mind to an intention. The intention is identified in order to achieve, control, or do something in the world. Once you have felt the desire of what you want and identified your intention or plan of action, all that is needed now is your willpower, your determination, and your steadfastness to make it happen. Have you ever felt a passion or a deep feeling for something? Maybe it is to help the homeless or write a book or save the whales. Your passion is an expression of a yearning for something beyond your perceived intention. You hope that this passionate yearning may give your life meaning. The process gives an illusionary sense that you have the power and you make change happen. The doer is now in power. Whether your intention has a positive effect or negative effect in the world depends on what that intention is.

When the passion and your fire are connected to the power of the constricted self, change comes from a different driving force. The fire driving force may be guilt or self-condemnation, which is the clue that the constricted self is in charge. What underlies the constricted self is "I have done something wrong." When you are driven by this force, it stimulates an illusion of unconscious behaviors and body sensations. The underlying desire is then driven by anger, jealousy, or competition or takes the form of helplessness, disempowerment, dependence, and control over others. The constricted self as a doer is now unconfident, blaming, and not good enough. When this doer is in charge, the tendency is to retreat and isolate yourself to protect from confrontation. The opposite may evolve in overcompensation in achievements, asserting power, or constantly questioning "How am I doing?" Another guilt approach is masked by the drive for accomplishments, financial gain, power, or recognition. Guilt intensely focuses on receiving acknowledgments that you should deserve.

Once attention is focused on the mind, the imagination can dig deeper into a lower frequency of alpha 2 brain waves, which increases despair, depression, and fear. The mind enfolds upon itself into a doing self with personal shielding: "I am a victim." You may notice that this constricted character continues in its competitive, arrogant, ambitious, hyperactive, stubborn, and driven self.

With too much drive, there is a pressure to discharge through angry responses. When anger arises, you will feel unloved. It is the depth of wanting to connect to others, to have something, wanting something to happen, wanting to be different, wanting to be seen, and wanting to be recognized. The mind encapsulates itself into a personal self with personal armoring and you then act like a victim. What happens in many cases is that in order to unwind from these qualities of mind, you are attracted to drugs. These drugs may be illegal or prescriptive to help numb and discharge the sense of negativity. The underlying dream is to raise your energy and to feel loved.

Step
3

Journey of the Mind Exercises

The Journey of the Mind brings more separation from the expanded self. With the addition of language and the mind being in control, you have moved your attention from your body to your head. To live in your head robs you of a vital, alive self. Many people who live active lives often comment that they feel "dead inside." What is missing is balance with the body, sensations, emotions, and mind in the moment. When the mind is the driver of the doer, there is an intense need to feel recognized, to be in power, and to be loved for the power and accomplishments. This craving overpowers the practical needs or emotions that allow life to flow. The goal of this strong desire is to be happy and to move out of the fear of survival and suffering, but instead it moves toward an excess of worldly pleasures. These come in all kinds of packages such as wealth, fame, sexual pleasure, food, and appearance.

The physical ramifications of being out of balance in this energy frequency are issues of digestion, liver, pancreas, spleen, stomach, gallbladder, kidneys, chronic fatigue, acidity, hypoglycemia, diabetes, and back pain.

Journey of the Mind Questions

Take a moment to ask yourself, before continuing to read, how the Journey of Mind affected your life during the ages eight to twelve, thirty-eight to forty-two, and sixty-eight to seventy-two.

- What age do you remember your mind running your life?

- How does the push of power affect your balance and flow?

- Are you aware of a focus on desire and sensory pleasures?

Exercise: *Brain Frequency Patterns*

Notice your energy patterns vibration especially at the developmental ages when there is an imbalance in the alpha 2 brain-wave frequency (7.8–13 Hz). In the following list of qualities and conditions, circle the ones you are currently

Step
3

experiencing. This will give you a sense of how active the constricted self is in your life.

Imbalanced Frequencies: Passivity, lack of energy, poor digestion, tendency to be cold, tendency to submission, blaming, low self-esteem, lack of confidence, weak will, poor self-discipline, use of stimulants, use of sedatives, dominating, controlling, competitive, arrogant, ambitious, hyperactive, stubborn, driven, and focused on goals.

Step 3

Exercise: *Enneagram Patterns*

The Enneagram exercises are to stimulate both your thinking and feelings about how your particular form of mental patterns developed throughout your life. Your reflection is in preparation for the meditations beginning on page 235.

Enneatype: Basic Desires

Check your Enneagram type in relation to your basic desire patterns. How do these patterns work in your life today?

Type One: To be good, to have integrity

Type Two: To feel love

Type Three: To feel valuable

Type Four: To be themselves

Type Five: To be capable and competent

Type Six: To be supported and guided

Type Seven: To be satisfied and complete

Type Eight: To protect themselves

Type Nine: To experience peace of mind and wholeness

Enneatype: Cognitive Patterns

Check your Enneagram type in relation to your basic cognitive pattern. How does your mental pattern work in your life today?

Type One: Identified with the moralizing self

Type Two: Value based on positive response from others

Type Three: Value based on "performance" external image

Type Four: Identify with their feeling and emotional states

Type Five: Think that they can understand by "witnessing"

Type Six: Look for guidance and security outside themselves

Type Seven: Anticipate the future, loss of immediacy

Type Eight: Feel that they are constantly working against something

Type Nine: Peace of mind by disengaging from instincts and reality

Enneatype: Doer Patterns

What kind of a doer are you in the world? How does that work for you?

Type One: Work hard, do everything perfectly

Type Two: Be generous, put others ahead of yourself

Type Three: Over succeed, over network, over work, keep climbing

Type Four: Be deep, dramatic, different, and experience life at its extremes

Type Five: Think smart, feel little, keep still, and think twice

Type Six: Be hyperalert, loyal, respectful of authority or challenge authority

Type Seven: Keep soaring, keep talking, keep planning, keep going, and be optimistic, cheerful, and entertaining

Type Eight: Stay on top, stay on the offensive, stay aggressive, take charge, full speed ahead

Type Nine: Stay calm, agreeable, never rock the boat, get rest, and let someone else row the boat

Journey of the Mind Meditations

Now you will take these exercises into meditation and ask some questions to help clarify your understanding of how your mind developed your constricted self. These meditations are a way you can explore this unique process of using your mental structure to create constriction in your life. The purpose of the questions before the guided meditations are to stimulate your memories of a particular age your mind was functioning in a certain way. Write your results in your notebook after the meditation.

The Journey of the Mind in the constricted self development is seen at ages eight to twelve, thirty-eight to forty-two, and sixty-eight to seventy-two. The patterns of this development relate to power, control, authority, and guilt.

Step 3

Exercise: *Meditation Ages Eight to Twelve*

Again, as with other exercises you've done before, please either pre-record this meditation in order to listen to it, or have a partner or friend read and guide you through it. Where there is a *(pause)* indicated, give yourself time to experience the instructions at that point. (If you want to use the bonus video for this meditation go to appendix D.)

Before beginning the guided meditation, I want you to focus on several questions in order to help you clarify your mental pattern at a deeper, and perhaps a more conscious, level. This reflection is in preparation for going deeper into the meditation. Write your results in your notebook after doing the meditations.

Questions on Ages Eight to Twelve

- Who did you blame at that time?
- Who held the power or authority in your family? Have you copied that pattern in your life?
- What changed in your life in relation to control?
- Were reading and studying important in your life?
- Were you shamed and who did it and what was it about?
- Did you stand your ground?
- What was so hard to digest about your family, school, and friends?
- What was your purpose in life?

Let's begin the meditation:

- Take three deep breaths and begin to let yourself relax into a safe, quiet, comfortable place with your back straight but not rigid or lie on a bed or a mat.

- Imagine the color yellow at your solar plexus like a yellow flower.

- With your eyes closed, feel the color yellow all around you and notice the movement of your breath and then the sounds in your environment. *(pause)*

- Recall the depth of your last meditation. Let yourself relax into that remembered state. What does that state of relaxation feel like inside you?

- Remember your marker. It was either a symbol, an image, or a word. Use your marker to return to that deep state of relaxation. As you move deeper into your marker, feel the tensions of your body letting go. *(pause)*

- Now take three deep breaths.

- Allow thoughts, feelings, or outside disturbances to simply float through your mind, emotions, and body without holding on to them.

- With your marker in mind, move down deeper inside yourself as though you were falling like a leaf through the air to the ground. Let yourself drift down and down and down within your body. *(pause)*

- As you move into that deeper state within you, feel yourself in a comfortable, safe place deep within your body.

- Now move through your body to your belly, right to the center of your body below your belly button. This is your healing center. Let yourself drop deeply into the center of this healing circle. Feel yourself resting in the center and opening and sinking deep into this healing place. *(pause)*

- In this center of this healing circle is a bright wood fire burning. It is radiating a healing energy of soft yellow light from the fire.

- Let yourself relax deeply as you gaze into the fire, having no worries or concerns.

Step

3

- Now as you let go to the entrancing and compelling movement of the fire imagine yourself going back in time to when you were between eight and twelve years old. *(pause)*

- I am going to ask you a series of questions about this period in your life. Try to respond to them with the first thought that comes to mind. Also, note any feelings that arise.

- Now take three deep breaths and slowly inhale and exhale. *(pause)*

- Who held the power or authority in your family?

- How has this family experience shaped your life? Do you exert power and authority in the same way?

- Did you feel shamed, disgraced, wronged, or humiliated in your family or by friends?

- If challenged by other kids did you stand your ground?

- Did you have eating problems? If so what was hard to digest in your family?

- Did you like school? Did you like to study, read, and get good grades?

- Did you have hobbies, sports, or some special purpose?

- Does relaxing in front of the fire bring up any other memories?

- As you feel the warmth of the fire, gently move back to the center of the healing circle and feel the fire begin to fade.

- Now allow yourself to come back to the healing circle right below your belly, having the feelings of peace, ease, and present awareness.

- Place your attention on the sensation of moving gently upward until you reach your chest.

- Notice your breath slowly moving in and out. Follow your breath for just a few moments.

- Let yourself integrate what you learned from your eight- to twelve-year-old time period. *(pause)*

- Notice your hands in your lap. Notice how heavy and relaxed they are. Begin to wiggle or stretch your fingers and hands and move your body.

- With a big inhale and exhale of breath, come back into the room.

- Please write in your journal what you learned and experienced.

Exercise: *Meditation Ages Thirty-Eight to Forty-Two*

Again, as with other exercises you've done before, please either pre-record this meditation in order to listen to it, or have a partner or friend read and guide you through it. Where there is a *(pause)* indicated, give yourself time to experience the instructions at that point. (If you want to use the bonus video for this meditation go to appendix D.)

As before, in beginning the guided meditation I want you to focus on several questions in order to help you clarify your mental pattern at a more conscious level. Consider these questions in preparation for going deeper into the meditation. Write your results in your notebook after doing the meditations.

Questions on Ages Thirty-Eight to Forty-Two

- Are you focused on your own needs or issues? What are they?

- What happens when you are not in control of yourself or others?

- Are there things about which you are ashamed?

- When have you been in a victim position?

- How do you express your power? What stops it? How do you get your recognition needs met?

- What is your purpose at this age?

- What is your attitude toward authority in your life?

Let's begin the meditation:

- Take three deep breaths and begin to let yourself relax into a safe, quite, comfortable place with your back straight but not rigid or lie on a bed or a mat. Be aware of the color yellow filling your solar plexus with energy.

Step 3

- With eyes closed, imagine yellow light filling the room you are in and notice the movement of your breath and then the sounds in your environment. *(pause)*

- Recall the depth of your last meditation. Let yourself relax into that remembered state. What does that state of relaxation feel like inside you?

- Remember your marker. It was either a symbol, an image, or a word. Use your marker to return to that deep state of relaxation. As you move deeper into your marker, feel the tensions of your body letting go. *(pause)*

- Now take three deep breaths.

- Allow thoughts, feelings, or outside disturbances to simply float through your mind, emotions, and body without holding on to them.

- With your marker in mind, move down deeper inside yourself as though you were falling like a leaf through the air to the ground. Let yourself drift down and down and down within your body. *(pause)*

- As you move into that deeper state within you, feel yourself in a comfortable, safe place deep within your body.

- Now move through your body to your belly, right to the center of your body below your belly button. This is your healing center. Let yourself drop deeply into the center of this healing circle. Feel yourself resting in the center and opening and sinking deep into this healing place. *(pause)*

- In this center of this healing circle you sit and gaze out onto a beautiful meadow. This meadow is filled with yellow sunlight, a soft breeze moves the green grasses in slow waves rippling out to the horizon.

- Let yourself relax deeply as you scan the beauty and radiance of the meadow with the yellow light, having no worries or concerns.

- Now as you let go to the entrancing and compelling movement of the ripples of grass in the meadow, imagine yourself going back in time to when you were between thirty-eight and forty-two years old. *(pause)*

- I am going to ask you a series of questions about this period in your life. Try to respond to them with the first thought that comes to mind. Also, note any feelings that arise.

- Now take three deep breaths and slowly inhale and exhale. *(pause)*

- Remembering when you were between thirty-eight and forty-two years old, become aware of any mental struggles in your work, personal life, or relationships.

- Did you mentally dwell on things that you did or did not do or become?

- Did you ever think that you were a victim? What thoughts brought you to this conclusion?

- Did you have thoughts of controlling or dominating others?

- Remember a time when you made plans but they fell through. What were the flaws in your thinking?

- Did you get overwhelmed in the "thinking" work you had to do in your job?

- Did you like detail thinking at this stage of your life or were you overwhelmed by detail?

- Did you get lost in thoughts and drift into daydreaming or did you discipline yourself to stay on your mental tasks? *(pause)*

- As you feel the sun and the breeze on you and watch the ripples running across the grass, gently move back to the center of the healing circle and see the meadow slowly fade.

- Now allow yourself to come back to the healing circle right below your belly, having the feelings of peace, ease, and present awareness.

- Place your attention on the sensation of moving gently upward until you reach your chest.

- Notice your breath slowly moving in and out. Follow your breath for just a few moments. Let yourself integrate what you learned from your thirty-eight- and forty-two-year-old time periods. *(pause)*

- Notice your hands in your lap. Notice how heavy and relaxed they are. Begin to wiggle or stretch your fingers and hands and move your body.

- With a big inhale and exhale of breath come back into the room.

- Please write in your journal what you learned and experienced.

Step 3

Exercise: *Meditation Ages Sixty-Eight to Seventy-Two*

Again, as with other exercises you've done before, please either pre-record this meditation in order to listen to it, or have a partner or friend read and guide you through it. Where there is a *(pause)* indicated, give yourself time to experience the instructions at that point. (If you want to use the bonus video for this meditation go to appendix D.)

The following questions are to help you clarify your mental process at a deeper level. This reflection is in preparation for going deeper into the guided meditation. Write your results in your notebook after doing the meditations.

Questions on Ages Sixty-Eight to Seventy-Two

- Are you in your head most of the time?

- What is your role in your life?

- How do you rely on your inner or outer authority?

- What happens when you deny yourself things?

- How has language played a role in your life?

- Have you been acknowledged for what you have done in your life?

- Do you shame yourself or do others shame you?

- What is the purpose at this time in your life?

- Do you approve of the way you handle authority now?

Let's begin the meditation:

- Take three deep breaths and begin to let yourself relax into a safe, quite comfortable place with your back straight but not rigid or lie on a bed or a mat. Be aware of the color yellow emerging from your solar plexus.

- Close your eyes and feel the yellow color shining like a gold ball resting now on your belly. Notice the movement of your breath and then the sounds in your environment. *(pause)*

- Recall the depth of your last meditation. Let yourself relax into that remembered state. What does that state of relaxation feel like inside you?

- Remember your marker. It was either a symbol, an image, or a word. Use your marker to return to that deep state of relaxation. As you move deeper into your marker, feel the tensions of your body letting go. *(pause)*

- Now take three deep breaths.

- Allow thoughts, feelings, or outside disturbances to simply float through your mind, emotions, and body without holding on to them.

- With your marker in mind, move down deeper inside yourself as though you were falling like a leaf through the air to the ground. Let yourself drift down and down and down within your body. *(pause)*

- As you move into that deeper state within you, feel yourself in a comfortable, safe place deep within your body.

- Now move through your body to your belly, right to the center of your body below your belly button. This is your healing center. Let yourself drop deeply into the center of this healing circle. Feel yourself resting in the center and opening and sinking deep into this healing place. *(pause)*

- In the center of this healing circle, you sit on a high bluff looking out over a vast forest. The view looks beyond the forest to a high range of mountains shining in the sunlight. A slight breeze is blowing and you see birds flying out over the forest.

- Let yourself relax deeply as you scan the beauty and radiance of the yellow sun bathing the forest and mountains in light, having no worries or concerns.

- Now as you let go to the entrancing and compelling movement of the breeze and the view of the forest and mountains, imagine yourself going back in time to when you were between sixty-eight and seventy-two years old. *(pause)*

Step 3

Step 3

- I am going to ask you a series of questions about this period in your life. Try to respond to them with the first thought that comes to mind. Note any feelings that arise as well.

- Now take three deep breaths and slowly inhale and exhale. *(pause)*

- What is it like to continually have thoughts coming and going in your mind?

- How has being in your head played a role in your life? What are its consequences? Has it contributed to your success in life?

- Have you tried to control your thoughts, or do you just let them come and go in you?

- Have you over the years focused on thinking what your purpose is in life?

- Through these years do you have negative or shameful thoughts?

- Do you try to control the negative, judgmental thoughts toward others? *(pause)*

- Does relaxing and sitting on the bluff looking out over the forest shining in the yellow sun bring up any other memories about these years?

- As you feel the gentle breeze and the sun shining on you, move back to the center of the healing circle and let the forest and mountains fade in your memories.

- Now allow yourself to come back to the healing circle right below your belly button, having the feelings of peace, ease, and present awareness.

- Place your attention on the sensation of moving gently upward until you reach your chest. Notice your breath slowly moving in and out. Follow your breath for just a few moments. Let yourself integrate what you learned from your sixty-eight- to seventy-two-year-old time periods. *(pause)*

- Notice your hands in your lap. Notice how heavy and relaxed they are. Begin to wiggle or stretch your fingers and hands and move your body.

- With a big inhale and exhale of breath come back into the room.

- Please write in your journal what you learned and experienced.

Chapter 15
Step 4:
Journey of Self-Identity

Every part of our personality that we do not love will become hostile to us.
—ROBERT BLY

In the Journey of Self-Identity we explore the explicit ages that shape your identity and what poet and author Robert Bly calls your shadow bag that you hide your true self within. We will also explore what your internal self-talk, or dialogue with yourself, does to reinforce your developing identity. Finally, you struggle to form your own identity with names like son, daughter, mother, boss, nurse, supervisor, etc., only to come to some point in your life where you feel lost and uncertain as to who you really are. We finish the chapter with the age activations, the Enneagram exercises, and the guided meditation.

Becoming an Identity

Adolescence, ages twelve to sixteen, is the time when the hormonal surge hits the constricted self. This is the next layer added to the structure of the constricted self. There is a temporary destabilization of mental focus because of the surprising disruption of body feelings. There is a shift of focus as you face new sexual feelings in your body. These sexual feelings take over your life. At this time, there is a remembrance of the intimacy with your mother when you were an infant. Sexual feelings arise in the renewed desire for intimacy with another.

This is a tumultuous time as the adolescent struggles between finding a sense of identity and a sense of worth. This tension creates an inner battle in the constricted self. Your newly formed identity is fragile, so you take it personally when others tease or criticize you. Taking things personally and taking yourself seriously is the central power of separation and constriction. In your adolescence, you are also dealing with the need to be accepted and to create an identity and a sense of value as you enter into the culture. If you feel unacceptable, it constricts you even more. Ultimately, you must hide this from the world so that you will be acceptable. The poet Robert Bly, in his book *A Little Book on the Human Shadow*, describes how we hide our unacceptable parts of ourselves into what he calls a "bag" we drag behind us all of our life. "Behind us we have an invisible bag, and the part of us our parents don't like, we, to keep our parents' love, put (these parts) in the bag. By the time we go to school our bag is quite large." [59]

Shadow Identity

This same issue of hiding what is unacceptable in your "bag" may occur again in midlife at ages forty-two to forty-six and again at seventy-two to seventy-six. What arises at these ages is the personal issue between your acceptable self-identity and what you try to hide so that you will be accepted. Swiss psychologist Carl Jung called the unacceptable self the "shadow." [60] The Jungian shadow concept consists of the traits, tendencies, and potentials with which you have

---

59. Robert Bly, *A Little Book on the Human Shadow* (New York: HarperOne, Reissue edition, 1988), 17.
60. Joseph Campbell, ed., *The Portable Jung*, translated by R. F. C. Hull (New York: Viking Press, 1971), 144–148.

lost contact and repressed. The shadow contains both shame and worth. Shame is when you feel you are bad, but as you look deeper into these traits, there are wonderful powerful aspects of worth in your shadow, even when you do not feel worthy. You have tucked inside the shadow qualities of value, excellence, and importance that the constricted self has hidden. The constricted self has hidden these qualities of worth to stay alive. These qualities may be hidden, but on some level you know and feel that you are accepted, worthy, and have value. When these potentials are repressed, you isolate yourself through anxiety and the fear of being bad. *Anxiety is the basic feeling of separation of the constricted self.* If you face your anxiety rather than avoiding or pushing it away, you will realize that anxiety does not exist. When faced, anxiety fades gently away because it is experienced in your mind. It fades away just like the air element of this frequency. When you face the constricted self's shadow traits, they dissolve as you embody your value and become more conscious, awake, and free.

Internal Dialogue

Another aspect of the constricted self is your internal dialogue. The brain frequencies related to the internal dialogue are higher alpha brain waves related to conscious states of stress, lack of connectedness with oneself, and mind/body disintegration. At this frequency, the struggle exists between finding connection and integration of your identity and the nature of the shadow within you. The constricted self's identity still exists in the body somewhere in this region of the brain and continues to grow in its mental ability. As the thinking ability grows, so does the incessant internal dialogue. This internal conversation gives you an identity that there is someone in you and that someone in there is real. The conversation is full of inner likes and dislikes, past memories, future possibilities, and opinions. In talking to yourself, the constricted self is constructing and monitoring layers of things you like or don't like about all of your different identities as woman, man, friend, teacher, parent, husband, wife, etc. *The constricted self continually talks to itself in order to establish a sense of reality and assure itself of its existence.*

The Struggle to Go Beyond the Constructed Identity

Now, once again, the constricted self continues to separate even more from the expanded self. It is amazing that most of us haven't examined the actuality of the constricted self's existence. If you did reflect on its existence, it could be so frightening that the fear of it might affect your survival.

You, like all of us, are strongly identified with our name, family, partners, history, job, and friends, etc., all of which we rely upon as our support system. However, there may come a point in your life when you feel empty or lost. This emptiness creates an urge to get away. If you listen to the urge and take a retreat, a rest, look inside, and reflect on your life, you may begin to wake up to your constricted identity. It is possible in the calm silence to gain insight on how incomplete, fragile, and illusory you are. In this silent reflection you may find that, within you, nobody exists. You may find that what you constructed as an identity is really just a compensation pattern to protect you from the early wounds of your life before you lost the connection and oneness to everything that was your state of being.

Unfortunately, these insights are quickly diverted by the chatter of the inner dialogue and the busyness of activities. You, like all of us, will move right on to the daily activities and barely miss a beat with the variety of identities we live within. If this continues in your early adulthood, you select many identities, but a main identity, such as parent, doctor, or gardener, becomes dominant. With that firm label, you have a stable personal identity and feel secure. This label is home for most of us. In midlife, the constricted self waves its magic wand and you look at what you have done in your life in terms of your talents and accomplishments and this confirms your identity once again. In later life it is looking back and trying to confirm meaning and purpose among the various identities that you have played out in the course of your life. The constricted self relies on these significant identity confirmations to stay alive.

Journey of Self-Identity Exercise

The development of the structure of the constricted self is quite a journey. You have just read and explored for yourself an incredible building project of the birthing and growing of your constricted self. First, you became aware of being separated at birth from the expanded self, then more separation by your emotions, then more separation by your mind, and finally you were separated by the development of your personal identities. The constricted self is very strong.

It is impossible for most of us even to consider looking at our inner self, let alone the possibility of dying. We are too frightened to confront our shadow, so it becomes what poet Robert Bly calls the black bag we all fill up and drag behind us throughout life. Anxiety turns you away from facing yourself. Our culture offers few models and little encouragement for tackling the constricted self. This challenge to face the constricted self is not widely supported. Thus, we maintain the illusion of separation because of fear that keeps us stuck where we are most familiar. So when death knocks on our door and we have to open it, we will probably defend ourselves by denying it. The strange reality is that we will probably be in shock that life is ending. Too many individuals facing this shock of dying go into isolation and depression. We resist and try to slam the door on death because our constricted self has built up a control process to isolate us and separate us from the truth of who we really are.

We live and die with air—the oxygen that gives life. The air element, which is your breath, is the connection to the touchstone of life's energy. At the level of this alpha 2 brain frequency, the air sustains your physical body and all parts of your life. As you take your last breath, the air element remains when you die. The air element is free; it is in unconfined space surrounding Earth with a mixture of oxygen and nitrogen. In each breath of air, there is a connection to that expanded space, which is the opposite of the constricted self that is filled with anxiety. But the air is also the element for awakening. In the meditative breathing process, it is possible to shift awareness to awaken the expanded self and breathe and merge with reality.

The physical issues that emerge in the imbalance of this alpha 2 brain frequency relate to the respiratory system as an aching in the chest or upper back. Also there can be problems with the lungs. You may have difficulty breathing and dysfunction of the thymus gland, which is an important part of the immune system. Other possible negative conditions include bronchitis, heart disease, circulation problems, and pericardium issues in which inner arms and hands are

Step
4

affected. If these conditions emerge in your life, use them as an opportunity to let go to that deep breath of the loving spirit that is your true inner guide to the truth of yourself.

Exercise: *Age Development*

Take a moment to ask yourself how the Journey of Self-Identity has affected your life during the ages twelve to sixteen, forty-two to forty-six, and seventy-two to seventy-six. Reflect and write about them in your notebook.

- As an adolescent, do you remember being shy or affected by peer talk about you?
- Have you been able to move beyond those and other issues as you matured?
- How do you express your worth and your value today?
- List ten things you like about yourself.

Step

4

Exercise: *Brain Frequency Patterns*

Observe what your energy patterns were, especially at the developmental ages when there is an imbalance in the alpha 2 brain-wave frequency (7.8–13 Hz). The following is a list of qualities that may reflect your imbalance. Circle the ones that you are currently experiencing. This will give you a sense of how active the constricted self is in your life.

Imbalanced Frequencies: Focusing on Self at the expense of others, seeking approval from others in order to receive love, being dependent on others, jealous, constant sufferer, being a pleaser to get love, antisocial and withdrawn, lonely, feeling isolated, and inability to share feelings.

Exercise: *Enneagram Patterns*

Structured personality patterns become familiar to you over the years. Once they become established, they are routine and they belong to you. The more you put your attention on them the more that confirms they are real. If, for example, you feel that nobody loves you, you then look for signs of that and the experience of nobody loving you will be everywhere. We can perform all kinds of tricks to finesse the data of our experience to keep us in alignment with who we believe we are not.

Your constricted self has an idealized image of you in order to make you feel good about yourself. The ideal image, however, grows into a grandiose imagining that has no relationship to who you really are. This image is born out of a driven inner necessity to create identity. The Enneagram labels these ideas as "prides." How does your ideal image fit for you? Reflect and write in your notebook.

Enneatype: Ideal Image

Type One: I am right, good.

Type Two: I am helpful.

Type Three: I am effective and successful.

Type Four: I am special, sensitive, and conform to elite standards.

Type Five: I am wise, perceptive.

Type Six: I am obedient, faithful, loyal; I do what I ought.

Type Seven: I am okay.

Type Eight: I am powerful; I can do.

Type Nine: I am settled.

Enneatype: Shadow Pattern

What shadows are you hiding that you do not want others to know about you? You might hide them so that they will not be challenged or experienced by others. Is that true for you?

Type One: Integrity and improvement

Type Two: Intimacy

Type Three: Acceptance and validation

Type Four: Identity

Step
4

Type Five: Mastery

Type Six: Security and safety

Type Seven: Satisfaction and fulfillment

Type Eight: Physical survival and legacy

Type Nine: Harmony and stability

Enneatype: Behavior Identity

How does your behavior fit your personal self-image? Does there need to be a change? Write about situations in which your identity manifests outwardly.

Type One: I am responsible in my job to fix things and repress anger.

Type Two: I need to be needed and give to others what I feel they need.

Type Three: I seek affirmation as an achiever, unaware of my feelings or value.

Type Four: I search for love and to be loved, addicted to emotional ups and downs.

Type Five: I am private, self-sufficient, accumulate knowledge, and limit desires.

Type Six: I am fearful, questioning, and vigilant for security.

Type Seven: I desire to plan pleasurable activities, new ideas, and possibilities.

Type Eight: I blame others and proclaim myself blame free.

Type Nine: I forget myself, merge with others, and devalue my priorities.

Enneatype: Avoidance Patterns

What is it you do to stay constricted in the shadow of your personal identity?

Type One: Avoid slacking off and taking play time so as not to reveal flaws and faults.

Type Two: Don't reveal your own needs and preference and don't say no.

Type Three: Don't notice your own feelings and wishes, avoid failure, and don't say no.

Type Four: Avoid being superficial, ordinary, and boring.

Type Five: Don't say anything you are not sure of and don't express feelings, intimacy, or being exposed.

Step

4

Type Six: Avoid being independent or too dependent.

Type Seven: Don't get emotionally down or pinned down, avoid pain, suffering, and boredom.

Type Eight: Avoid weakness in yourself, being vulnerable, being nice, and being sucked in with kindness.

Type Nine: Avoid conflict, your own agenda, and don't waste energy or get
too enthused.

Step

4

Journey of Self-Identity Meditations

Once again, use the Enneagram exercises on the previous pages to stimulate
both your thinking and feelings about how your particular identity patterns developed throughout your life. Your reflection is in preparation for the following
meditations. These guided meditations are a way you can continue to explore
this unique process of using your identity structure to create constriction in
your life.

Again, there is a set of questions before each of the three meditations. Read
the questions first and reflect on them before doing the meditations. The purpose of the questions before the meditations is to stimulate your memories of
a particular age the meditation focuses on. Write your results in your notebook
after the meditation.

The following guided meditations examine patterns of the Journey of Self
Identity in the constricted self's development at ages twelve to sixteen, forty-two
to forty-six, and seventy-two to seventy-six years. The patterns identify issues of
worth, shame, and value. Your self-identity is built around these concepts. It is
for you to discovery how these issues evolved in your life.

Exercise: *Meditation Ages Twelve to Sixteen*

Again, as with other exercises you've done before, please either pre-record this
meditation in order to listen to it or have a partner or friend read and guide you
through it. Where there is a *(pause)* indicated, give yourself time to experience

the instructions at that point. (If you want to use the bonus video for this meditation go to appendix D.)

Continue the practice to focus on several questions in order to help you clarify your identity pattern at a deeper, and perhaps a more unconscious, level. This reflection is in preparation for going deeper into the meditation. Write your results in your notebook after doing the meditations.

Questions on Ages Twelve to Sixteen

- How do you hide your shame?
- In what ways do you feel unworthy?
- How do you define your identity?
- What behaviors do you display and put on to get love?
- How much do you give to others of what you are wanting for yourself?
- What are you hiding in your shadow personality?
- What gives you value?

Let's begin the meditation:

- Once again take several deep breaths and take them with a long inhale and exhale. Permit yourself to relax into a safe, comfortable place with your back straight but not rigid or lie on a bed or a mat. Bring to your awareness the color green filling the room you are in.
- Close your eyes and imagine a beautiful emerald jewel sitting on the top of your heart. As you see in your mind's eye this emerald stone on your heart, notice the sounds in your environment. Take three deep breaths and feel your body relaxing. *(pause)*
- Recall the depth of relaxation in your last meditation. Let the body memory relax your body right now. Notice how you feel mentally, physically, and emotionally inside yourself as you relax.
- What does that state of relaxation feel like inside you?

Step
4

- Remember your marker. It was either a symbol, an image, or a word. Use your marker to return to that deep state of relaxation. As you move deeper into your marker, feel the tensions of your body letting go. *(pause)*

- Now take three deep breaths. Slowly inhale and exhale.

- Allow thoughts, feelings, or outside disturbances to float through you without holding on to them.

- With your marker in mind, move down deeper inside yourself as though you were falling like a leaf through the air to the ground. Let yourself drift down and down and down within your body. *(pause)*

- As you move into that deeper state within you, feel yourself in a comfortable, safe place deep within your body.

- As in other meditations now move through your body to your belly, right to the center of your body below your belly button. This is your healing center. Let yourself drop deeply into the center of this healing circle. Feel yourself resting in the center and opening and sinking deep into this healing place. *(pause)*

- Resting in the center opening, sink deeply into your healing place.

- Imagine as you are in this healing place that you are sitting in a beautiful glass atrium. All around you are beautiful, colorful flowers. The sun is filtered through the taller emerald green foliage around you. The fragrances relax you deeply as you take easy, gentle inhales. Notice the beautiful blue sky above you through the glass. From somewhere there is a gentle breeze that caresses your body as you sit and look about you. *(pause)*

- In this beautiful and restful place you have no worries and no concerns, with a feeling of safety and rest.

- As you feel this deep, restful place in the atrium go back in time and remember your ages twelve to sixteen. *(pause)*

- I am now going to ask you a series of questions about this period in your life. Try to respond to them with the first thought that comes to mind. Also, note any feelings that arise.

Step

4

Step

4

- Now take three deep breaths and slowly inhale and exhale. *(pause)*
- At this period of time in your life are you flowing or struggling with life?
- In the time period of twelve years old to around sixteen years what was going on in your life?
- What kind of a person were you at this age?
- How did you value your self?
- Who supported your self-worth?
- Did you feel worthy?
- When did you feel you were not good enough?
- How did you hide negative feelings about yourself?
- Were you sensitive to how people treated you?
- What was your behavior, attitudes, and reactions like to others?
- Were you anxious about sex, school, or your future?
- What were your sexual concerns?
- Who were the ones you shared your personal feelings and thoughts with? Was that difficult, satisfying, or vulnerable for you?
- Continue to stay in the warmth of your heart connection as you come back to your breath and feel your heart beat.
- See yourself now back in the atrium. As you relax in the midst of the beautiful flowers and smells, reflect on what was important to you at this time of your life.
- Now allow yourself to come back to the healing circle right below your belly button, having the feelings of peace, ease, and present awareness.
- Place your attention on the sensation of moving gently upward until you reach your chest. Notice your breath slowly moving in and out. Follow your breath for just a few moments. Let yourself integrate what you learned from your twelve- to sixteen-year-old time period.
- Notice your hands in your lap. Notice how heavy and relaxed they are. Begin to wiggle or stretch your fingers and hands and move your body.

• With a big inhale and exhale of breath come back into the room.

• Please write in your journal what you learned and experienced.

Exercise: *Meditation Ages Forty-Two to Forty-Six*

Again, as with other exercises you've done before, please either pre-record this meditation in order to listen to it or have a partner or friend read and guide you through it. Where there is a *(pause)* indicated, give yourself time to experience the instructions at that point. (If you want to use the bonus video for this meditation go to appendix D.)

Focus now on the following questions in order to help you clarify your identity pattern at a deeper level in the next guided meditation. This journey is to help you find how you created your shadow identity. Write your results in your notebook after doing the meditations.

Questions on Ages Forty-Two to Forty-Six

• How do you react to unpleasant situations?

• What gives you your worth?

• How do you respond when your identity has been stepped upon?

• What conditions do you have in order for you to receive love?

• What happens to you with others when you establish your boundaries?

• What are your fears about opening your heart?

Let's begin the meditation:

• Once again take several deep breaths and take them with a long inhale and exhale. Permit yourself to relax into a safe, comfortable place with your back straight but not rigid or lie on a bed or a mat. Bring to your awareness the color green filling the room you are in.

Step

4

Step

4

- Close your eyes and imagine a green spotlight focused on your heart. The green light is soft and your heart seems to fill your entire body. As you see in your mind's eye this green light shining on your heart, notice the sounds in your environment. Take three deep breaths and feel your body relaxing. *(pause)*

- Recall the depth of relaxation in your last meditation. Let the body memory relax your body right now. Notice how you feel mentally, physically, and emotionally inside yourself as you relax.

- What does that state of relaxation feel like inside you?

- Remember your marker. It was either a symbol, an image, or a word. Use your marker to return to that deep state of relaxation. As you move deeper into your marker, feel the tensions of your body letting go. *(pause)*

- Now take three deep breaths. Slowly inhale and exhale.

- Allow thoughts, feelings, or outside disturbances to float through you without holding on to them.

- With your marker in mind, move down deeper inside yourself as though you were falling like a leaf through the air to the ground. Let yourself drift down and down and down within your body. *(pause)*

- As you move into that deeper state within you, feel yourself in a comfortable, safe place deep within your body.

- As in other meditations now move through your body to your belly, right to the center of your body below your belly button. This is your healing center.

- Let yourself drop deeply into the center of this healing circle. Feel yourself resting in the center and opening and sinking deep into this healing place. *(pause)*

- Imagine as you are in this healing place that you are sitting in a beautiful field of tall, wavy green grass. The mid-morning sun warms you as you sit looking out toward some mountains. The fragrances of the field with wildflowers relaxes you deeply as you take easy, gentle inhales. Notice the beautiful blue sky above you as you see birds gliding through the sky. From somewhere there is a gentle breeze that caresses your body as you sit and look about you. *(pause)*

• In this beautiful and restful place you have no worries and no concerns, with a feeling of safety and rest.

• As you feel this deep, restful place in the atrium go back in time and remember yourself at ages forty-two to forty-six. *(pause)*

• I am now going to ask you a series of questions about this period in your life. Try to respond to them with the first thought that comes to mind. Note any feelings that arise as well.

• Now take three deep breaths and slowly inhale and exhale. *(pause)*

• What are you ashamed of in this period of your life? How do you hide it?

• About what do you feel unworthy?

• At this age, what roles define your identity?

• What do you do and how do you act to get love?

• How much do you give to others of what you are wanting for yourself?

• What are you hiding that you do not tell anyone?

• What are the things you do, think, or feel that give you value?

• Continue to stay in the warmth of your heart connection as you come back to your breath and feel your heart beat.

• See yourself now back sitting in the tall green grass on the hill. As you relax in the midst of the beautiful flowers and smells, reflect on what was important to you at this time of your life.

• Now allow yourself to come back to the healing circle right below your belly button, having the feelings of peace, ease, and present awareness.

• Place your attention on the sensation of moving gently upward until you reach your chest. Notice your breath slowly moving in and out. Follow your breath for just a few moments. Let yourself integrate what you learned from your forty-two- to forty-six-year-old time period.

Step 4

- Notice your hands in your lap. Notice how heavy and relaxed they are. Begin to wiggle or stretch your fingers and hands and move your body.

- With a big inhale and exhale of breath, come back into the room.

- Please write in your journal what you learned and experienced.

Step 4

Exercise: *Meditation Ages Seventy-Two to Seventy-Six*

Again, as with other exercises you've done before, please either pre-record this meditation in order to listen to it or have a partner or friend read and guide you through it. Where there is a *(pause)* indicated, give yourself time to experience the instructions at that point. (If you want to use the bonus video for this meditation go to appendix D.)

Again, there are several questions below to help you clarify your identity pattern at a deeper, and perhaps a more conscious, level. This guided journey is to help you understand more clearly your shadow identity. Write your results in your notebook after doing the meditations.

Questions on Ages Seventy-Two to Seventy-Six

- How did you form your personal identity of yourself?

- Did you value yourself?

- Who supported your self-worth?

- Did you feel worthy?

- How did you hide your shame?

- What were your fears?

- What were your sexual concerns?

- Were there family and friends with whom you shared your heart?

Let's begin the meditation:

- Once again take several deep breaths and take them with a long inhale and exhale. Permit yourself to relax into a safe, comfortable place with your back straight but not rigid or lie on a bed or a mat. Imagine the color green filling the walls of the room you are in.

- Close your eyes and imagine a young green plant resting on your heart. The green plant seems to arise from your heart, and the green of the plant seems to fill your entire body. As you see in your mind's eye this green plant growing from your heart, notice the sounds in your environment. Take three deep breaths and feel your body relaxing. *(pause)*

- Recall the depth of relaxation in your last meditation. Let the body memory relax your body right now. Notice how you feel mentally, physically, and emotionally inside yourself as you relax.

- What does that state of relaxation feel like inside you?

- Remember your marker. It was either a symbol, an image, or a word. Use your marker to return to that deep state of relaxation. As you move deeper into your marker, feel the tensions of your body letting go. *(pause)*

- Now take three deep breaths. Slowly inhale and exhale.

- Allow thoughts, feelings, or outside disturbances to float through you without holding on to them.

- With your marker in mind, move down deeper inside yourself as though you were falling like a leaf through the air to the ground. Let yourself drift down and down and down within your body. *(pause)*

- As you move into that deeper state within you, feel yourself in a comfortable, safe place deep within your body.

- As in other meditations, now move through your body to your belly, right to the center of your body below your belly button. This is your healing center.

- Let yourself drop deeply into the center of this healing circle. Feel yourself resting in the center and opening and sinking deep into this healing place. *(pause)*

- Imagine as you are in this healing place that you are holding a beautiful green plant in your hands. The mid-morning sun warms you as you sit admiring

Step 4

the beauty of the plant. There is a fragrance from the plant and it relaxes you deeply as you take easy, gentle inhales. Notice the beautiful blue sky above you as you see birds gliding through the sky. From somewhere there is a gentle breeze that caresses your body as you sit with the plant resting in your hands. *(pause)*

- In this beautiful and restful place you have no worries and no concerns, with a feeling of safety and rest.

- As you feel this deep restful place, go back in time and remember your ages seventy-two to seventy-six. *(pause)*

- I am now going to ask you a series of questions about this period in your life. Try to respond to them with the first thought that comes to mind. Also, note any feelings that arise.

- Now take three deep breaths and slowly inhale and exhale. *(pause)*

- Let yourself go back to when you were seventy-two years old to around seventy-six years old.

- How do you react to unpleasant situations?

- What gives you your worth at this age?

- How do you respond when your identity as a person is not recognized?

- How do you receive love from others?

- What happens when you put up your boundaries with people and situations?

- What are your fears about opening your heart at this stage of your life?

- Continue to stay in the warmth of your heart connection as you come back to your breath and heartbeat as you integrate these memories of your past.

- See yourself now back sitting with the green plant in your hands. As you relax in the mid-morning sun and smell the delicate fragrance of the plant, reflect on what was important to you at this time of your life between ages seventy-two to seventy-six.

- Now, allow yourself to come back to the healing circle right below your belly button, having the feelings of peace, ease, and present awareness.

Step

4

- Place your attention on the sensation of moving gently upward until you reach your chest. Notice your breath slowly moving in and out. Follow your breath for just a few moments. Let yourself integrate what you learned from your seventy-two- to seventy-six-year-old time period.

- Notice your hands in your lap. Notice how heavy and relaxed they are. Begin to wiggle or stretch your fingers and hands and move your body.

- With a big inhale and exhale of breath come back into the room.

- Please write in your journal what you learned and experienced.

Step
4

Part III
The Path of Freedom

A man with outward courage dares to die; a man with inner courage dares to live.
—LAO TZU, *TAO TE CHING*

To come face-to-face with your constricted self is to face your death. As you recall from the information and exercises you've worked through, this is what happens when you die. You face the challenge of letting go into the unknown. Letting go shifts your attention from what appears to be constricted reality and opens you to expanded reality. This shifting takes courage and a genuine achievement of perseverance and strength.

As I described earlier, I was overwhelmingly surprised when I faced death one night while on a meditation retreat. The next day, I made an appointment with my teacher and told her what had happened the night before. I was shocked when the first thing she said to me was, "That took courage." I knew I had experienced a shift in my awareness of who I was, but I didn't know how courageous I had been. I thought I had no choice but to face what was creating terror in me. It took months to untangle the repercussions from my confrontation with death. It wasn't until I began studying, reflecting, and writing about the death process that I realized how strongly attached I had become to my constricted self. So for me to just "let it all go" did take courage and strength. As I now reflect on the attributes of the constricted self, I realize how big a process it is to release this self.

What I realized, however, is that the constricted self is not my separate body, my feelings, my reactions, my need to control, or my desire to be someone. This someone I am with a personality seems remarkably complete with mind, body, sensations, emotions, perceptions, and consciousness. The question becomes what is wrong with being "constricted"?

Remember how the personality of the constricted self tricks us into believing it is who we are? You learned its ways in the step-by-step strategically developed person that you've become. From working through how your constricted self is constructed, you know its formation, structure, and control over you. But now you are about to embark on the journey to face and detach from it.

The next hurdle for you is to surrender or let go of your constricted self. What a scary thing to ask you to do. Yet it is the same thing that happens when we die. When you surrender the constricted self, it will not vanish or go away, but it will no longer be in control of your life. Your constricted mind appears to be continuous as it goes from one moment to the next. Your brain/mind links your thoughts, your emotions, and your experiences so that there is an appearance of an uninterrupted flow in your life. You will not be unconscious of your constricted self's behaviors and actions. The great blessing of letting go is that you will have a choice of what behaviors and actions you will choose.

The purpose of the exercises and guided meditations (and the video journeys, if you chose to also incorporate them) has been to help you understand how your constricted self is constructed and how it developed. Now we are to begin on the path of action to change your perception or detach from the constricted self to the awareness of the expanded self. The objective of this next phase of your journey is to live your life in this freedom of awareness of the expanded self before you die. Remember, at your last moment before your death, you want to be in the quality of mind of expanded awareness. While you are alive, you also want to be free and independent of the rise and fall of life's situations and challenges.

Attention and intention is the practice you will use to begin this new path. Your attention will be placed on who you really are. Your intention is to practice awareness of the expanded self daily. Your daily practice will be instrumental for the fundamental change on the path to freedom. Freedom is being free from reacting to life's ups and downs and being relaxed, calm, open, spontaneous, and playful.

As you engage in the practices of attention, you will not be engaged in the default mode network (DMN) in your brain. As you recall, DMN is the internal wondering brain that envisions your future, memories, and daydreams. The DMN's neuronal pathways are the neuronal construct of the constricted self. By the use of focused attention with these practices, you will no longer be creating the DMN. When your mind is focused with attention, you increase the neuronal networks of the task-positive network (TPN). This TPN shifts and generates an evolutionary change in the brain, which will affect the clarity and aliveness of your entire body, mind, and emotional system. You will be at the point where there is "no you," only a loving awareness. Life will continue to unfold as it always has with its distractions and problems, but you will respond differently.

Chapter 16
Step 5:
Freedom from Personal Identity

*The moment we choose to love we begin to move against domination,
against oppression. The moment we choose to love we begin to move towards freedom,
to act in ways that liberate ourselves and others.*

—BELL HOOKS

The inner psychospiritual freedom has already begun for you with the understanding of how your constricted self was constructed. Now the intention is to disengage from your self-absorbed personal identities so you can focus on your heart center energy frequency. This path to freedom allows you to embody, accept, and open to all the aspects of your separation without self-judgment. Now you will begin to disconnect from your separation. The objective on this path is to work your way back to the first energy frequency where you began in the Journey of Separation. Each stage has practices that will shift your perception so you can be present with reality as it actually is for you. The strange truth is that a practice doesn't truly evoke reality because reality is always present in you; it never goes away. The nature of awareness is like space, but it is not physical space. This awareness of reality is what you will discover as you progress through the various steps I will lay out for you.

You will begin to change the reference point from constriction to expansion in which your daily experiences arise in you. Also, the research suggests the heart affects intelligence, physiology, emotions, and awareness. As you think of awareness, think of space as expansiveness because it is a container for birds, airplanes, bees, the wind, and so on to move, flow, and exist, but the awareness you can experience is beyond this physical concept. This space of awareness is like your breath. As long as you are aware of your breath, you are alive. This awareness of the expanded self is consistent, always there, nonbiased, unconditional, and non-conceptual. As I described earlier, this space awareness is the quality of consciousness in which you die. Hopefully, you can begin to understand the importance of shifting your perception to this different quality of expanded awareness. Remember, where you place your attention is who you are. As you place your attention on your expanded self, this deeper awareness will grow in you.

In this journey toward inner freedom we will explore how your heart generates a tremendous amount of power. The HeartMath Institute in California has done research and measurements of the electromagnetic energy that your heart can produce. They have also demonstrated how negative emotions alter your heart rhythm and effect your nervous system. What you will find is that your love for yourself and forgiveness is the core energy that removes feeling of being a victim and opens the door to inner freedom. The exercises and meditations of this chapter work with the power and grace of forgiveness as the key to releasing your constricted self.

The Power of Your Heart

To begin to experience this expanded self of awareness you will start by placing your attention on your heart. This is the first way to disengage the constricted self's hold on you and to shift your perception to your expanded self. The heart generates an incredible amount of electromagnetic energy, five thousand times greater in strength than the electromagnetic field generated by the brain. It can be detected a number of feet away from your body in all directions and is an important carrier of information for you. The electromagnetic signals generated by the heart have the capacity to affect others around you. Over the years, scientists have experimented with different psychological and physiological measures of heart function. Heart rhythms reflect inner emotional states and stress. Focusing on the heart alters your emotional state via the neurological input from the heart to the brain.

The HeartMath Institute has the mission to create research, training, and technologies focused on bridging the connection between heart and mind and teaching people how to grow heart connections with others. The HeartMath Institute has conducted extensive research on heart-brain interactions, heart-rate variability and autonomic functions, emotional physiology and energetics, and a variety of other workplace and clinical research projects. The Institute has also conducted research on how the heart's magnetic field radiates beyond the body and can affect other people. Their research has demonstrated that when you experience positive feeling states, the heart's rhythms become more coherent and the interactions between "the brain and heart maintain a continuous two-way dialogue, each influencing the other's functioning." [61] Neurocardiology researchers view this as a "heart brain." When this happens, the brain can modify cortical functions and influence your performance at many levels. This may help explain the increased mental clarity and heightened intuitive awareness individuals experience in this state of heart coherence.

Step
5

The Power of Negative Emotions

It is clear that negative emotions lead to increased disorder in the heart's rhythms and in the autonomic nervous system. Disorder adversely affects the rest of your body. In contrast, positive emotions create increased harmony and coherence in heart rhythms and improve balance in the nervous system. The health implications are easy to understand. Disharmony in the nervous system leads to inefficiency and increased stress on the heart and other organs while harmonious rhythms are more efficient and less stressful to the body's systems. It is as though the heart is acting as if it has a mind of its own. Your heart profoundly influences the way you perceive and respond to the world.

---

61. Rollin McCarty, PhD, *Science of the Heart: Exploring the Role of the Heart in Human Performance* (Boulder Creek, CA: HeartMath e-book, 2015), 5.

From the HeartMath research, there is now a scientific basis to explain how and why the heart affects mental clarity, creativity, emotional balance, and personal effectiveness. Thus the heart is far more than a simple pump. Your heart is, in fact, a highly complex, self-organized information processing center with its own functional "brain" that communicates with and influences the cranial brain via the nervous system, hormonal system, and other pathways. This is why you will begin the shift of perception of the constricted self with the heart to balance disharmony or incoherence in the mind and the body. This powerful organ helps release the pathways of fear that separate you from your expanded self by the opening of your heart's love.

Love Dissolves Victim Identity

The heart's coherence of love opens the way to dismantling your many clinging victim self-identities. The victim hides under the cover of needing and wanting pleasure and establishing a justification for its position in the world. But beneath this cover is fear, anxiety of being unworthy, suffering, and creating pain. Attention from the heart energy reduces tension spent holding pain down and denying parts of yourself as unworthy and shameful. You are here to relax, open your heart, and extend outwardly with the eternal awareness of the expanded self, not to live in the false desires of the constricted self. This awareness of expanded self will be your focus as it dissolves the illusion of separateness and opens you to connectedness and freedom.

The Practice of Forgiveness

Hafiz, the thirteenth-century Sufi master, said, "Fear is the cheapest room in the house, I would like to see you in better living conditions." [62] Forgiveness is what enables us to release the deepest fears of our life. From these fears, the constricted self continues to weave an energetic pattern, using the thoughts, experiences, attitudes, behaviors, and emotional projections you put on yourself and that others project onto you. These projections comprise your constricted

---

62. Hafiz, *The Gift: Poems by Hafiz The Great Sufi Master,* translated by Daniel Ladinsky (New York: Penguin Putnam, 1999), 39.

self. Projections are mental images placed on you with picture-feelings of being a victim, being unworthy, being angry, or filled with terror, guilt, shame, and fear. Your constricted self is this woven pattern of inner and outer projections. As you've observed, you hide these projected feelings behind a mask of outward personality, as your Enneagram structures revealed to you. What exploration of the building process of your constricted self taught you, however, is that your personality is not who you really are!

Forgiveness is the energy of the heart that releases the binding structure of projections that have been woven together as your self-identity. The manner in which forgiveness releases the bindings of projections is by releasing the energy within the binding process itself. The bindings will naturally dissipate if not held together by your mind. If you release the projections, you allow the energy to dissipate and merge again into the vast energy of existence. Through forgiveness, the constricted self begins to dissolve and evaporate. This is what happens in the dying process when the mind/heart is attempting to dissolve all the projections woven into the tapestry of the constricted self that you created over a lifetime. Forgiveness practice is the means to begin to dissolve the woven tapestry of this self before you die. This is the beginning of waking up now!

Step 5

Exercise: *Working with Forgiveness*

Take some time to review the beliefs about who you are and your self-identity. Narrow the review down to the following three elements.

- What form of your identity are you strongly holding on to for which you need to forgive yourself? You will know the right one because it will be a pattern of events that goes back throughout your life. You may have already done some forgiveness on yourself and this issue, but now is the time for a deeper release.

- Who is the key person in your life that shaped your victim identity and toward whom you hold anger, fear, or deep shame? It could be a parent, friend, spouse, colleague, or coworker. You know when you've picked the right person because you will feel it in your body. That person will be like a spider in a web that spins you out to other similar people with whom you have the same kind of feelings.

- What group(s) do you have negative attitudes, beliefs, or prejudices toward that affect your view of the world? The group could be political, religious, educational, the media, etc. Again you will know it by the physical reaction in your body. The feeling can run from mild dislike to outright hatred.

Each of these three elements is a focus point that, as you start the forgiveness process, will spread to different but similar beliefs, feelings, and reactions. Sit with each of these three areas and ask internally and intuitively what area in your life, what person, and what group become your starting point.

Remember, forgiveness is the surrendering process that begins the transformation and opening of your heart. This leads ultimately to awakening to the light of your own true nature.

So how do you forgive yourself, the other person, and groups?

The first step is to recognize that some form of forgiveness and inner reconciliation is needed for yourself and between you and others.

The second step is being objective about what and who is being forgiven. This requires being in a quiet place of receptivity and asking yourself to see clearly the situation without trying to sugarcoat the truth of the situation. The third step is a form of meditation. It is a repetitive set of simple phases you can use after you've identified what your forgiveness practice needs.

A friend and meditation teacher, Doug Kraft, suggests that there are three drivers that generate our need for forgiveness:

- *When you do not fully understand a situation.* This happens when you do not understand your impulsive need to build an identity to protect yourself. The desire to protect yourself blocks your heart from opening.

- *When you are overcome by remorse and guilt.* This reaction happens if you've harmed others or yourself when no harm actually resulted.

- *When your behavior violates your values.* This is when your inner shadow is in charge.

Step

5

Kraft suggests that each of these three drivers—lack of understanding, reactions of remorse and guilt, and the violation of your values—leads you to four simple forgiveness meditation phrases. As with any meditation, as you repeat the phrases notice the feelings in your body. Let insight and new consciousness arise in you. This forgiveness practice is a healing of deep unconscious patterns that will open you to the great liberation and freedom you are seeking. When you are in the quiet, it is the expanded self that is saying these phrases to your constricted self. Take the people and issues you identified and place them in the appropriate phrases for you, for others, and for groups. In each parenthesis, place your name or that of the other person or group.

- I forgive *(myself, the other, or group)* for not understanding.
- I forgive *(myself, the other, or group)* for making mistakes.
- I forgive *(myself, the other, or group)* for hurting *(myself, the other, or group)*.
- I forgive *(myself, the other, or group)* for not following *(my, your, their)* deepest values. Say the four statements first for yourself and then in turn do them for the other and for the group you've chosen. I did a meditation retreat at which I spent two days on the part for myself. It took that long to open the many aspects of myself that needed forgiveness.

When you are forgiving others, you may experience an inner turnaround such that you are looking into the eyes of the other and asking for their forgiveness. This was very powerful for me and broke open my heart. The phrases are the same but take on a new meaning and feeling. You keep repeating them until you can actually hear the person or group forgive you.

Please forgive me for not understanding you. Please forgive me for making mistakes with you. Please forgive me for hurting you.

Exercise: *Forgiveness Meditation*

Again, as with other meditations you've done before, please either pre-record this meditation in order to listen to it or have a partner or friend read and guide you through it. Where there is a *(pause)* indicated, give yourself time to experience the instructions at that point. (If you want to use the bonus video for this meditation go to appendix D.)

In this meditation, you will experience forgiveness as a thought and as an energy form that is connected to a higher frequency of energy. The frequency acts like a laser beam that melts and dissolves your inner projections, such as shame. It also dissolves your constricted self's negativity toward others when you act as being special or self-justifying and when you hurt others or yourself. Forgiveness can dissolve these energetic projections whether they are positive or negative projections of your self-identity. In this meditation, the way forgiveness works is that it raises the awareness of feeling and thought to a much higher frequency so that it becomes laser-like in its ability to project energy into a situation of feeling or thought. This forgiveness energy's use of projected intention releases the bindings of your woven thoughts and feelings so an expansion of awareness naturally opens within you.

Step
5

Let's begin the meditation:

- Let yourself relax into a safe, quiet, comfortable place with your back straight but not rigid or lie on a bed or a mat.

- Close your eyes and imagine a green color at your heart. Notice the sounds in your environment.

- Recall the depth of your last meditation and take several deep breaths and relax into all parts of your body. *(pause)*

- What does the relaxation feel like inside you?

- Remember the feeling of deep relaxation when using your marker. Return to that place. As you move deeper into recalling the symbol, image, or word of your marker that you created in the first meditation, feel the tensions of your body letting go.

- Now take three deep breaths. As you take them, observe your breath. Is it shallow? Labored? What is the quality of your inhale and exhale? Does one seem easier or fuller? Is there a natural pause when your breath is full or empty? Feel the sensations of the belly, as well as the cool and warmth of your nostrils. *(pause)*

- If your inhale is pronounced are you holding your energy in too much? If you are, then lengthen the exhale. If the exhale is pronounced, you need to give away some of your energy. Don't push yourself for not letting yourself receive. Sink deeper into your body and notice sensations. Move down into your inner ground of sensations. *(pause)*

- Put your hand over your heart, feel your heart beat. From your belly or womb, notice that breath and heartbeat never stop; feel this increase. Allow thoughts, feelings, or outside disturbances to float through without holding on to them.

- Again with your marker, let yourself relax and move down and in, down deep into your heart as if falling down like a leaf to the ground. Go down and in, down and in, deep inside yourself, moving toward your heart. *(pause)*

- As you move into this deeper state within, move through to your heart, right to the center of your chest. Feel a warmth, a caring of being inside yourself. Rest in the opening and sink deep into this warm, caring place.

- Let yourself continue to relax and be held in this caring connection. In this caring place you have no worries or concerns.

- Now place an intention, a feeling, a thought of acceptance to release that I am someone, that I have these identities that create pain, rejection, hurt, and anger within me. Notice your body and breathe into any tense areas that may have arisen. Let yourself relax and go even deeper into yourself.

- As you relax, the warmth gets deeper. As you relax, your breath merges into your heart. Notice and feel its warming, pulsating, and tingling sensations. *(pause)*

- As you feel the relaxation, be aware of the sensations moving from your heart center up through your body and moving up and out of the top of your head.

Step

5

- At the top of your head, in the crown, the heart energy merges with a higher frequency. This frequency is always present and waiting for this pathway connection.

- This emergence of higher frequency energy begins a natural forgiveness and releasing of the projections and bindings that hold your identity pattern together.

- Notice as you forgive yourself from holding on to all your identities the energy expands out from all around you.

- As these patterns of your thoughts, emotions, sensations, and feelings dissolve, a quiet peace, tranquility, and a deepening awareness arises in you.

- Rest in this awareness and observe the difference in your thoughts and feelings as your patterns dissolve. *(pause)*

- Love energy is doing its work in you. Trust that this high frequency energy will dissolve what is needed at this time in your life.

Step 5

- Now move your attention downward to your heart very gently.

- Continue to stay in the warmth of your heart connection as you come back to your breath and heartbeat as you integrate these memories of your past. *(pause)*

- Allow yourself to inhale and exhale, feeling the sensations of your belly and the air in your nostrils. Feel now the grounded sensations in your body as you rest in the gentle movement of your breath. *(pause)*

- Place your attention now on the sensation of moving gently upward until you reach your chest. Notice your breath slowly moving in and out. Follow your breath for just a few moments. Let yourself integrate what you learned from letting forgiveness release your identity patterns.

- Notice your hands in your lap. Notice how heavy and relaxed they are. Begin to wiggle or stretch your fingers and hands and move your body.

- With a big inhale and exhale of breath come back into the room.

- Remember as you return, that after you've entered the high-frequency state where you released the constricted self identify, you may have difficulty with a feeling of overwhelm or being lost. If you stay with an inner focus on the expanded energy you experienced, you will find a great release and freedom. Trust that as you continue to attune to the heart energy of forgiveness, you will dissolve your constricted identity and open to your natural awakening.

• Be gentle and loving to yourself and know that the energy source is guiding you.

• Trust also that there is your unique timing that brings you to full forgiveness and awakening

• Please write in your journal what you learned and experienced.

Chapter 17
Step 6:
Freedom from the Mental Self

Old power is replaced by being the observer of awareness
from a place of space not thinking.
—KATHLEEN DOWLING SINGH

The next step is for you to disconnect from the "chief" that thinks it is in control, your mental self. The power of the thinking mind controls and separates you from your body, sensations, and feelings. Its power is to take the driver seat and control your intention to direct, plan, and set goals. The script that controls you every day is written and directed by your thinking mind. Your mind does not allow for an energy flow to let go or allow things to orchestrate themselves in a natural process. Everything is thought through and composed by the constricted mind, both conscious and unconscious. The constricted self's need to control is driven by fear, desire, and survival. Your sense of survival thinks you need your mind to figure out everything in order to stay in control.

In this step of confronting your mind, you come face-to-face with the behavior of wanting life to be the way you want it, no matter the impact on others or even yourself. Your mind attempts to control the force of your life, others, and the world. The chatter in your mind can become so intense that you are often overcome and dismayed by the tight grip it has on you. If you try to let go of this tight grip of your mind, there is an immediate challenge to the mind's authority that fills you with fear. This tightness from fear competes, drives, and creates an emotional and behavioral imbalance in you. The imbalance can be marked by believing you are better than others, that you have more than others, and that in every way you control your own life. Or it runs the opposite direction with your mind telling you "I can't control myself or others" or "I have nothing to show for my life." Your control one way or the other is so convincing that it is difficult to see clearly what is really happening to you. Everything around you seems so real. Your will focuses energy on your desires, wants, and fears and repeats them in your mind until the brain forms a comprehensive neuronal circuitry pattern that runs on its own without you needing to even think about it. The neuronal pattern is a strong fire-type energy that, with the repetition of focused attention, develops the personal power behavior of the constricted self. This is a familiar performance you see in you and in others.

This chapter will show you ways to relax and open your heart to find freedom and release from the mental pattern that constricts you. The two keys is to expand beyond being "someone" to become "everything." But the importance of this chapter is to experience the expansion that gratitude brings to you. Gratitude increases the neuronal pathways that generate joy, happiness, freedom, and contentment. Finally, in this chapter I provide to you a number of gratitude practices that will enrich you daily and then finish this chapter with a gratitude meditation that you can practice many times to release the constriction of your mind and heart.

Releasing the Mental Pattern

At this step in your journey, your goal is to release the grip of this repeated pattern so that you can relax into the awareness of the expanded self. When this pattern of the mental constricted self is not in control, your heart can open. As it opens, you become more aware of the expanded self. You begin to be more conscious of not being so contained. You are more expanded in your body and you include more heart expression in your life. Love plus awareness expands you to raise your consciousness so that there is not just "me" in the world. This expansive realization shouts out clearly, "I am not the doer. There is something more powerful than me running my show." The awareness of the expanded self then begins to discover its potential. This potential can manifest in many ways, including prosperity.

Your Potential Expansion

The release of your potential moves your energy frequency into being more alive with greater awareness, but it does not become dominating or controlling. This extension of alive energy will take you out of your habits, break through conformity, and open you to more individuality and greater authenticity. But most of all, it releases your wanting and your desire to be "someone" and have "everything" because you already are someone and truly have everything as an expanded self. You have value and worth in being who you are. The adjustment of your attention is focused back in your body and not focused in your mind or outward into the world. You allow the world to pass by without judgment or bias. Therefore, you don't become attached to it.

One of my teachers would say, "Your mind is not your friend, so stay out of the world." The idea for you to evolve and live an expanded life is not to stay attached to your outer world of mental constructs. The expanded self is the new reference point, not your mind clinging to the old patterns. As you focus your consciousness on the expanded awareness of love, the love energy is then used for your further evolution. The practice that unfolds the process of unifying the mind and body toward your dynamic evolution of expansion is gratitude.

The Frequency of Gratitude

The energy of gratitude shatters the illusion of reality. Gratitude penetrates and throws open to the light of day what you think is running the world. Gratitude is an energy that alters how you perceive the world. Gratitude is the unification of the mind/body awareness so that it is available for a fuller, more conscious, and deliberate expression of you.

Step
6

When you don't live from a place of gratitude, you contract into a narrow focus. That contraction moves you toward desire and wanting what actually can't fulfill you. When this happens, the flow and magic of existence shut down. With gratitude, you open naturally to the magic. You will also be aware and alert when desire and wanting sneak into your life as a substitute for the authentic flow of your existence. The integration of your awareness with gratitude stimulates aliveness in you as a living organism.

Gratitude shapes your life into a rhythm and harmony that expands you into all of life's experiences. Gratitude lightens up every person and event you encounter. When gratitude is present, you are patient. Gratitude reveals the gifts in everything you experience. It slows you down to see, feel, and experience depth and clarity and have an understanding of any person, event, or experience you encounter.

Gratitude is an important teaching gift for emerging from the illusion of your mental existence. Gratitude opens you to experience reality as it actually is, not as it may appear in your mental construct. In this respect, gratitude is "magic" because it shows you that love holds both the positive and negative, the dark and the light, the male and the female, the earth and the sky. Gratitude weaves opposites together to reveal how the illusionary force holds everything together.

Step 6

Gratitude Increases the Energy of the Heart

Gratitude increases the vibration and energy of the heart center and increases the pulsation of the nervous system as neurons fire off in new patterns that generate joy, happiness, freedom, and inner contentment. Gratitude catalyzes the field of energy in a person by radiating a higher frequency of light photons within the body. The greater the gratitude the more your mind becomes illuminated, the mind chatter dies away, and clarity of awareness of your expanded self continually opens. When you live in a constant state of gratitude, you are awake to the light of who you truly are.

Gratitude Practices

Brother David Steindl-Rast, a true ambassador of gratitude, says, "There are degrees of grateful wakefulness. Our intellect, our will, our emotions must wake up. Let us take a closer look at this process of awakening. It is the growth process of gratefulness." [63] The transformational reality of gratitude is that it opens the door of awareness and awakening within us. Gratitude is the key transformer of reality perception. In the perception of reality, nothing needs to change in your life for you to feel fulfilled, complete, and at peace. Everything that you feel, see, and understand becomes transformed into beauty, clarity, and a more holistic and integrated reality that continues to grow and expand into every area of your life. Awareness with gratitude is the gift of the integrated mind/body. This is the first expanded level of consciousness in your entry into transpersonal realms.

If there is only one practice that you do, giving gratitude for everything would be the doorway to freedom. It will sharpen what you resist by being grateful for those daily experiences for which you don't naturally feel grateful. You may be surprised at what you experience.

First Gratitude Practice

This is a simple practice that keeps gratitude at the forefront of your consciousness. This practice will slow down the awareness and sharpen your observation and insight.

Step
6

- Make a list of all the things you are grateful for.

- Make another list of all the things you are not grateful for.

- Keep adding to the lists for a few days.

- Say the words "thank you" for both the positive and negative people, situations, and events you experience.

- A few days later, touch your heart area when you say "thank you" for both positive and negative events. The physical touch and feeling will begin to open the love doorway wider and wider.

---

63. David Steindl-Rast, *Gratefulness, the Heart of Prayer: An Approach to Life in Fullness* (Ramsey, NJ: Paulist Press, 1984), 10.

- Soon become aware of any feelings of lightness and sensations of warmth associated with the positive and the negative experiences you listed.

- Keep this practice going until you begin to feel and see the light in all things through this lens of gratitude. In reality, there is no positive or negative. There is only one thing for which you will be grateful: *all the experiences that make up your life!*

Second Gratitude Practice

- Make a list of all the things, people, events, situations, and experiences in your life that have supported, inspired, and motivated you over the past three to five years.

- As you write and review the list, feel in your heart center gratitude for each one of them.

Third Gratitude Practice

- When you take a walk, name and acknowledge the trees, clouds, animals, flowers, people, etc., that you see. As you name them, place a hand over your heart area and feel the gratitude in your heart.

- At every meal, thank the food and all the people and beings that are nourishing your body to stay alive.

Fourth Gratitude Practice

- Make a list of the key positive and key negative people in your life. Thank both for being your teachers.

- List key family and friends and every day feel gratitude that they are part of your life.

Fifth Gratitude Practice

Be grateful daily as you see expressions of the four elements.

Water: Rain, facet water, pond, river, stream, etc.

Earth: Rock, dirt, the land you walk on, mountains, etc.

Step 6

Fire: Flames, wood burning, the sun, candles, etc.

Air: The wind, breeze smells, breathing in your lungs, etc.

- Be grateful for your experience of nature's manifest forms and the spirits that embody them: the sounds of birds and animals, sunsets and full moons, snowstorms and fierce winds, forest fires and calm waters, and on and on.

Exercise: *Gratitude Meditation*

Your awareness expands as gratitude increases within you in this meditation. Naturally, there is a new energy vitality in and coherence between the mind, the body, and the heart. *Gratitude is the jewel that every being at all levels of existence comes to finally experience, as it is the doorway to the expansion of the love that is at the heart of all existence.* The nature of gratitude is more than a concept. It is one of the Universal Principles that begins and extends the expanded perception of awareness. Gratitude is what opens you toward full realization of freedom.

Again, as with other exercises you've done before, please either pre-record this meditation in order to listen to it or have a partner or friend read and guide you through it. Where there is a *(pause)* indicated, give yourself time to experience the instructions at that point. (If you want to use the bonus video for this meditation go to appendix D.)

Let's begin the meditation:

- Let yourself relax into a safe, quiet, comfortable place with your back straight but not rigid or lie on a bed or a mat.
- Close your eyes and imagine a yellow color filling your belly area. Notice the sounds in your environment. *(pause)*
- Recall the depth of your last meditation and take several deep breaths and relax into all parts of your body. *(pause)*
- What does the relaxation feel like inside you?

Step
6

- Remember the feeling of deep relaxation when using your marker. Recall how you created your marker as a symbol, an image, or a word and you felt your marker at a particular place on your body. Return to that inner feeling of relaxation spreading through your body. *(pause)*

- As you move deeper into recalling the symbol, image, or word of your marker feel the tensions of your body letting go.

- Now, take three deep breaths. As you take them, observe your breath. Is it shallow? Labored? What is the quality of your inhale and exhale? Does one seem easier or fuller? Is there a natural pause when your breath is full or empty? Feel the sensations of the belly, as well as the cool and warmth of your nostrils. *(pause)*

- If your inhale is pronounced are you holding your energy in too much? If you are, then lengthen the exhale. If the exhale is pronounced, you need to give away some of your energy. Don't push yourself for not letting yourself receive. Sink deeper into your body, notice sensations. Move down into your inner ground of sensations. *(pause)*

- Put your hand over your belly; feel your breath move in and out. From your belly or womb, notice that breath and heartbeat never stops. Allow thoughts, feelings, or outside disturbances to float through you without holding on to them.

- Again with your marker, let yourself relax and move down and in, down deep into your heart as if falling down like a leaf to the ground. Go down and in, down and in deep inside yourself, moving toward your belly. *(pause)*

- As you move into this deeper state within, move through to your heart, and then down into your belly. Feel a yellow warmth, a caring of being inside yourself. Rest in the opening and sink deep into this warm, caring place.

- Let yourself continue to relax and be held in this caring connection. In this caring place you have no worries or concerns.

- Now place an intention, a feeling, a thought of acceptance to release that I am someone, that I have these identities that create pain, rejection, hurt, and anger within me. Notice your body and breathe into any tense areas

Step 6

that may have arisen. Let yourself relax and go even deeper into yourself. *(pause)*

• Move through any tension to be deeper within your belly; deep into the center of your warm, glowing yellow belly.

• Feel a warmth and light opening into an expansion of gratitude. Let your gratitude be for this deep relaxation and caring of being inside yourself. *(pause)*

• Let your caring awareness for yourself be fully open. Be aware now of your efforts in trying to control your life. Trying to control your behavior, emotions, and thoughts.

• And trying to control others in your life. *(pause)*

• Feel grateful for all your trying.

• What would it be like if you let it go of all your trying? What happens in your life?

• What trait or behavior do you have that you do not like? Do you identify yourself as that trait or behavior?

• Whatever you perceive in yourself feel grateful for who you are. *(pause)*

• Imagine now the feeling of yourself to be a beautiful bouquet of flowers. You release the tie around the bouquet and the flowers fall outward in a beautiful circle of expansion of the bouquet. Let yourself be that bouquet opening into gratitude, into expansive love for yourself, and opening far and wide for everything in your life. *(pause)*

• Begin now to slowly return to an awareness of your body and the room, but stay in the warmth of your connection to gratitude as you come back to your breath and heartbeat knowing who you truly are in deep beauty and caring for yourself.

• Allow yourself to inhale and exhale, feeling the sensations of your breath in your belly and your nostrils. Feel grounded in your body, just resting in this place of gratitude for yourself. *(pause)*

Step

6

- Place your attention now on the sensation of moving gently upward until you reach your chest. Notice your breath slowly moving in and out. Follow your breath for just a few moments. Let yourself integrate what you learned from feeling gratitude for who you are.

- Notice your hands in your lap. Notice how heavy and relaxed they are. Begin to wiggle or stretch your fingers and hands and move your body.

- With a big inhale and exhale of breath come back into the room.

- As you relax and feel the experience of this meditation, trust that as you continue to attune to the belly energy of gratitude you will dissolve your constricted identity more and more, opening to your natural awakening.

- Be gentle and loving to yourself and know that a higher energy source is guiding you.

- Trust also that there is your unique timing that brings you to a full state of gratitude.

- Please write in your journal what you learned and experienced.

Step

6

Chapter 18
Step 7:
Freedom from the Emotional Self

You have to just stand by the side and watch whatsoever is passing,
with no judgment, with no evaluation. Just a silent mirror reflecting
whatsoever is passing by … without any commentary, just watching …
just a little patience, sitting silently, doing nothing, just watching as it comes.
And when it comes it opens a totally new dimension.

—OSHO RAJNEESH

Your journey moves down the road of discovery as you continue to detach from the illusionary hold of your constricted self. The constricted self's personal identity is being released by the dismantling strength of the practice of forgiveness. Next your controlling mind is being released by the powerful energy of awareness while practicing gratitude. In repeating these two practices, you will notice a release of tightness and tension held in you by the constricted self. You will begin to relax and become more unbiased and nonconceptual as you experience the world. The practice of gratitude revealed that you are not the "doer" of the self-centered constricted self.

Your new awareness begins to shed light on anything and everything on which you place your attention. This is the beginning of letting go of the constricted self's need to be someone. Your perceptions of the world will change as you continue the practice of living in this greater context of awareness, rather than in the content of your constricted self. The gift of openness and expansion begins to make this new awareness your home base. You continue now with this expansion by taking the journey of detaching from your emotional self.

For this chapter, your focus is how to detach from your emotional self. We will consider the emotional drivers in your life that are at the heart of your emotional fear. This fear is, of course, all of our fears of confronting our death. This fear of death is what shapes your emotional future. What needs to be learned to escape this emotional future is how to surrender your fear. The healing of fear is to develop the practice of presence or mindfulness in your daily life and to discover the power of appreciation that changes your perception of your world. Appreciation gives you "new eyes" and the power to a new awareness in you. Both of these practices of presence and appreciation will open your emotional self to a potential place of new expansion in you. We will conclude the chapter with a heart-filled meditation of presence and appreciation.

Your Emotional Drivers

The first thing as you awake in the morning is to get your emotional, hectic, and clock-driven life in gear. Your schedule is filled with appointments, activities, and meetings. On top of that, as you move through your day, your mind is busy with the inner dialogue that keeps you racing in fear, anger, judgment, confusion, pleasure, uncertainty, and so on as you process your own thoughts, sensations, feelings, and emotions as well as from the people and situations around you. As you focus on where all those thoughts and emotional feelings come from, they just seem to be there, no matter what is happening in your life. What you notice is that they never stop. Because they never stop, your external world and internal world keep you emotionally strung out and at the edge of exhaustion most of the time.

The mental and the emotional world is conditioned by whatever awful or wonderful thing is going to happen in the future or by what awful or wonderful thing that happened in your past. You live in a conditional world where one thing leads to another. This past and hopeful future makes your world seemingly predictable and somewhat known, but basically unconsciously unsteady and uncertain. You hear yourself say "When is the next shoe going to drop?" or "What can I expect from my next encounter with so and so?" Thus you live with an unconscious, underlying anxiety of what is going to happen next to you. This underlying fear is part of the constant clock-driven busyness you face daily. If you stop your activities for a while, you may begin to feel the emotions that are driving you.

As I described in the first half of the book, you are most likely unconsciously driven by fear of the possibility of death, but it is unspoken and you avoid the fear mentally and emotionally. You do not know the time of your death, so you keep your time filled up so as not to face it. Meanwhile, you spend your thoughts, feelings, and energies working, playing, hoping, worrying, evaluating, judging, criticizing, gossiping, and planning about everything in your life until death arrives suddenly at your door.

Fear of Death: Will I Survive?

The constricted self has you in an emotional turmoil of anxiety and fear most of the time. This turmoil keeps the unconscious question churning in you, "Will I survive?" No matter what the outer questions of survival are, the unconscious question is "Will I die?" This question of survival/death is a dance between past and future to the point that you can't be here right now. The biggest terror of the future is trying to avoid the possibility of death. You avoid it for yourself but focus the concern on your partner, family, and friends. This concern keeps your emotions raw and your mind tense. It does not have to be this way, but the constricted self says, "This is the only way you can live." It is your fear that unconsciously overwhelms you and sustains your personal constricted self in continual avoidance. It gets to a point that you have to surrender the state of wanting it to be the way you want it to be. You are not aware that you can change this feeling. Many of us long for a life without judgment and evaluation of self and others. Living in that way means "simply" observing the movements and the changes that constantly move through your life.

Step
7

Learning to Surrender the Fear

What would your life be like if you lived in a state of awareness and observing what is going on right here, right now, instead of living with the fear of the past and future?

Without this fear, you would be free. From your expanded background, the context of your life, you as the observer would more easily surrender to the process of your death. As you die, letting go of all the activity in the foreground—the content of your life—is the heart of the surrender process. Surrender of the past and future, whether now in this instant or at your death, brings you to what is going on in the present moment. The present moment is not governed by the past or the future or by trying to change others, so life will appear perfect to you. Living right here in the moment is the greatest gift you can give yourself. It is called *presence.*

Presence and Appreciation

Presence is what the Buddhists call mindfulness. Mindfulness is being attentive to just what is in front of you, and not letting the mind emotionally worry or wander to past or future people, situations, or events. With mindfulness, you don't let your mind react to outer or inner experience. You stay focused right here in the moment. The practice of appreciation trains your reactive mind to stay focused in the present moment. The motivational writer and speaker Alan Cohen says, "Appreciation is the highest form of prayer, for it acknowledges the presence of good wherever you shine the light of your thankful thoughts."

Appreciation releases the attachment to your emotional reactions of fear and being a prisoner of time. Appreciation is another energy component of love that is connected to your perception of time and releases the reaction of push or pull in you. *Appreciation changes the focal length of the depth of perception.*

Perception gives us our ability to recognize, to have conscious awareness of, and to grasp an understanding of life. If appreciation changes the focal length of perception or your awareness, then you are again releasing tension and expanding even more. This means that when you wake in the morning, awareness is that consciousness that wakes you up. It is the awareness that opens you to observe what life is going to offer you today. This awareness does not react to the world nor is it controlled by time. As thoughts come and thoughts go, the background of awareness is stable and remains continuous during all your waking hours.

Awareness is conscious observation—watching, looking, seeing, and concentrating. Your awareness, just your awareness, is looking through your eyes right now. As you extend your perception inward, it allows you to contact an inner awareness that is looking through your eyes at what you are aware of in the outside world. *When you are both aware of your inner and outer awareness at the same time, you are living in the moment.* To appreciate whatever is in your experience is to connect both the inner and outer awareness. When you make this connection, you are truly right here right now.

Appreciation and Awareness

Appreciation both changes and charges your energy field pattern. You have more energy because you are connected directly to the expanded self. The more you are aware from this inner vantage point of appreciation you will see the good and the beautiful and consciously look at the essence of the person, situation, or encounter. Appreciation opens the doorway of awareness of the awareness. The contact with this awareness essence creates a field of energy and of light through connection. This field of energy "bridges" and creates an enfolding field between you and the other that "strikes a bell" of a positive energy. This field charges both your energy field and that of the other. The result is that, in this moment of appreciation, you open to a higher frequency.

The Power of Appreciation

As you begin to be in the appreciation field, your focal point shifts from inner awareness to being aware in the outer world and then back to awareness of what is real inside you. The energy charge of appreciation activates the feeling state within you, and shifts your moods, attitudes, and beliefs. In the moment of appreciation, you perceive the reality of love that directly eliminates judgment or preconception. At this point, things are as they are and there is no need to react.

Step
7

You have accessed an energy that lets you penetrate directly to the essence of your awareness. As you rest in your awareness through appreciation, you can be fully present with others. You can see in the other what is actually present, unique, expressive, and expansive. In the same way, you can also be appreciative of the qualities and capabilities in you. With this focused attention, we transcend time by entering the present.

When we lose appreciation, the focal length of our seeing becomes short, close to us, and broken up by our beliefs, judgments, fears, and conditioning. Thus, when we judge people, animals, and situations, we close down our focal length of appreciative perception. Practicing appreciation daily releases your close-in perception of self-protection and brings you into the present moment of joy, freedom, and lightness of being.

Appreciation Practices

The following appreciation practice and meditation are incredibly important for your preparation of death and your freedom now. They give you a focus to recognize that you are always aware right now. When you are aware of your awareness, you are integrated in both inner and outer worlds. You are also integrated in the power of presence.

On some level, these practices are not really necessary because awareness is already within you. At the same time, these exercises are necessary to create an environment in which your perception shifts, dropping you into the depth of expanded higher consciousness and enabling you to experience your inner awareness. The presence of awareness is a moment of exhilaration in being fully alive, of being a true living organism. Relaxation and expansion deepen you to experience and reveal this energy of life. This is the same energy of grace that is felt as you draw closer to dying.

Remember, do these practices with a sense of curiosity and wonder but with nothing to achieve, only to appreciate what is happening right here, right now. As you continue your practice of appreciation and presence, a unity of feeling emerges in you with the capacity to be present. This is the next step in the journey into the freedom of the expanded self.

Step 7

Exercise: *Appreciation Practice*

- Every day, look for people and situations to express your appreciation. Simply see who or what they are or what they are doing and acknowledge what you see. For example, I see a cat stretched out on a windowsill and I say, "You look beautiful in your relaxation," or I am in the office and observe someone working late and speak my appreciation to his or her effort. Or I hear a beautiful piece of music with a string solo and appreciate the talent playing the violin. As you see the element in a person or situation, appreciate it by speaking out loud; don't think about it or evaluate it.

- As you speak your appreciation, feel the energy speaking from your heart. The awareness of your awareness builds an energy charge between you and the other.

- If you find you are focused on judging someone or something, shift your focus and look for something that you can appreciate in the person or situation you are judging. By interrupting the cycle of judging with appreciation, you generate a strong awareness and build your energy rather than contract it.

- Keep the appreciation going throughout the day. The more you appreciate consistently throughout the day the more the energy will increase the clarity of your awareness. Practice this for two to three weeks and you will find your perception and awareness has changed.

Step 7

Exercise: *Presence and Appreciation Meditation*

As with other exercises you've done before, please either pre-record this meditation in order to listen to it or have a partner or friend read and guide you through it. Where there is a *(pause)* indicated, give yourself time to experience the instructions at that point. (If you want to use the bonus video for this meditation go to appendix D.)

Let's begin the meditation:

- Let yourself relax into a safe, quiet, comfortable place with your back straight but not rigid or lie on a bed or a mat.

- Close your eyes and imagine an orange color filling your lower spine area. Notice the sounds in your environment. *(pause)*

- Recall the depth of your last meditation and take several deep breaths and relax into all parts of your body. *(pause)*

- What does the relaxation feel like inside you?

- Remember the feeling of deep relaxation when using your marker. Recall how you created your marker as a symbol, an image, or a word and you felt your marker at a particular place on your body. Return to that inner feeling of relaxation spreading through your body. *(pause)*

- As you move deeper into recalling the symbol, image, or word of your marker, feel the tensions of your body letting go.

- Now, take three deep breaths. As you take them, observe your breath. Is it shallow? Labored? What is the quality of your inhale and exhale? Does one seem easier or fuller? Is there a natural pause when your breath is full or empty? Feel the sensations of the belly, as well as the cool and warmth of your nostrils. *(pause)*

- If your inhale is pronounced are you holding your energy in too much? If you are, then lengthen the exhale. If the exhale is pronounced, you need to give away some of your energy. Don't push yourself for not letting yourself receive. Sink deeper into your body, notice sensations. Move down into your inner ground of sensations. *(pause)*

- Put your hand over your belly, feel your breath move in and out. From your belly or womb, notice that breath and heartbeat never stops. Allow thoughts, feelings, or outside disturbances to float through you without holding on to them.

Step

7

- Again with your marker, let yourself relax and move down and in, down deep into your heart as if falling down like a leaf to the ground. Go down and in, down and in deep inside yourself, moving toward your belly. *(pause)*

- Place your attention deep inside, back near your spinal cord as you observe your breath.

- Notice as you inhale you take in air from the outside air and it mixes with the air in the space of your lungs inside of you.

- As the air merges between inside and outside of you, become even more relaxed. Let yourself fall down deeper inside you like a falling leaf. With this feeling of gliding down like a leaf, your mind begins to move downward as the space and air on the outside and the space and air on the inside come together, allowing the boundaries of the body to dissolve and the movement of the breath flows easefully and naturally back and forth within you. *(pause)*

- You are moving deeper into a space where there is a softness and warmth.

- Now as you rest your mind back into this soft, warm space, feel a gentle movement continue downward as if you are on an escalator gently sliding downward softly, slowly, and gently.

- As you feel yourself coming to rest near the bottom of your spine, let yourself be held in this place and appreciate yourself just being held for who you are. Let yourself feel that deep appreciation for yourself. *(pause)*

- Be aware of being appreciated right here in the present moment.

- Let the focus of your awareness be on whatever arises as you imagine the color orange. Let your awareness not rush after the various appearances of thoughts, sensations, or memories. As they appear, just appreciate them as they are appearing and then disappearing. Let your awareness become still, unattached, and nonreactive to what is arising within you. *(pause)*

- Stay engaged with your awareness and don't space out but be still with the comings and goings of the mind.

Step

7

- Now, turn your awareness inward away from the comings and goings of the mind and notice what is there in the space of stillness. What is the quality of this space? Is there movement, is there life, is there some type of feeling, or is there nothing at all in the space of silence? *(pause)*

- Observe the comings and goings of your mind and the stillness itself from within this space. Do you notice a difference?

- Relax more deeply with what appears in the mind but don't get carried away by grasping or reacting to the stream of thoughts, images, and memories. Just be present within this expanded space that is beyond your mind. In this space you are the observer.

- Continue to stay in the warmth of being held in this awareness that is beyond time.

- The power of awareness itself catalyzes the difference between life and death.

- Appreciate these precious moments of being present in awareness.

- Now use your breath to bring presence in to your entire body and being.

- Allow yourself to inhale and exhale, feeling the sensations of your breath in your belly and your nostrils. Feel grounded in your body, just resting in this place of appreciation and presence for yourself. *(pause)*

Step 7

- Place your attention now on the sensation of moving gently upward until you reach your chest. Notice your breath slowly moving in and out. Follow your breath for just a few moments. Let yourself integrate what you learned from letting forgiveness release your identity patterns.

- Notice your hands in your lap. Notice how heavy and relaxed they are. Begin to wiggle or stretch your fingers and hands and move your body.

- With a big inhale and exhale of breath, come back into the room.

- As you relax and feel the experience of this meditation, trust that as you continue to attune to the belly energy of gratitude, you will dissolve your constricted identity more and more, opening to your natural awakening.

- Be gentle and loving to yourself and know that a higher energy source is guiding you.

- Trust also that there is your unique timing that brings you to a full state of appreciation and presence.

- Please write in your journal what you learned and experienced.

Step

7

Chapter 19
Step 8:
Freedom from Separation

It is a wonderful day in a life when one is finally able to stand before the long,
deep mirror of one's own reflection and view oneself with appreciation, acceptance,
and forgiveness. On that day one breaks through the falsity of images and expectations
which have blinded one's spirit. One can only learn to see who one is when one learns to
view oneself with the most intimate and forgiving compassion.

—JOHN O'DONOHUE

Your journey continues to release the constricted self from its illusionary hold on you. You have used the practice of forgiveness to release how you identify yourself. Each release with a different pillar of love opens and expands your true expression of yourself. The heart opened in you to reveal the self-centered constricted self, to reveal a gentleness of knowing that you are not the doer. The convincing constricted self cajoled you to be in charge of a false awareness of reality. The awakening of an inner awareness enabled you to acknowledge your hectic and pressure-cooker–driven life. Through the love frequency of openhearted appreciation, you experienced the deepening of your focal length perception moving from the inside to the outside. Appreciation expanded you even more to be aware of what you are capable of experiencing and how to have inner freedom at all times. Amazingly, awareness transformed and went beyond time to being you right in the moment. Appreciation brings awareness so you know that presence looks through your eyes.

We come in this chapter, finally, to face the possibility of you becoming free of this constricted separation from your expanded self. We first will examine what I call the "ground of your being," which is the essence of your true self. We will explore the reality that you've never been separated from this essence and that what you've lived in is a "false home" of illusion and can return to your "real home" as a complete human being. The means to return home to yourself as a complete human is through kindness and compassion for yourself and others. These two practices plus those of forgiveness, gratitude, appreciation, and presence provide the pathway for your inner and outer freedom. Both the kindness and compassion meditations opens fully your heart to embrace your expanded self.

Finally, in this chapter we put all the pieces together with an integration meditation. This meditation uses the brain frequency of gamma to take you through all of the chakra color energies I've asked you to visualize with each meditation. The gamma frequency will take you up and out the top of your head into the pure white light, which is the energy that the brain research says we die in. In this meditation, it is to know and experience that this high level gamma frequency is the access point to experiencing your expanded self now in your life today.

The Ground of Your Being

Now you come to the eighth and final step of the detachment journey of your constricted self. This final step takes you back to the beginning of your life journey many years ago. In your journey, you come now to the *ground of your being* with awareness in a different capacity and with a capability to see your constricted self in a purer light. The time from your birth to today has been a continuous experience of living out your primal catastrophe. Now is the time to look at what has kept you captured in your constricted self. As you look at the

Step

8

"catastrophe" of pain and separation, you find that the solution is really quite simple.

The truth is that you have never been separate or separated at all from your essential self. If this isolated psychological space were removed between you and others, you would experience you and others as one being. As you look deeper at being one individual, there is a key similarity in everything that exists on this planet. Everything is alive with energy. All matter can be turned into energy, and energy can be turned into matter, so anything made of matter contains energy. For example, if you hold a bowling ball in your hand and combine it with a bowling ball's worth of antimatter, the matter and antimatter will destroy each other and simply become energy. It would be a stupendous amount of energy, since the equation that tells us how much energy we get from matter is Einstein's equation, $e = mc^2$ or energy = mass times the speed of light squared. In simple terms this is a correlation of energy to matter and how powerful energy becomes when we bring the two together at the speed of light!

There Is No Separation

You are a combination of many energy frequencies. In reality, the space or separation between you and everything is in the mind and emotions of your constricted self. There really is no separation between you and everything else. There is no space between or around this self. It is the woven tapestry of your ego that separates you in your mind. The constricted self made it up. We are all connected energy in this life and everything and everyone is a different frequency whether it is an object, a mountain, a tree, another person, or an animal. It is all you too.

The Illusion of the False Home

It is actually quite simple how you came to this experience of feeling separated and alone, abandoned, betrayed, and not belonging. Remember our earlier description that at birth you chose (not consciously) to leave your inner home to move into your outer physical earthbound "body home." You left your inner

Step
8

home. You chose to make your physical world home. This is the home of objects, bodies, feelings, emotions, and perceptions. You left home and tried to create a new home that was an illusion, a dream, and not reality. At death, you leave this false home and return to your expanded self's home. Gradually, the recognition dawns in you that you are not contemplating someone else as the Divine. It is like a mirror and the Divine you are contemplating is yourself. *You are the Divine.* There is no difference between the seer, the scenery, and the scene (seen).

Your Real Home

When you separate from the constricted self, it relaxes its contraction finally and fully. You are then in the midst of a present vastness. Your identity explodes into everything that is empty and where ignorance and desire are gone. As the sense of self dissolves, so do the body and the experience of the "other." Your mind becomes like the sky where it is open, free, limitless, and not complicated, corrupted, or stained. A more powerful integration of the constricted self merges into the expanded self as you move deeply into the interior of awareness. This awareness is quiet, more centered, and with an experience of grace and stillness that rests in the sacred. You then become filled with love, openness, acceptance, and wholeness. Now you are really home!

The Complete Human

As you may recall, the last stage of human life is where you as a human become whole and integrated. Transpersonal integration is where the heart is open, where the mind is clear and knowing, and where grace exists. At this stage, you become completely human. Completely human is the integration of pain to transform suffering into joy. It is the constricted self merging into the expansion of a nonself. Trying to be a self is all that holds you back from becoming who you really are as "one consciousness." Once the illusory sense of the constricted self surrenders, unity envelops you. Your sense of identity shifts to become the entire universe. This is what happens when you die. You merge with the pure light and become the Universe. But this is also what can happen for you now, today.

Step
8

This is the transcendent process; it is the last stage of dying. This last stage is where the dissipation of the "other" dissolves. The process of dying is like a clay vase that holds the ordinary mind. When you die, the expanded self is freed as the vase shatters. At that moment, you realize that there never was any separation or difference with "another." It is when you surrender that you let go to the expansion. At this point, it is impossible to continue with the identity of the constricted self. The constricted self crumbles and is no longer manifest in you. The pure mind clears and the heart of kindness and compassion opens. This is the place of awakening to your essential human self in this lifetime.

Kindness

Kindness is an energy that is always noticing and looking for ways to act in order that the heart energy can expand more and mutually connect with all beings in the world. It is looking to be kind to yourself, other humans, animals, plants, trees, birds, and so on, as well as made objects such as tools, cars, and homes. Kindness increases the energetic connection within the web of existence. Kindness moves you into heart connection and weaves you into the mystery of unity with everything you confront in your life. The ancient Chinese writer Lao Tzu said in the Tao Te Ching, "In dealing with others, be gentle and kind. In speech, be true." [64]

The energy of kindness is the foundation of True Reality. The Dalai Lama says that his religion is kindness. He knows from inner knowledge that kindness is the outer action that shifts patterns and that opens new awareness. It is kindness that takes you to the heart of love's power, healing, knowledge, creativity, and revelation. The energy of kindness is transforming not only for you expressing it, but also for those receiving it. Kindness generates energy and creates a higher vibration frequency. This frequency moves quickly toward the spectrum of light. With kindness, things "lighten up!" Your constricted self does not drive kindness because it isn't about actions; it is about intent. The action of kindness is not about what you do, but rather the focus of intent in your heart. It is

Step

8

---

64. Gia-Fu Feng and Jane English, *Lao Tsu, Tao Te Ching: A New Translation* (New York: Vintage Books, Random House, 1972), 12.

the frequency of the kindness intent that motivates your action. The energy of kindness is an attitude of acceptance and recognition that there is no difference between you or anything else in the world or the part of you that receives the kindness from yourself. Kindness prepares you for closing the door of separation, which is the space that separates you from everything and everyone.

Kindness Practices

All around you are opportunities to express kindness. All it requires is a deeper perceiving energetically.

- To develop an awareness of kindness, you can attune to the frequency of the forehead and the top of your head at the crown area. During meditation, walking, or sitting, quietly focus your attention on the forehead and the crown simultaneously. Hold your attention until you feel warmth, buzzing, pulsation, or whatever sensation begins to shift your awareness at these two points. At first, you will need to be conscious of these points. In time, they will be a natural radar for actions of kindness. You will begin to see people and situations in new ways. When the seeing opens, notice what would be appropriate to do. Now bring your attention down into your heart and intuitively ask if you are to do some outward action or not to respond to what you see. The heart will channel the energy of your insight and love in the appropriate act of kindness.

- The more you hold these two points and focus them at your heart the more naturally you will live in the kindness of oneness.

- Practice this frequency of kindness every day and it will open and release your sense of separation.

Step 8

Compassion

In compassion, you attune to the frequency of the "other." Compassion is not really a feeling or an emotion. Compassion is becoming unified with the energetic field of the other. Thus, in compassion you let go of the self-concern and you align and become one with the movement, drive, energy, and experience of the other. So when we say you feel compassion for another, what you feel is the core essence of their energy condition, but your feelings are matching their energy feeling. The difference is that responding in compassion to another holds the awareness of a larger context for the energy condition of the other as you together align with the higher frequency that can transform the quality and condition of the other's experience.

To have compassion for a person, animal, country, tree, weather, and so on is to hold a context in which the higher frequency energy of love "stands under" and holds both of you. Being with the other in the same frequency while holding the larger frequency of the essence of reality is love without separation, judgment, or a sense of fundamental difference between you and the other.

Being in the same higher energy frequency with the other is to stand together with their true nature and in your own true nature. When being together in the one expanded self, both of you experience an aligned frequency that is higher, larger, and stronger than any condition, circumstances, or environment either of you are facing in a particular time and space. The Dalai Lama, who is considered the embodiment of compassion, holds for his people a higher frequency that permits him to hold the pain, suffering, and destruction of Tibet without separating himself from the Chinese. He has understanding and experience of their frequency, just as he does for his own people. His role in exhibiting compassion is not just to hold the frequency of pain and suffering, but also to be in a higher-level frequency for his people and the Chinese at the same time.

Compassion is a transformation of the deep mother quality that respects and understands all of her children and does not hold back from her caring and actions to redeem, save, or protect all beings in her frequency of the supreme energy of love. Compassion, as an unknown author has said, "Is lack of love for ourselves that inhibits our compassion toward others. If we make friends with ourselves, then there is no obstacle to opening our hearts and minds to others." [65]

And so to you, I would say, may you wake up to your essence—your true essence—that essence that holds your destiny in this life and that wakes you up

Step
8

---

65. Unknown Author, cited at http://quotesweliveby.blogspot.com/2009/09/lend-helping-hand
-compassion-quotes.html.

to walk through the door of your heart to sublime compassion for yourself. It is truly the door of your compassion that will wake you up!

Compassion Practices

To deepen your compassion is increasingly to shift your perception away from separation. For your compassion to grow, you need to know that you are the source of all that is holding, protecting, and caring for you and others.

- The first practice is to acknowledge the frequency of your own pain and suffering. Literally name it, understand it, shift your awareness and focus to the frequency of your heart, and bring the specific issues and experiences that cause you pain and suffering to that place.

- As you hold these conditions in your heart, feel a warming, a pulsing, an electrical feeling, or any other sensation of energy increase, then move this heart energy to the crown of your head. Feel the sensation of energy building in you like you did at the heart.

- Then let this energy go out the top of your head and experience the expansion of your being of the love that you truly are. In this expanded space, let yourself see, feel, and experience your pain and suffering dissolving in the greater frequency of expansion.

- You may have to do this practice again and again as new issues of pain and suffering emerge from your awareness.

- After you have worked with your self-compassion, turn your attention toward other people. Another practice is to first connect to the highest frequency you know from the expanded frequency you have practiced for yourself and reach out mentally and with your feelings from your heart/mind to the other.

- Let that frequency connect with and understand—stand with—the frequency of the other.

- As you practice this extending to another, it will be similar to how you have been working with your own self-compassion.

Step
8

- Extending toward another in this way, you will find that it is easier to connect to their frequency than you realize.

- It is moving from focusing on yourself to focusing on matching your frequency with that of the other and then expanding to the larger, higher, and more expansive frequency that encompasses you both.

- This is when you will experience true and deep connection of love with another that holds no judgment of what they or you are experiencing.

- You see and know in the other what you have seen and known in yourself. And you know that whatever is the pain and suffering of the other can be healed in them.

- Start practicing with animals, trees, family, and friends close to you.

- All you have to do is inwardly ask if you can connect with them. Simply extending to them is to understand from their point of reference. This shifts you and their frequency and opens the connection of understanding as to who and what they are experiencing.

- You then expand together to a higher frequency that brings caring, comfort, and a sense of their true nature as a being. If something concretely and practically needs to be done for that other person as part of the act of compassion, it will be done with an equality of mutual love rather than with condescension. This is called love in action and it releases the separateness of life.

Exercise: *Kindness and Compassion Meditation*

The final step of the journey is to release the constricted self by opening and expanding your heart with kindness and compassion. These meditations offer an expansion of giving what releases the constricted self into a free, expanded, light mind. This mind of loving awareness prepares you to live an amazing full life now as well as at the last moment of your life on earth. Through each step of the journey, you have released your attachments and have left your baggage behind. As you practice these exercises and meditate, you will be supported to

Step 8

release and move forward in your evolution. I bless you on this journey as you eliminate anxiety, avoidance, and resistance. With open arms and open heart, the next step of this journey is the most important sacred experience of your life.

Again, as with other exercises you've done before, please either pre-record this meditation in order to listen to it or have a partner or friend read and guide you through it. Where there is a *(pause)* indicated, give yourself time to experience the instructions at that point. (If you want to use the bonus video for this meditation go to appendix D.)

Let's begin the meditation:

- Let yourself relax into a safe, quiet, comfortable place with your back straight but not rigid or lie on a bed or a mat.
- Close your eyes and imagine a red color filling your lower heart area. Notice the sounds in your environment. *(pause)*
- Recall the depth of your last meditation and take several deep breaths and relax into all parts of your body. *(pause)*
- What does the relaxation feel like inside you?
- Remember the feeling of deep relaxation when using your marker. Recall how you created your marker as a symbol, an image, or a word and how you felt your marker at a particular place on your body. Return to that inner feeling of relaxation spreading through your body. *(pause)*
- As you move deeper into recalling the symbol, image, or word of your marker, feel the tensions of your body letting go.
- Now, take three deep breaths. As you take them, observe your breath. Is it shallow? Labored? What is the quality of your inhale and exhale? Does one seem easier or fuller? Is there a natural pause when your breath is full or empty? Feel the sensations of the belly, as well as the cool and warmth of your nostrils. *(pause)*
- Place your attention deep inside, back near your spinal cord as you observe your breath.

Step

8

- Notice as you inhale that you take in oxygen from the outside air and it mixes with the air in the space inside your body.

- As the air merges inside and outside you become even more relaxed, like a falling leaf your mind gently begins to fall down, moving deep inside your heart space. The air on the outside space and air on the inside are merging, allowing the boundaries of the body to dissolve and the movement of the breath to flow easefully and naturally back and forth in and out in an even rhythm. *(pause)*

- Feel the softness, warmth, caring, openness of your heart quality as you are deep inside your heart. Imagine yourself being held by your heart as you move downward, slowly, gently down all the way to the base of your spine.

- With this heart quality, feel the energy tingling or the energy sensation building in your heart and deep within your body.

- Being held in the gentle softness of your heart, let yourself become open to any current or past pain, issue, or sadness in your life. Be gentle with yourself and let it all rest there in your heart. Compassion is letting it all rest in your heart and your heart will recognize your suffering, pain, and sorrow. *(pause)*

- Move into this inner knowing and go deeper into this heart space without judgment or condemnation. Let there be acceptance and give this acceptance softness, caring, warmth, and kindness.

- Now, feel kindness for yourself. Feel yourself being held by kindness. Feel what kindness is like within the pain of your suffering.

- Rest your mind back into this soft, warm space of kindness and feel a gentle movement upward as if an escalator is gently sliding you upward softly, slowly, gently.

- Feel yourself rising upward until you come to the top of your head and let this heart energy move out through the top of your head into the space above you, into a vastness. Experience the expansion of the vastness of space. Let yourself move out into this vastness. *(pause)*

Step

8

- Now remember your pain, your suffering, and your sadness. Move all of these feelings into this vast space to disappear into the greater energy frequency that you've moved into.

- Also become aware of being held by compassion right here in the present moment of letting go and notice the space of love and acceptance you feel in this vastness of heart energy.

- Let go of your holding of pain, suffering, and hurt. Put your attention and focus on the dissolving of all the hurt; let it fade away. Know that it is gone. Let your awareness remain still unattached and nonreactive. Just rest, rest, rest in this vast peace. *(pause)*

- Stay engaged in your awareness of this resting and not space out with the comings and goings of the mind. The gift is to let go to compassion and love for yourself.

- Claim within you that in this vastness you can forever know that compassion is always present for you. *(pause)*

- Now, turn your awareness inward, away, backward from the comings and goings of your mind and notice what is there in this vast space. In this quality of space, there is movement, life, feeling, or nothing at all.

- Relaxing more deeply but not getting carried away with what appears in your mind without grasping or reacting, just being present, being in the self-compassion, in this bright higher frequency. Continue to stay in the warmth of being held in expanded love. *(pause)*

- Now move back downward, gently to your heart. Notice in this vast space a presence of your being—of who you truly are.

- Now use your breath to bring presence into your entire body and being.

- Allow yourself to inhale and exhale, feeling the sensations of your breath in your belly and your nostrils. Feel grounded in your body, just resting in this place of appreciation and presence for yourself. *(pause)*

- Place your attention now on the sensation of moving gently upward until you reach your chest. Notice your breath slowly moving in and out. Follow your breath for just a few moments integrating what you learned in how

Step
8

you became aware of your kindness and compassion for yourself, and your willingness to release all your pain and suffering. *(pause)*

- Notice now your hands in your lap. Notice how heavy and relaxed they are. Begin to wiggle or stretch your fingers and hands and move your body.

- With a big inhale and exhale of breath, come back into the room.

- As you relax and feel the experience of this meditation, and trust that as you continue to attune to the heart energy of kindness and compassion, you will dissolve your constricted identity more and more, opening to move into your natural awakening.

- Be gentle and loving to yourself and know that a higher energy source is guiding you and that you can return to this vast space of energy, love, acceptance, kindness, and compassion.

- Trust also that there is your unique timing that brings you to a full state of integration.

- Please write in your journal what you learned and experienced.

Integration Process

The Journey of Freedom is to heighten and raise our consciousness. You come now to the place of integration to combine all the qualities of the heart to become whole within you. The integration process is important because it shifts you from the Journey of Separation, where you faced not belonging, resistance, control, and your many identities, all of which have been given to you by others. The integration process creates the potential to shift you into being free of all that creates tension, pain, and fear within you to a quality of expansion and acceptance of your true self. The late Terence McKenna once said to us, "You are a divine being. You matter, you count. You come from realms of unimaginable power and light, and you will return to those realms." [66] You will be able to experience the heart of this powerful light in the Integration Meditation.

Step
8

66. Terence McKenna, "Unfolding the Stone," 1991, YouTube: Fractal Youniverse.

In this meditation, you will experience each step of the Journey of Freedom moving from the Freedom of Separation to the Freedom of Identities. This will then take you step-by-step to your heart and raise your energy to the top of your head. At the top of your head, you will experience a white light and the frequency of gamma brain waves.

It is in the gamma brain waves that you both awake in this life and die into the next passage of being. You will notice that the frequencies in the meditation build upon each other to open an energetic flow similar to when you die. It is like a rainbow ladder of inner awakening. When the meditation and energy reaches the top of your head, you will experience an awareness of merging into the oneness of a loving white light of high frequency. As you practice this meditation, you will experience the beginning of an inner awakening that may occur at the moment of your death.

Exercise: *Integration Meditation*

Again, as with other exercises you've done before, please either pre-record this meditation in order to listen to it, or have a partner or friend read and guide you through it. Where there is a *(pause)* indicated, give yourself time to experience the instructions at that point. (If you want to use the bonus video for this meditation go to appendix D.)

Let's begin the meditation:

- Let yourself relax into a safe, quiet, comfortable place with your back straight but not rigid or lie on a bed or a mat.
- Close your eyes and imagine a red color filling your lower heart area. Notice the sounds in your environment. *(pause)*
- Recall the depth of your last meditation and take several deep breaths and relax into all parts of your body. *(pause)*
- What does the relaxation feel like inside you?

Step

8

- Remember the feeling of deep relaxation when using your marker. Recall how you created your marker as a symbol, an image, or a word and where you felt your marker at a particular place on your body. Return to that inner feeling of relaxation spreading through your body. *(pause)*

- As you move deeper into recalling the symbol, image, or word of your marker, feel the tensions of your body letting go.

- Now, take three deep breaths. As you take them, observe your breath. Is it shallow? Labored? What is the quality of your inhale and exhale? Does one seem easier or fuller? Is there a natural pause when your breath is full or empty? Feel the sensations of the belly, as well as the cool and warmth of your nostrils. *(pause)*

- Place your attention deep inside, back near your spinal cord, as you observe your breath.

- Notice as you inhale that you take in oxygen from the outside air and it mixes with the air in the space inside your body.

- As the air merges inside and outside you, become even more relaxed, like a falling leaf, your mind gently begins to fall down moving deep inside your heart space. The air on the outside space and air on the inside are merging, allowing the boundaries of the body to dissolve and the movement of the breath to flow easefully and naturally back and forth in and out in an even rhythm. *(pause)*

- You are moving deeper in this space where there is a softness and a warmth.

- Now as you rest your mind back into this soft, warm space, feel a gentle movement downward as if on an escalator, gently sliding downward softly, slowly, and gently, moving down to the base of your spine.

- Let yourself be held here, right in the very base of your body, and imagine the color red. As you imagine the red color, you let yourself rest in this energy frequency of red as it moves you into a vast space in which you are held by the energy of who you truly are. Let yourself rest in this loving space, totally belonging and filled with self-compassion. In this space of

Step

8

self-compassion, many thoughts and feelings may be passing through your mind/body/heart. *(pause)*

- Open even more as you now imagine and let go to the orange color. Imagine the orange color move into your sacrum. Open yourself, open your mind and heart now, right here in the present moment. Be absolutely here now. Be aware of inner stillness. Be aware of deep appreciation for yourself. *(pause)*

- Remember to be aware and mindful of whatever arises as you now imagine and view in your mind's eye the color yellow. Feel the energy, the frequency of yellow, as you move up into your belly. Notice within you and be aware of the energies building into calm gratefulness. Let your awareness remain still, unattached, and nonreactive, just receiving this feeling and awareness of gratefulness for yourself, your life, and all that you've been given. *(pause)*

- Stay engaged, stay present, bring your mind to full focus as the color green appears in your mind's awareness. The green color and its frequency opens and moves you into your heart area. Your mind and heart becoming one in gentle, loving peace and a feeling of openheartedness. Stay focused, not spacing out but still observing the comings and goings of the mind yet not grasping at anything. *(pause)*

- Notice the color white emerging in your mind. It is naturally moving upward. The energy and frequency of the color white is moving upward to your throat and then upward to your forehead. The color white pulls you upward to the top of your head. As you rest here at the top of your head, feel the sensations. It may feel like buzzing, tingling, or warmth moving energies about your head. Within your own sensations notice that there is movement and energies coming toward you above your head. Let yourself open and merge with this white light of healing energy and stay as long as you like, continuing to let go and merge with it. *(pause)*

- When you are ready, turn your awareness and move downward from above your head and the white light, down to your heart. Notice that the light has subsided, allowing for your breath to appear. Rest from the comings

Step 8

and goings of your mind and thoughts. Notice what is in the space of your heart. What is the quality of this heart space? Is there movement, life, or the feeling of nothing at all? *(pause)*

• Observe the movement of your breath as you come back into your body. Continue to notice each breath relaxing into a natural flow of inhale and exhale.

• Feel in yourself and appreciate these precious moments of being present in awareness to the energies and the movement in and beyond yourself with the white light.

• Now use your breath to bring presence into your entire body and being.

• Allow yourself to inhale and exhale, feeling the sensations of your breath in your belly and your nostrils. Feel grounded in your body, just resting in this place of love and presence for yourself. *(pause)*

• Place your attention now on the sensation of moving gently upward until you reach your chest. Notice your breath slowly moving in and out. Follow your breath for just a few moments, integrating what you learned in how you became aware of your integration for yourself, and your willingness to experience that this movement up and out of your body into this place of freedom is always available to you. You know now that freedom from fear and separation is alive and present in you both in your present life and when you die. *(pause)*

• Notice now your hands in your lap. Notice how heavy and relaxed they are. Begin to wiggle or stretch your fingers and hands and move your body.

• With a big inhale and exhale of breath, come back into the room.

• As you relax and feel the experience of this meditation you know that you can come back to this experience again and again to attune your heart and mind energy to this expansion and that you will dissolve your constricted identity more and more opening to your natural awakening.

Step
8

- Be gentle and loving to yourself and know that a higher energy source is guiding you and that you can return to this vast space of energy, love, acceptance, kindness, and compassion because you are all alive now in freedom.

- Trust also that there is your unique timing that brings you to a full state of integration.

- Please write in your journal what you learned and experienced.

Step
8

Afterword

This has been quite a journey for me writing this book, as I am sure it was for you to read and work with it. The event of our death is shrouded in hidden fear. Bringing our fear into the open confronts us with many things. From the time I confronted my death, as I wrote in the beginning of the book, I have had a passion to know what is needed to prepare for the most important event of our lifetime, but it was not an easy book for me to write.

Going through the writing process, I uncovered something very important and revealing for me. What I uncovered and deeply learned was to put everything in place for my family and not to leave any broken emotional ties with others unresolved. It became very clear that I could not leave this life without all those relationships healed. I learned that I want to be clear with my caregivers on what I need during the death process and after I die. Most important, I came to understand the practices that will prepare my mind to be in a place of open awareness without distractions as I am dying. I am now actually curious about the final step of my death, rather than being driven by fear and avoiding it. However, beyond this openness to face my death without fear was the wonderful discovery that I could live in freedom from fear now in my life. The practices that enabled me to face my constricted self governed by fear was also the practices that could awaken me to my expanded true self.

If you read the book and did not do any of the exercises, you may have missed the point of the book. This is not a book just for the cognitive mind. Yes, it is filled with information, but it is for you to experience the meditations and practice the exercises. These experiences will give you the unique understanding of preparing you for your death as well as how to live a more expanded life today. The exercises can be practiced many times to help you to release from your constricted self and awaken you to your expanded self so that you can live a life of love and joy now as well as when you pass through the transition from this life to beyond. Practice the exercises in order to keep questioning and to uncover more about yourself so that you can open more into your heart. Your heart is your "home base" for living your life in freedom.

As you know now from reading the book, death is not easily faced alone, so my vision is that you work in groups to encourage each other to move forward in the process. Bring a group of your friends or family together. Take the book into your religious and spiritual communities, into men and women's circles, or social groups to find people who would work as a group. In such a group, share, learn, and support each other in this amazing adventure of a heart and mind that is courageous, curious, and embracing both your death and the vitality of your life.

The process of preparing for your death and awakening to a more vital life now is a gift to your community. Be a light wherever you find yourself. You can share your life and the end of your life with a circle of family and friends so they will be aware of your preferences and how you want to die with all the practical considerations about caregivers to legal concerns, so when it is your time to die you will feel confident that your wishes will be fulfilled. As you may recall, my first intention in writing this book was for my family. I wanted my family members, individually and together, to be prepared for each of our deaths. I am committed to my family and to help each other to awaken now and in our dying. Your willingness to prepare for your death is a gift to yourself, but it is also a gift to your family and friends. To embrace your end of life and to awaken to your expanded self is the great journey of our life. I truly wish you well and hope this book has been a useful guide for you whatever your path or beliefs.

Appendix A
Resources

Below are some recommendations before removing the body, including washing the body, applying body oils, and shrouding the body. Other resources are for gravesite preparation and organizing memorials and ceremonies. You can find more discussion on these topics in chapters 8 and 9.

Methods of Preparing the Body
During the Three-Day Period After Death

Preparation of the Body

http://immarama.faithweb.com/preparation.htm

Care of the Body for a Home Funeral

www.thresholdcarecircle.org/caring-for-our-own/care-of-the-body

The Vigil and the Three Days after Death

www.thresholdcarecircle.org/caring-for-our-own/vigils

Gravesite, Memorial, and Ceremony Preparation

Thirteen Religious Perspectives on Mourning and Memorials

www.everplans.com/articles/13-religious-perspectives-on-mourning-and
-memorial-events

Funeral and Religious Customs

www.a-to-z-of-manners-and-etiquette.com/funeral-and-religious-customs.html

Jewish Belief That the Spirit Lingers for Three Days

http://peopleof.oureverydaylife.com/jewish-belief-spirit-lingers-three
-days-9380.html

Full Circle Living & Dying Collective

www.fullcirclelivingdyingcollective.com

Dying Consciously—The Greatest Journey (Based in Shamanic Tradition)

www.dyingconsciously.org

Appendix B
Legal Documents

There are many legal documents that relate to preparing for your own death. As I indicated in chapter 9, I want to provide access to information that helps you make appropriate end-of-life legal decisions for yourself. Listed below are Internet sites that can provide specific information about the topics I discussed. Many of these sites are specific to the United States. For readers from other countries, please search these topics for your country, states, or principalities.

Wills and Living Trusts

Will
www.lawdepot.com/contracts/last-will-and-testament-usa/#.WAU3j6O-IUF

Living Trusts
www.uslegalforms.com/livingtrusts

Ethical Will
www.everplans.com/articles/ethical-will-worksheet

Medical Directives and Power of Attorney

Advance Health Care Directive

http://uslwr.com/formslist.shtm

Do Not Resuscitate (DNR) / Do Not Intubate (ADNI)

www.lincoln.ne.gov/city/fire/emsoa/pdf/dnr.pdf

Cardiopulmonary Resuscitation (CPR) Directive

www.chaclaplata.org/PDF/CPR%20Directive%20Form.pdf

Physician's Orders for Life-Sustaining Treatment (POLST)

http://polst.org/programs-in-your-state/

Organ Donation Directive

www.organdonor.gov/register.html?gclid=CKzulvaD5c8CFYOFaQodCiAL0g

Medical School Body Donation

www.livingbank.org/whole-body-donation

Death Certificates

www.cdc.gov/nchs/data/dvs/death11-03final-acc.pdf

Durable Power of Attorney

www.12law.com/engine/start.aspx?rgp_key=4a736dbe-2c14-479c-ac9d
-6bc367d2eef0

Medical Power of Attorney

www.expertlaw.com/library/estate_planning/medical_power_of_attorney
.html

www.wvlegalservices.org/medpoa.pdf

Burial and Cremation

Burial at a Conventional Cemetery

www.consumer.ftc.gov/articles/0301-funeral-costs-and-pricing-checklist

Green Burials

www.greenburialcouncil.org

Cremation

www.neptunesociety.com/cremation-process

Additional Book Resource

A Graceful Farewell: Putting Your Affairs in Order by Maggie Watson
www.agracefulfarewell.com

The documents in the book, along with the documents I've listed, provide everything that your family and friends need to resolve the practicalities of your life after you die. The book includes a wide range of topics that only you know about and others might find difficult to discover. The book covers such topics as where your critical documents are to be found, all your money placements (banks, credit cards, investments, loans, real estate, etc., as well as antiques), different types of insurance, property you own, business contracts and partners, document checklist, farewell wishes, and much more. This is a gift that will keep on giving as you "gracefully" prepare your farewell!

Appendix C
Enneagram

In chapter 11, you were invited to discover your Enneagram type. Here are some additional resources to explore this topic even further.

The Enneagram Institute

www.enneagraminstitute.com
You can take the longer Enneagram type indicator test for free at this source to get a better understanding of your type. A complete listing of the Enneagram Institute's books, audio tapes, printed Enneagram tests, and other Enneagram materials can be found on their website.

Additional Book Resource

In addition to the Enneagram Institute website, I recommend a book by Riso and Hudson that specifically focuses the use of the Enneagram on the spiritual development of your life: *The Wisdom of the Enneagram: The Complete Guide to Psychological and Spiritual Growth for the Nine Personality Types.*

Appendix D
Bonus Meditation Videos

I created the sixteen video meditations that are used in part 2 of the book to assist you, the reader, to have a deeper experience of the meditations than what are written in the text. The intent of each video is to guide you into a relaxed state, with color that matches the particular chakra of the body for a particular meditation. I am reading the meditation from the text with the background sound of the frequency of a particular color and with binaural beats embedded in the sound track in order to put you into a particular brain wave pattern. The combination of the color, sound, binaural beats, and my voice give you the experience of all the sensory aspects of your brain, mind, and body as the meditation takes you into a deep place within you. The following material is presented in the introduction video by me if you choose to go directly to that at this time. To access this introductory video simply put www.PattLindKyle .com/meditations into your computer browser and click on Introduction. If you are reading from an ebook, click on the URL and then click on the Introduction.

In each video track there are binaural beats that correspond to the particular brain wave for that meditation. Binaural beats in the beta frequency range create increased concentration, alertness, vividness, and clarity. Binaural beats in the alpha range can improve concentration and memory. Binaural beats in the theta and delta ranges are associated with deepened, relaxed creativity and deeper meditative states. Each meditation indicates what brain frequency each meditation is accessing. For more detailed information about brain frequencies, go to my book, *Heal Your Mind, Rewire Your Brain*. Visit my website, www.pattlindkyle.com, for other information and to follow my blog.

Headphones or ear pods with a frequency response of 20–20k Hz will serve you best in receiving the greatest benefit from the binaural beats in each video. If you don't have ear pods or you are using the video in a group setting, try to have two speakers spaced on either side of the group so that you can experience the binaural beats that accompany a particular video. One of my purposes of creating the videos is to use them in groups that are meeting together to discuss and do the exercises in the book. Watching the guided meditation videos together and then sharing their experience proves to be an invaluable experience for people. Classes I've taught using the videos in this way have provided great value listening to each other and supporting each other's experience from the shared video experience.

Each written meditation in the text stands alone and you can receive great value experiencing it, as I've written it without using the videos if you so choose. The bonus video meditations are for those who have access to the Internet and are interested in using the videos to work with the meditations separate from the text in the book. As indicated below, you will access the videos by putting www.PattLindKyle.com/meditations into your browser window and then clicking the appropriate video.

The first four chapters of part 2 of the book use the videos from:
Chapter 12 – Journey of Separation
Chapter 13 – Journey of Emotions
Chapter 14 – Journey of the Mind
Chapter 15 – Journey of Self-Identity

The last four chapters of the book use the videos from:
Chapter 16 – Forgiveness Meditation
Chapter 17 – Gratitude Meditation
Chapter 18 – Presence and Appreciation Meditations

Chapter 19 – Kindness and Compassion Meditations
Chapter 19 – Integration Meditation

How to Practice with the Video Color

As you chose to access each video meditation for a particular chapter, I give you information on the particular color for a meditation, the brain wave frequency embedded in the sound of the frequency of the color itself, what chakra it is focused on, the element it represents, and some basic information and questions related to your life ages. To access a particular video simply put www.PattLind Kyle.com/meditations into your computer browser and click on the appropriate meditation you want. If you are reading from an ebook click on the URL and then click on the appropriate meditation you want.

Color is included as an aspect of these meditations. To watch the color of the video as you listen to the guided questions have your eyes half open. Put your attention and focus on listening to what you are experiencing inside yourself as the questions are being asked. This will allow the color to naturally enter into your unconscious as you have your eyes slightly open. If after a period of time your eyes close that is okay. The sound in the background is the frequency sound of the particular color you are watching.

If you have any questions or technical problems related to the videos, you can contact me at my website, www.PattLindKyle.com

Journey of Separation Videos (for Chapter 12)

To access these two videos, put into your computer browser the following URL www.PattLindKyle.com/meditations. It will take you to a menu. Click on either Red 1 or Red 2.

As you work with the videos, the energetic beginning of the constricted self begins with a slow delta brain-wave frequency pattern, with a red vibration and a sound frequency of C. The solidness of the element earth grounds the constricted self here. Thus, at these ages your constricted self is born and repeats at a variety of different stages in your life. You will find it fascinating how all these characteristics affect you. The personality is so beautifully developed it is difficult not to believe that you are a real self.

Video Summary

Brain-Wave Frequency: Delta, 0.5–4 Hz

Chakra: Root   **Color:** Red   **Sound:** C

Element: Earth, your foundation of sensations

Age Development Stages: Birth to four, thirty to thirty-four, sixty to sixty-four, and ninety to ninety-four

If you have not reached the age of sixty, just do the first two ages. Do all three if you are sixty or beyond. The Video Red 1 is 17 minutes, it should be used for ages birth to four years old; Red 2 is 12+ minutes and should be used for both ages thirty to thirty-four years old and sixty to sixty-four years old. Repeat these videos at least two or three times to go deeper into this early stage of your life.

Journey of Separation—Red Color

Now we will take this information from the Journey of Separation section and use the video to ask some questions to clarify so you may experience at a deeper level. These questions will be on the video. However, read the questions first and then turn on the video to the appropriate age Red track(s) of the videos. Write your results in your notebook after using the video.

Questions on Video: Red 1: Ages Birth to Four Years Old

- What is the result of being separated in your life? Did you feel lonely, have connection needs, or did it seem okay and supportive to you?
- What did you need from your parents that you did or did not get—such as security or feeling grounded and at home in yourself and with others?
- When did you have an unstable time of feeling ungrounded and fearful?
- Throughout your life, did you feel safe and did you trust your environment? Were there perceived times when you did not feel safe?

Questions on Video: Red 2: Ages Thirty to Thirty-four Years Old and Ages Sixty to Sixty-Four Years Old

- Did you feel alone and separate at this time in your life?

- What is your behavior like when feeling separate?

- What triggers your anxiety and fear?

- What is it like for you when you try to connect to others and the world around you?

- What is it like not to be safe or trusting?

- What does separation or loneliness feel like for you?

- What gives you security?

Journey of Emotions Videos (for Chapter 13)

To access these two videos, put www.PattLindKyle.com/meditations into your computer browser. Click on either Orange 1 or Orange 2 based on the age of the meditation.

How to Practice with the Video Color

To watch the color of the video as you listen to the guided questions, have your eyes half open. Put your attention and focus on listening to what you are experiencing inside yourself as the questions are being asked. This will allow the color to naturally enter into your unconscious as you have your eyes slightly open. Remember also that the sound in the background is the frequency of the particular color you are watching.

Video Summary
Brain-Wave Frequency: Theta, 4–7.8 Hz
Chakra: Sacral, two inches below the navel
Color: Orange   **Sound:** D   **Element:** Water
Age Development Stages: Ages four to eight, thirty-four to thirty-eight, and sixty-four to sixty-eight

If you have not reached the age of sixty-four just do the first two ages. Do all three if you are sixty-four or beyond. The Three Video URLs: Orange 1 is 13 minutes for ages four to eight years old, Orange 2 is 13+ minutes for ages thirty-four to thirty-eight years old, and Orange 3 is 16+ minutes for sixty-four to sixty-eight years old. Work with these videos once a day as you explore the core issues.

Journey of Emotions—Orange Color

Now we will take this information from the Journey of Emotions section and use the video to ask some questions to clarify so you may experience at a deeper level. These questions will be on the video. However, read the questions first and then turn on the video to the appropriate age orange track(s) of the videos. Write your results in your notebook after using the video.

Prepare yourself for the videos by reflecting on the questions below.

Questions on Video: Orange 1: Ages Four to Eight

- What kinds of moods or emotional reactions did you have to people and situations?
- What were the interests that you were excited or even passionate about?
- How did you resist change in your life? For example, did you move a lot? Were you forced to eat things you didn't like?
- Do you remember having pleasant/strong or unpleasant/weak feelings about yourself, friends, teachers, parents, activities, etc.?
- How did you protect yourself from bad or unpleasant feelings?
- Do you remember being scared of dying or something negative and bad happening to you?

Questions on Video: Orange 2: Ages Thirty-Four to Thirty-Eight

- Are you aware of the type of dominant emotions or feelings you have or had?
- How did you react to them? How do you usually react?

- Were you aware of your sexual attractions? Did you act on them, sublimate them, or what did you do? Were you excited, guilty, or self-shaming, etc.?

- What is your fundamental fear of not getting what you want in your life?

- How much do your past experiences influence you today? Which ones?

- What are your deep interests and passions at this age, if any?

- What causes you to be fearful of death?

Questions on Video: Orange 3: Ages Sixty-Four to Sixty-Eight

- How would you describe what it is to flow with life?

- What emotions do you respond to when you resist life?

- What pleases you in life?

- Do you have a strong interest or passion in your life at this time?

- What are the sensualities in your life? How do you express them?

- What are the routine emotions you fall back on in tense situations?

- How do you protect yourself from the feelings of fear and anger?

- What are your fears about dying?

Journey of the Mind Videos (for Chapter 14)

To access these three videos, put into your computer browser the URL www.PattLindKyle.com/meditations. Click on either Yellow 1, Yellow 2 or Yellow 3, based on the age of the meditation.

How to Practice with the Video Color

To watch the color of the video as you listen to the guided questions, have your eyes half open. Put your attention and focus on listening to what you are experiencing inside yourself as the questions are being asked. This will allow the color to naturally enter into your unconscious as you have your eyes slightly open. Remember also that the sound in the background is the frequency of the particular color you are watching.

Video Summary
Brain-Wave Frequency: Alpha 2, 7.8–13 Hz
Chakra: Solar Plexus   **Color:** Yellow   **Sound:** E
Element: Fire
Age Development Stages: Eight to twelve, thirty-eight to forty-two, and sixty-eight to seventy-two

If you have not reached the age of sixty-eight, just do the first two ages. Do all three if you are sixty-eight or beyond. The Three Videos: Yellow 1 is 19+ minutes for ages eight to twelve years old, Yellow 2 is 16+ minutes for ages thirty-eight to forty-two years old, and Yellow 3 is 28 minutes for ages sixty-eight to seventy-two years old. These videos have a yellow color with its vibrational sound D and binaural beats of alpha 2 brain waves. Work with these videos once a day as you explore the core issues.

Journey of the Mind—Yellow Color
Now we will take this into meditation and ask some questions to clarify at a deeper level. These questions will be on the video. Read the questions first and turn on the videos to the yellow track. Write your results in your notebook after using the video. You will examine your frequency patterns of the Journey of the Mind in the constricted self development at ages eight to twelve, thirty-eight to forty-two, and sixty-eight to seventy-two. The patterns identified are shame, purpose, and craving for power. The mental self is likened to a house we do not want to be locked into all of the time. We need to go out in the world too. We are larger than our inner house.

Questions on the Video: Yellow 1: Ages Eight to Twelve
- Who did you blame at that time?
- Who held the power or authority in your family? Have you copied that pattern in your life?
- What changed in your life in relation to control?

- Were reading and studying important in your life?

- Were you shamed and who did it and what was it about?

- Did you stand your ground?

- What was so hard to digest about your family, school, and friends?

- What was your purpose in life?

Questions on the Video: Yellow 2: Ages Thirty-Eight to Forty-Two

- Are you focused on your own needs or issues? What are they?

- What happens when you are not in control of yourself or others?

- Are there things about which you are ashamed?

- When have you been in a victim position?

- How do you express your power? What stops it? How do you get your recognition needs met?

- What is your purpose at this age?

- What is your attitude toward authority in your life?

Questions on the Video: Yellow 3: Ages Sixty-Eight to Seventy-Two

- Are you in your head most of the time?

- What is your role in your life?

- How do you rely on your inner or outer authority?

- What happens when you deny yourself things?

- How has language played a role in your life?

- Have you been acknowledged for what you have done in your life?

- Do you shame yourself or do others shame you?

- What is the purpose at this time in your life?

- Do you approve of the way you handle authority now?

Journey of Self Identity Videos (for Chapter 15)

To access these two videos, put the URL www.PattLindKyle.com/meditations into your computer browser. Click on either Green 1, Green 2, or Green 3, based on the ages of the meditation.

How to Practice with the Video Color

To watch the color of the video as you listen to the guided questions, have your eyes half open. Put your attention and focus on listening to what you are experiencing inside yourself as the questions are being asked. This will allow the color to naturally enter into your unconscious as you have your eyes slightly open. Remember also that the sound in the background is the frequency of the particular color you are watching.

> **Video Summary**
> **Brain-Wave Frequency:** Alpha 1 (7.8–13 Hz)
> **Color:** Green   **Sound:** F   **Element:** Air
> **Age Development Stages:** Twelve to sixteen, forty-two to forty-six, and seventy-two to seventy-six

If you have not reached the age of seventy-two, just do the first two ages. Do all three if you are seventy-two or beyond. The Three Videos: Green 1 is 19+ minutes for ages twelve to sixteen years old, Green 2 is 16+ minutes for ages forty-two to forty-six years old, and Green 3 is 28 minutes for seventy-two to seventy-six years old. Work with these videos once a day as you explore the core issues.

Journey of Self-Identity—Green Color

There are a set of question before each of the three meditations. Read the questions first and reflect on them before doing the meditations. The purpose of the questions before the meditations are to stimulate your memories of a particular age the meditation focuses on. Write your results in your notebook after the meditation.

You will now examine patterns of the Journey of Self-Identity in the constricted self development at ages twelve to sixteen, forty-two to forty-six, and seventy-two to seventy-six years old. The patterns identified are worth, shame, and value.

Questions on Video: Green 1: Ages Twelve to Sixteen

- How did you form your personal identity of yourself?
- Did you value yourself?
- Who supported your self-worth?
- Did you feel worthy?
- How did you hide your shame?
- What were your fears?
- What were your sexual concerns?
- Were there family and friends with whom you shared your heart?

Questions on Video: Green 2: Ages Forty-Two to Forty-Six

- How do you hide your shame?
- In what ways do you feel unworthy?
- How do you define your identity?
- What behaviors do you display and put on to get love?
- How much do you give to others of what you are wanting for yourself?
- What are you hiding in your shadow personality?
- What gives you value?

Questions on the Video: Green 3: Ages Seventy-Two to Seventy-Six

- How do you react to unpleasant situations?
- What gives you your worth?
- How do you respond when your identity has been stepped upon?
- What conditions do you have in order for you to receive love?

- What happens to you with others when you establish your boundaries?
- What are your fears about opening your heart?

Forgiveness Meditation (for Chapter 16)

To access the forgiveness meditation video, put into your computer browser the following URL: www.PattLindKyle.com/meditations. Click on Green 4

Gratitude Meditation (for Chapter 17)

To access the gratitude meditation video, put www.PattLindKyle.com /meditations into your computer browser. Click on Yellow 4

How to Practice with the Video Color

This video is a yellow color with the vibration sound color and binaural beats. This is the gratitude meditation. This journey is to liberate you, bringing more awareness to letting go of control of your mental life. The intention of this meditation is to relax into the experimental space of this sixth step in order to detach the mental hold of the constricted self and open to the awareness of the expanded self.

Presence and Appreciation Meditation (for Chapter 18)

To access the presence and appreciation meditation video, put the URL www.PattLindKyle.com/meditations into your computer browser. Click on Or-ange 4.

How to Practice with the Video Color

The video session for this meditation uses an orange color with the vibration sound of the color orange and binaural beats of the brain waves. This medita-tion is to free you from your emotions and to shift your perception of time. The intention is to relax into the experimental space of the seventh step of detach-ment from the constricted self's emotional control by waking up to the power of presence and appreciation. To watch the orange color of the video as you listen to the guided questions, have your eyes half open. Put your attention and focus on listening to what you are experiencing inside yourself as the questions are being asked. This will allow the color to naturally enter into your unconscious as you have your eyes slightly open. Remember also that the sound in the background is the frequency of the particular color you are watching.

Kindness and Compassion Meditation (for Chapter 19)

To access the kindness and compassion meditation video, put the following URL into your computer browser: www.PattLindKyle.com/meditations. Click on Red 3.

This video is a red color with the vibration sound color and binaural beats. The meditation is called the kindness and compassion meditation. This meditation is to detach from constricted self's separation to enter into the true nature of your being. The intention is to relax into the experimental space of the eighth step of the constricted self's detachment. After the meditation, write in your journal what you learned and experienced.

How to Practice with the Video Color

To watch the color of the video as you listen to the guided questions, have your eyes half open. Put your attention and focus on listening to what you are experiencing inside yourself as the questions are being asked. This will allow the color to naturally enter into your unconscious as you have your eyes slightly open. Remember also that the sound in the background is the frequency of the particular color you are watching.

Integration Meditation (for Chapter 19)

To access the presence and appreciation meditation video, put into your computer browser the URL www.PattLindKyle.com/meditations. Click on Gamma.

How to Practice with the Video Color

This video is in all the colors plus the color white. The video has the frequencies of sound of each color energy, and binaural beats of all brain waves plus gamma brain waves.

To watch the color of the video as you listen to the guided questions have your eyes half open. Put your attention and focus on listening to what you are experiencing inside yourself as the questions are being asked. This will allow the color to naturally enter into your unconscious as you have your eyes slightly open. Remember also that the sound in the background is the frequency of the particular color you are watching.

Bibliography

Academy of Achievement. "Edward Albee—Academy of Achievement." http://www.achievement.org/achiever/edward-albee/#biography.

Anyen Rinpoche. *Dying with Confidence: A Tibetan Buddhist Guide to Preparing for Death*. Boston: Wisdom Publications, 2010.

Asimov, Isaac. *Fantastic Voyage II: Destination Brain*. Vol. 2. London: Grafton, 1988.

Bishops' Committee on the Liturgy. *Catholic Household Blessings and Prayer*. Revised edition edited by United States Conference of Catholic Bishops. Washington, DC: USCCB Publishing, 2007.

Blackman, Sushila. *Graceful Exits: How Great Beings Die*. Boston: Shambhala, 1997.

Bly, Robert. *A Little Book on the Human Shadow*. New York: HarperOne, Reissue edition, 1988.

Borjigin, Jimo, UnCheol Lee, Tiecheng Liu, Dinesh Pal, et al. "Surge of neurophysiological coherence and connectivity in the dying brain." *Proceedings of the National Academy of Sciences* 110, no. 35 (2013): 14432–14437.

Brill, Marla. *If Something Should Happen*. Great Barrington, MA: American Institute for Economic Research, 2010.

Campbell, Joseph, ed. *The Portable Jung*. Translated by R. F. C. Hull. New York: Viking Press, 1971.

Carlson, Lisa. *Caring for the Dead: Your Final Act of Love*. Hinesburg, VT: Upper Access Books, 1998.

Chogyam Trungpa and Francesca Fremantle. *The Tibetan Book of the Dead: The Great Liberation Through Hearing in the Bardo*. Boston: Shambhala, 2000.

Church Publishing. *Book of Common Prayer*. New York: Church Publishing, 1979.

Coberly, Margaret. *Sacred Passage*. Boston: Shambhala, 2013.

Coelho, Paulo. *The Alchemist*. San Francisco: HarperOne, 2014.

Dalai Lama. *Advice on Dying*. London: Random House, 2002.

———. *The Good Heart: A Buddist Perspective on the Teachings of Jesus*. Edited by Robert Kiely. Somerville, MA: Wisdom Publications, 1996, 2016.

———. *How to Practice: The Way to a Meaningful Life*. Translated and edited by Jeffrey Hopkins. New York: Pocket Books, 2002.

———. *Kindness, Clarity, and Insight*. Translated and edited by Jeffrey Hopkins. Ithaca, NY: Snow Lion Publications, 1984.

———. *The Path to Tranquility: Daily Wisdom*. Edited by Renuka Singh. New York: Penguin Books, Reprint edition,1999.

Deutsch, Eliot, translator. *The Bhagavad Gita*. New York: Holt, Rinehart and Winston, 1968.

Dowling Singh, Kathleen. *The Grace in Aging*. Boston: Wisdom Publications, 2014.

———. *The Grace in Dying*. New York: Harper Collins, 2000.

Edward Jones, Inc. *Steps to Take When a Loved One Dies*. Edward Jones Pamphlet, 2015.

Elias, Mufti Afzal Hoosen. *Qur'an Made Easy*. Lenasia, South Africa: Electronic Dawah Institute, 2012.

Feng, Gia-Fu, and Jane English. *Lao Tsu, Tao Te Ching: A New Translation*. New York: Vintage Books, Random House, 1972.

Frankl, Viktor. *Man's Search for Meaning.* New York: Simon and Schuster, 1984.

Gallo, Joseph J. "Life-sustaining treatments: What do physicians want and do they express their wishes to others?" *Journal of the American Geriatrics Society* 51, no. 7, (July 2003): 961–969.

Gawande, Atul. *Being Mortal: Medicine and What Matters in the End.* New York: Henry Holt, 2015.

Gibran, Kahlil. *The Prophet.* New York: Alfred A. Knopf, 1923.

Gilford, Bill. *Spring Chicken.* New York: Grand Central, 2015.

Griffith, Ralph. *The Rig Veda (Unabridged, English Translation).* Classic Century Works, 2012.

Hafiz. *The Gift: Poems by Hafiz The Great Sufi Master.* Translated by Daniel Ladinsky. New York: Penguin Putnam, 1999.

Halifax, Joan. *Being with Dying: Cultivating Compassion and Fearlessness in the Presence of Death.* Boston: Shambhala, 2011.

Hawkins, David R. *Dissolving the Ego, Realizing the Self.* New York: Hay House, 2011.

Hoffmann, Erik C. *New Brain, New World.* London: Hay House UK, 2012.

Holecek, Andrew. *Preparing to Die.* Boston: Snow Lion, 2013.

Holy Bible: Contemporary English Version. New York: American Bible Society, 1995.

Howe-Murphy, Roxanne. *Deep Coaching: Using the Enneagram as a Catalyst for Profound Change.* El Granada, CA: Enneagram Press, 2007.

Jenkinson, Stephen. *Die Wise: A Manifesto for Sanity and Soul.* Berkeley, CA: North Atlantic Books, 2015.

Johnson, Robert A. *The Fisher King and the Handless Maiden.* San Francisco: HarperSanFrancisco, 1993.

Joyce, James. *Dubliners.* New York: Penguin Classics, 1993.

Judith, Anodea. *Chakra Activation: An Online Course for Empowerment through Your Body's Energy Centers.* Boulder, CO: Sounds True, 2012. http://www.soundstrue.com/store/chakra-activation-2251.html.

Jung, C. G. *Memories, Dreams, Reflections.* Edited by Aniela Jaffe. New York: Vintage Books, Random House, 1989.

———. *Psychological Types.* Edited by R. F. C. Hull. Princeton, NJ: Princeton University Press, 1974.

———. *Selected Letters of C. G. Jung, 1909–1961.* Edited by Gerhard Adler and Aniela Jaffé. Princeton, NJ: Princeton Legacy Library, 1984.

Kalina, Kathy. *Midwife for Souls: Spiritual Care for the Dying.* Boston: Pauline Books and Media, 1993.

Kübler-Ross, Elisabeth. *On Death and Dying.* New York: Simon and Schuster, 1970.

Lachard, James L. *An Interview with God.* Unpublished work.

Lama Surya Das. *Awakening the Buddha Within.* New York: Harmony, 2009.

Levine, Stephen. *Guided Meditations, Explorations, and Healings.* New York: Doubleday, 1991.

———. *Who Dies?: An investigation of conscious Living and Conscious Dying.* New York: Doubleday Anchor Books, 1982.

———. *A Year to Live: How to Live This Year as If It Were Your Last.* New York: Bell Tower, 1998.

Lind-Kyle, Patricia. *Heal Your Mind, Rewire Your Brain.* Santa Rosa, CA: Energy Psychology Press, 2010.

———. *When Sleeping Beauty Wakes Up: A Woman's Tale of Healing the Immune System and Awakening the Feminine.* Columbus, NC: Swan-Raven, 1992.

Longaker, Christine. *Facing Death and Finding Hope.* New York: Doubleday Dell, 1997.

Maitri, Sandra. *The Enneagram of Passions and Virtues.* New York: Penguin, 2005.

Maslow, Abraham H. *Motivation and Personality.* New York: Harper & Row, 1954.

McCarty, Rollin, PhD. *Science of the Heart: Exploring the Role of the Heart in Human Performance.* Boulder Creek, CA: HeartMath e-book, 2015.

McKenna, Terence. "Unfolding the Stone," 1991, YouTube: Fractal Youniverse.

Merton, Thomas. *The Asian Journal of Thomas Merton*. New York: New Directions, 1973.

———. *The Way of Chuang Tzu*. New York: New Directions, 2010.

Miller, Henry. *The Wisdom of the Heart*. New York: New Directions, 1960.

Mitchell, Stephen, trans. *Bhagavad Gita: A New Translation*. New York: Harmony, 2000.

Moody, Raymond. *Life After Life*. St. Simons Island, GA: Mockingbird Press, 1975.

Moorjani, Anita. *Dying to Be Me*. Carlsbad, CA: Hay House, 2012.

New Revised Standard Version of the Bible. Nashville, TN: HarperCollins Christian Publishing, 1989.

Nisargadatta Maharaj. *I Am That,* 2nd American edition (revised) edition. Translated by Maurice Frydman. Durham, NC: The Acorn Press, 2012.

Nulman, Macy. *The Encyclopedia of Jewish Prayers*. Lanham, MD: Jason Aronson, 1993.

Nyoshul Khenpo and Lama Surya Das. *Natural Great Perfection: Dzogchen Teachings and Vajra Songs*. Ithaca, NY: Snow Lion, 2009.

Osho, Rajneesh. *Meditation: The Art of Ecstasy*. New York: Osho International, 1992.

Palmar, Parker. "A Friendship, A Love, A Rescue." *On Being, Letter from Loring Park,* January 7, 2015. http://onbeing.org/blog/a-friendship-a-love-a-rescue/.

Poinier, Anne C., and Shelly R. Garnone. "Palliative medicine—physical and emotional changes as death approaches." WebMD Medical Reference from Healthwise, 2014. http://www.webmd.com/palliative-care/emotional-changes-as-death-approaches.

Raymond, Chris, "Coping with End of Life Issues," Verywell.com. Accessed September 2016. https://www.verywell.com/end-of-life-4014730.

Ring, Kenneth. *Life at Death*. New York: Coward McCann, 1980.

Riso, Don Richard, and Russ Hudson. *The Wisdom of the Enneagram*. New York: Bantam Books,1999.

Romer, John, ed. *The Egyptian Book of the Dead*. Translated by E. A. Wallis Budge. London: Penguin, 2008.

Rumi, Jalaluddin. *The Soul of Rumi*. Translated by Coleman Barks. New York: HarperCollins, 2001.

Sacks, Oliver. *Musicophilia: Tales of Music and the Brain*. New York: Knopf, 2007.

St. John of the Cross. *Dark Night of the Soul*. Radner, VA: Wilder Publications, 2008.

Schroeder-Sheker, Therese. *Chalice of Repose: A Contemplative Musician's Approach to Death and Dying* (VHS). Boulder, CO: Sounds True, 2007.

Seton, Ernest Thompson. *The Gospel of the Red Man: An Indian Bible*. San Diego, CA: The Book Tree, 2006.

Shah, Idries. *The Pleasantries of the Incredible Mulla Nasrudin*. New York: Penguin, 1993.

Sogyal Rinpoche. *The Tibetan Book of Living and Dying*. San Francisco: Harper Collins, 1994.

Steindl-Rast, David. *Gratefulness, the Heart of Prayer: An Approach to Life in Fullness*. Ramsey, NJ: Paulist Press, 1984.

Tagore, Rabindranath. *Vedanta Monthly: Message of the East*, vol. 36 (1947).

Tart, Charles. *Waking Up: Overcoming Obstacles to Human Potential*. Boston: Shambhala, 1986.

Tolle, Eckhart. "Living in Presence with Your Emotional Pain Body." Huffington Post (blog), March 10, 2014. http://www.huffingtonpost.com/eckhart-tolle/living-in-presence-with-y_b_753114.html.

———. *A New Earth: Awakening to Your Life's Purpose*. New York: Penguin, 2008.

———. *The Power of Now*. Novoto, CA: New World Library, 1999.

Trungpa, Chogyam. *Cutting Through Spiritual Materialism*. Boston: Shambhala, 1973.

Trungpa, Chogyam, and Francesca Fremantle. *The Tibetan Book of the Dead: The Great Liberation through Hearing in the Bardo*. Boston: Shambhala, 2000.

Van Lommel, Pim, MD. *Consciousness Beyond Life: The Science of the Near-Death Experience*. New York: HarperCollins, 2010.

Villoldo, Alberto. *Shaman, Healer, Sage*. New York: Harmony Books, 2000.

Wagner, Jerome. *Nine Lenses of the World: The Enneagram Perspective*. Evanston, IL: NineLens Press, 2010.

Watson, Maggie. *A Graceful Farewell*. Fort Bragg, CA: Cypress House, 2006.

Wilber, Ken. *The Eye of Spirit*. Boston: Shambhala, 1997.

———. *One Taste*. Boston: Shambhala, 1999.

Williams, Margery, and William Nicholson (illustrator). *The Velveteen Rabbit*. New York: Doubleday, 1991.

Yeshe, Lama Thubten, and Thubten Zopa Rinpoche. *Wisdom Energy: Basic Buddhist Teachings*. Somerville, MA: Wisdom Publications, 2012.

Acknowledgments

I did not choose to write this book. As I describe in the book I received a surprising nudge that opened within me an explosive interest in discovering how to prepare for the end of my life. The other books I've written have also been a surprise for me, but this is the biggest one. The journey of this book has taken several years and the support and help of many people.

The book would never have been born to the world without the work of my remarkable literary agent Steve Harris. His visionary ability saw the uniqueness and the "first of a kind work" that he said would heal many people. He worked tirelessly to find just the right publisher, and it was Llewellyn Worldwide. Without David Kyle, my husband, this book would never have been introduced to Steve Harris. David's encouragement and supportive love and care opened me up to seeing that this book was for the world, not just our family.

A big thank you to Robin Milam, who is a bright, stable, and loving force in my life. She is a gift beyond words. Her assistance created a successful introductory class to present the book to twelve courageous people and continues to support me in many ways. My deep bow to Ann Deden, Janaia Donaldson, Rhonda Clark, Maggie Cull, Bonnie Hensel, Carol Nimick, Connie Parsons, Linsey Richards, Lew Sitzer, Kate Stewart, and Jacque Weills. You all indicated at the end of the course that you had faced death and no longer feared the process. Thank you all so much. Your involvement and energy gave flight to this book. A big hand for Michael Logue, who recorded and created the video and audio on the sixteen bonus video meditations. I so appreciate his knowledge and understanding of the art. Along with Michael was Adam Verhasselt, who filmed and orchestrated the introduction to the videos. I couldn't have done it without them.

I have so appreciated the many people who read the manuscript and gave strong endorsements for this work. Stephanie Moran, an incredible editor, was the first to bless and encourage me to bring the book out into the world. Lastly, I am grateful for Llewellyn Worldwide's publisher, Bill Krause, for his commitment to the book and to my editor Angela Wix, who touched my heart when she said that she had been looking for a book like this one. Her commitment to make the book "sing" and her attention to detail gave the book a deep clarity. The staff at Llewellyn, including Stephanie Finne, who did an amazing job fine-tuning the manuscript, Lynne Menturweck, and Vanessa Wright, whose enthusiasm and skill pushed the book out into the world, have worked hard to make the book better and valued the importance of how we view our end of life process. I am truly grateful to all who have helped me at Llewellyn.

And to you, my readers, I am grateful that you are willing to take this journey of facing your own death and learning that it can create freedom and more vitality in your life now.

To Write to the Author

If you wish to contact the author or would like more information about this book, please write to the author in care of Llewellyn Worldwide Ltd. and we will forward your request. Both the author and the publisher appreciate hearing from you and learning of your enjoyment of this book and how it has helped you. Llewellyn Worldwide Ltd. cannot guarantee that every letter written to the author can be answered, but all will be forwarded. Please write to:

Patt Lind-Kyle
℅ Llewellyn Worldwide
2143 Wooddale Drive
Woodbury, MN 55125-2989

Please enclose a self-addressed stamped envelope for reply,
or $1.00 to cover costs. If outside the USA, enclose
an international postal reply coupon.

Many of Llewellyn's authors have websites with additional information and resources. For more information, please visit our website at

http://www.llewellyn.com

GET MORE AT LLEWELLYN.COM

Visit us online to browse hundreds of our books and decks, plus sign up to receive our e-newsletters and exclusive online offers.

- Free tarot readings • Spell-a-Day • Moon phases
- Recipes, spells, and tips • Blogs • Encyclopedia
- Author interviews, articles, and upcoming events

GET SOCIAL WITH LLEWELLYN

Find us on

www.Facebook.com/LlewellynBooks

Follow us on

www.Twitter.com/Llewellynbooks

GET BOOKS AT LLEWELLYN

LLEWELLYN ORDERING INFORMATION

 Order online: Visit our website at www.llewellyn.com to select your books and place an order on our secure server.

 Order by phone:
- Call toll free within the U.S. at 1-877-NEW-WRLD (1-877-639-9753)
- Call toll free within Canada at 1-866-NEW-WRLD (1-866-639-9753)
- We accept VISA, MasterCard, American Express and Discover

 Order by mail:
Send the full price of your order (MN residents add 6.875% sales tax) in U.S. funds, plus postage and handling to: Llewellyn Worldwide, 2143 Wooddale Drive Woodbury, MN 55125-2989

POSTAGE AND HANDLING
STANDARD (U.S. & Canada):
(Please allow 12 business days)
$30.00 and under, add $4.00.
$30.01 and over, FREE SHIPPING.

INTERNATIONAL ORDERS:
$16.00 for one book, plus $3.00 for each additional book.

Visit us online for more shipping options. Prices subject to change.

FREE CATALOG!

To order, call 1-877-NEW-WRLD ext. 8236 or visit our website

Guidance, Comfort, and Healing at the End of Life

"Superb..."
—Library Journal (starred review)

dreams
at the
threshold

Jeanne
Van Bronkhorst

Dreams at the Threshold
Guidance, Comfort, and Healing at the End of Life
JEANNE VAN BRONKHORST

At the end of life dreams can help start important conversations and encourage the resolution of old wounds. They provide a welcome sense of dignity in their sharing and often help those who are dying move confidently toward an unknown future.

Dreams at the Threshold provides simple instructions on how to listen with a caring, respectful curiosity to our own dreams and the dreams of others. Discover how these important messages can provide the gift of peace and the courage to say goodbye. Just one shared dream can bring lasting comfort to those who are dying and to the community around them.

978-0-7387-4234-2, 288 pp., 5 ³⁄₁₆ x 8   **$15.99**